CIVIL
AIRCRAFT

CIVIL AIRCRAFT

ROBERT JACKSON

BARNES
&NOBLE
BOOKS
NEW YORK

This edition published by Barnes & Noble, Inc.,
by arrangement with Amber Books Ltd
2001 Barnes & Noble Books

M 10 9 8 7 6 5 4 3 2 1

ISBN 0-7607-2405-9

Editorial and design by
Amber Books Ltd
Bradley's Close
74–77 White Lion Street
London N1 9PF

Project Editor: Naomi Waters
Design: Hawes Design

Printed in Singapore

PICTURE CREDITS
TRH Pictures

ARTWORK CREDITS
All artworks Istituto Geografico De Agostini S.p.A.

CONTENTS

Introduction

More than any other form of transport, aircraft have revolutionized commercial travel, making the world a much smaller place. Within a few decades of the pioneering flight of the Wright brothers, passengers could make long-haul flights as a matter of routine. Today's civil aircraft can carry just one or many hundreds of passengers, and a wide range of cargoes, representing a remarkable diversity in aviation technology.

At 10am on New Year's Day, 1914, a Benoist XIV flying boat flown by Antony Jannus, an instructor pilot with the Benoist Aircraft Company, took off from St Petersburg, Florida. With him was a solitary passenger, the Mayor of St Petersburg. Twenty three minutes later, at the end of a 35km (22 mile) overwater flight across Tampa Bay, Jannus alighted, having inaugurated the first scheduled, aerial passenger service in the world.

The St Petersburg and Tampa Airboat Line, as the service became known, operated for nearly four months, with the aircraft making two round trips per

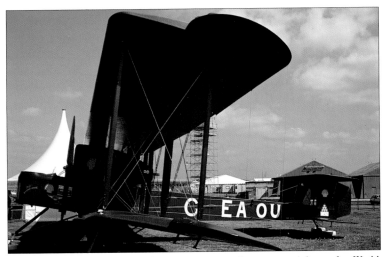

Above: Many Vickers Vimy bombers were converted to commercial use after World War I. Alcock and Brown made the first transatlantic crossing in such a craft.

day. The fare was $5, provided the passenger weighed no more than 91kg (200lb). Heavier people were charged extra. During its short career, the Airboat Line covered some 17,700km (11,000 miles), only 22 flights were cancelled through bad weather or other reasons, and the total number of passengers carried was 1205.

By 1918, only 15 years after the Wright brothers had made their historic flight at Kitty Hawk, aviation was no longer in its infancy. The demands of total war had turned the aircraft into a killing machine of awesome potential. On the other hand, apart from limited ventures like the Tampa Airboat Line – which had ceased to operate because it was not economically viable – the aircraft's usefulness as a source of commercial revenue had yet to be explored; and in this context the obstacles seemed almost insurmountable. Commercial aircraft had to have range, speed and adequate capacity; they had to be able to fly in all kinds of climatic conditions; and they had to transport their payloads efficiently, and in safety.

At the end of World War I, no such aircraft existed. Yet a mere decade later, a new generation of airliners was already plying the embryonic air routes of the world, while new and exciting machines capable of spanning the world's great oceans were on the drawing boards. It was one of mankind's greatest technological triumphs, and would not have been possible without the courage and determination of a relatively small band of men: the aircrews, the managers of the world's pioneer airlines, and the financiers who were prepared to stake fortunes on such an unknown quantity.

THE DAWN OF COMMERCIAL AVIATION

Ironically, the first regular, commercial air service after World War I was inaugurated in a defeated Germany. It began on 5 February 1919, when aircraft of Deutsche Luft-Reederei started carrying mail, newspapers and passengers between Berlin-Johannisthal and Weimar on a regular, daily schedule. DLR, which had been formed the previous year, had rapidly risen to prominence among the spattering of fledgling aviation companies that had emerged in Germany after the Armistice; and its expansion was rapid. In March 1919, it inaugurated a second service, between Berlin and Hamburg, and opened a third route to Warnemünde in April. By mid-1920, the DLR fleet comprised 71 single-engined aircraft, almost all of them ex-military types such as the LVG and AEG, and 13 twin-engined Friedrichshafen FF45 and GIIIA machines, the latter capable of carrying up to six passengers as well as two crew, mail and cargo. In August that year, in co-operation with KLM and DDL, the Dutch and Danish airlines, the airline inaugurated its first international route from Malmî to Amsterdam, via Warnemünde, Hamburg and Bremen.

The organization of Germany's early air services was a world apart from the situation pertaining in France, which had been both the cradle and hub of civil aviation before the 1914–18 war. After the war, although the widespread destruction of surface communication led to the rapid establishment of airmail services, involving half a dozen companies, France's attitude towards civil aviation was shaped, in essence, by the past. Prior to 1914, France's aviators and aircraft constructors were world leaders, and her air aces global legends by 1918. Consequently, the actions of those responsible for furthering French aviation during the years that followed were, in essence, shaped by a profound desire to recapture former glories. Everything, it appeared, was devoted to the creation of more heroes, with huge funds allocated to record-breaking attempts by intrepid young men in stripped-down, ex-military machines; there was no attempt at co-ordinating civil flying, as there was in Germany and elsewhere. Not until the formation of Air France, in 1933, would order begin to emerge from the confusion that attended France's post-World War I civil

Above: The Douglas DC-3 was arguably the most famous commercial aircraft of all time. Thousands were built, serving with numerous airlines worldwide.

aviation industry, even though, in the interim, French airmen achieved amazing successes in long-range, pioneer flights to Africa, the Far East and Latin America. Yet it took French commercial aviation a long time to recover from the wasteful diversification of the 15 years immediately following World War I. One consequence of the lack of a coherent civil-aviation programme and a shortage of financial support was that French designers tended to concentrate on the development of short- and medium-capacity aircraft. Large, commercial designs rarely received government backing, although when such aircraft proved successful, French governments were not slow to exploit them for propaganda purposes. When the big, six-engined flying boat Lieutenent de Vaisseau Paris flew the Atlantic via the Azores on 30 August 1938, for example, much was made of the event; yet no appreciable payload was carried, and, in any case, the British, Americans and Germans had already done it.

In these three countries, the impetus behind the development of long-range, commercial air transport was the carriage of mail. The British government, in particular, had been quick to recognize the aircraft's potential as a means of communication across the routes of its vast empire. As early as 1925, the decision had been made that responsibility for the carriage of mail to the

Above: The Vickers-Viscount, the world's first turboprop-powered airliner, was a real success story for British commercial aviation.

Middle East and India should pass from the Royal Air Force to the newly established Imperial Airways. However, the scheme had been slow to start because of a lack of suitable equipment; the aircraft types that then formed the fleet of Imperial Airways would not stand up to the rigours of continual operation over long distances in tropical climates. What was needed was an entirely new type, specifically designed for long-range operations. The machine that was to fulfil this need was the de Havilland DH66 Hercules. Other purpose-built, commercial designs quickly followed, eventually culminating in the types that symbolized Britain's long-range, commercial air operations in the 1930s: the Handley Page HP42 and the magnificent Short 'C' class flying boats.

Yet, behind all this growing commercial success in the two decades following the end of Word War I, all the major air arms of the world took part in record-breaking exercises that pushed range, endurance, altitude and speed to the limits of known technology. Such exercises were to have a profound effect on the development of future aircraft, both military and civil, some of which were directly descended from machines produced solely for record-breaking purposes.

TECHNOLOGICAL INNOVATIONS

In the early days, the US Navy was at the forefront of range and endurance flying. On 27 May 1919, a Curtiss NC-4 flying boat became the first to make a transatlantic flight, from Newfoundland to Lisbon via the Azores. Yet, just under three weeks later, the honour of making the first non-stop, transatlantic crossing fell to two RAF officers, Captain John Alcock and Lieutenant Arthur Whitten Brown, who completed the journey in a converted Vickers Vimy bomber. On 6 July 1919, the British military rigid airship R34 completed the first non-stop, east–west flight. But it was the US Navy that, in 1924, successfully completed the first round-the-world flight, using Douglas DT-2 biplanes that were externally similar to those in service as torpedo-bombers. Apart from bringing well-deserved honour to their crews, this epic voyage brought home a number of lessons that were to make their mark on the design of future aircraft and equipment. One such lesson was that wood and fabric were far from suitable materials for use in hot and humid conditions; another was that the flight would not have been possible without massive support and organization, with US warships carrying spares, fuel and technicians positioned along the route. Logistical support of long-range air operations was something the Americans would come to excel at over the next 20 years.

Above: The first of the high-capacity, wide-bodied airliners, the Boeing 747 'Jumbo Jet' underpinned America's lead in commercial aircraft design.

The key to the whole problem of improving all-round aircraft performance was the aero-engine, and in this respect the record-breaking efforts of the 1920s produced an important spin-off. For much of that decade, it seemed, the French and Americans, whose high-performance aircraft virtually swept the trophy board, had established a commanding lead; but these successes spurred leading British aero-engine manufacturers into reappraising their engine design philosophy. From three firms in particular, Rolls-Royce, Bristol and Napier, came a new generation of powerful aero-engines that would change the face of British aviation, both commercial and military. In Germany, aero-engine development would not gain momentum until the early 1930s when the facade of disarmament was stripped away, and massive funds were diverted to the industry.

By the late 1930s, the invention that would revolutionize air travel, the jet engine, was beginning to take shape. In 1937, when Frank Whittle tested the first turbojet designed specifically to power an aircraft, the reaction engine was still a novelty; less than a decade later, it was a practicality, having been blooded in action in World War II in Germany's Me 262 and Britain's Gloster Meteor. In 1952, the British Overseas Airways Corporation inaugurated the world's first jet airliner services, using the de Havilland Comet. Unfortunately, this venture was curtailed following a series of fatal accidents, attributed, eventually, to structural fatigue. Despite this setback, it was a 'stretched' version of the Comet, the Mk 4, that inaugurated the first fare-paying jet service across the Atlantic in October 1957, some three weeks before its US rival, the Boeing 707. The Russians, meanwhile, had begun their own scheduled jet airliner services in September 1956, with the Tupolev Tu-104, and in 1959, France entered the running with the Sud-Aviation Caravelle.

Aero-engine developments generated other success stories in the 1950s. At the forefront was the Vickers Viscount, powered by the revolutionary Rolls-Royce Dart turboprop. The turboprop, which was both economical and efficient, was the engine destined to power future generations of short- and medium-haul 'feeder' airliners operating at medium level, far below the altitudes at which the turbojet engine is at its most effective. And the turbojet has given way to the powerful and more fuel-efficient turbofan, the engine that today powers jet airliners of all sizes the world over. The advent of the turbofan, together with new construction materials, made it possible for aircraft designers to take the next step up the technological ladder: the development of the 'wide-body' airliner, with its much-increased seating capacity. The first in the field was the Boeing 747, followed by the Lockheed TriStar and the McDonnell Douglas DC10 – all-American in origin, but soon to be challenged by the European Airbus.

SUPERSONIC FLIGHT AND BEYOND

In the 1950s and 1960s, considerable thought was given to the development of supersonic transports for long-range airline services. Seen as an irrelevance by many, commercial supersonic flight has not been an economic success. Only two supersonic transports (SSTs) have seen service. The first was Russia's Tu-144, a technological and commercial disaster; and the other the Anglo-French Concorde, a technological success that was beginning to be commercially viable only after a quarter of a century of operation.

But the notion of supersonic passenger flight is by no means dead. Advanced SSTs are still being studied, as are hypersonic, sub-orbital transports, which, skimming the upper reaches of the atmosphere, would be capable of circumnavigating half the globe in 30 minutes. The technology to build such creations, a mixture of aircraft and spacecraft, is here today; they may be a reality tomorrow. They are part of an an ongoing quest, the fruits of which are already visible throughout the world today, in the vapour trails of the great jetliners as they carve their way through the stratosphere, six miles and more above the earth. And it should never be forgotten that in the shadow of those contrails fly the ghosts of airliners of times long past, and of the gallant pioneers who flew them.

Aerospatiale (Sud-Aviation) Caravelle Series III

The Caravelle III was the second production version of this French airliner. It first flew on 30 December 1959, and the first delivery was made in April 1960 to Alitalia, which later converted its four Series III aircraft to VI-N standard. FGAA Type Approval was gained on 12 July 1960. One Caravelle III, airframe number 42, was fitted with General Electric CJ805-23C turbofan engines; in this guise, it was designated Caravelle VII. It flew for the first time on 29 December 1960, but was later restored to Series III standard. The Société Tunisienne de l'Air (Tunis Air) operated nine assorted Caravelles from 1961 to 1977. A number were leased from other airlines, but the example shown (TS-TAR, No 178) was a Series III ordered new by the airline and delivered in March 1964. It was finally withdrawn from use at Tunis in August 1977.

Country of origin:	France
Engines:	two Rolls-Royce Avon 527 turbojets of 5171kg (11,400lb) thrust each
Wingspan:	34.3m (112ft 6in)
Length:	32m (105ft)
Height:	8.69m (28ft 6in)
Weight loaded:	46,000kg (101,413lb)
Cruising speed:	779km/h (484mph) at 10,670m (35,000ft)
Service ceiling:	10,000m (32,808ft)
Range:	1740km (1081 miles)
Passengers + crew:	80 + 4

Aerospatiale Caravelle III

The Italian airline Alitalia was one of the largest operators of the Caravelle, with some 21 aircraft on strength during 1965. This aircraft, I-DAXA, was a Series III that received the fleet name Altair and first entered service in April 1960. It later became a Series VIN with Rolls-Royce Avon RA.29/6 Mk 531 engines, and was used by SAM, Alitalia's charter subsidiary, in the late 1960s. I-DAXA was finally sold to the Ecuadorian operator SAWTA as HC-BAD, and flew until it was withdrawn from use at Quito. The Caravelle VIN was the first variant to have engines fitted with noise-suppression equipment. The Caravelle III's sea-level take-off distance at maximum take-off weight was 1830m (6000ft), and its landing run at maximum landing weight was 1800m (5900ft). Eight Caravelles were lost in fatal accidents during this remarkable aircraft's lengthy operational career.

Country of origin:	France
Engines:	two Rolls-Royce Avon 527 turbojets of 5171kg (11,400lb) thrust each
Wingspan:	34.3m (112ft 6in)
Length:	32.01m (105ft)
Height:	8.69m (28ft 6in)
Weight loaded:	46,000kg (101,413lb)
Cruising speed:	779km/h (484mph) at 10,670m (35,000ft)
Service ceiling:	10,000m (32,808ft)
Range:	1740km (1081 miles)
Passengers + crew:	80 + 4

Aerospatiale Caravelle III (Military Conversion)

Two Caravelle IIIs were purchased from SAS by the Royal Swedish Air Force in 1971. This machine was formerly SE-DAG Dag Viking, and was extensively modified with nose radar and electronic equipment in a large radome under the forward fuselage. As illustrated, it flew with the Forsokscentralen (Research Centre) but was later used by Squadron F13, coded '81'. Its task was electronic countermeasures (ECM) and the gathering of electronic intelligence (Elint). The Swedish Air Force's other Caravelle III was used as a VIP transport, serving with F13M Wing as part of Military Air Command, North Norrland, but this too was converted to the electronic intelligence role in the 1980s. Both aircraft were later replaced in the ECM role by specially modified variants of the SAAB J32 Lansen and the Grumman Gulfstream.

Country of origin:	France
Engines:	two Rolls-Royce Avon 527 turbojets of 5171kg (11,400lb) thrust each
Wingspan:	34.3m (112ft 6in)
Length:	32.01m (105ft)
Height:	8.69m (28ft 6in)
Weight loaded:	46,000kg (101,413lb)
Cruising speed:	779km/h (484mph) at 10,670m (35,000ft)
Service ceiling:	10,000m (32,808ft)
Range:	1740km (1081 miles)
Passengers + crew:	dependent on mission

Aerospatiale Caravelle VI-R

One of the reasons why Sud-Aviation did not proceed with the General Electric engine project was that the uprated Avon Mk 532R engine became available, and the much improved Caravelle VI was introduced. It featured an enlarged cockpit area, which resulted in a slightly bulged roof contour, and side windows of greater area. The Caravelle VI was the subject of the first American order when United Airlines purchased 20 aircraft. These were fitted with Avon 533 engines, which were fitted with reverse thrust, and were designated Caravelle VI-R. Four VI-Rs were sold to Panair do Brasil. The first was this aircraft, PP-PDU (No 118), which was named Antao Leme da Silva and delivered in July 1962. The following year, it was forced into violent manoeuvres to avoid a light aircraft while it was approaching Recife. It was subsequently declared unairworthy and written off.

Country of origin:	France
Engines:	two Rolls-Royce Avon 533 engines of 5725kg (12,620lb) thrust each
Wingspan:	34.3m (112ft 6in)
Length:	32.01m (105ft)
Height:	8.69m (28ft 6in)
Weight loaded:	50,000kg (110,230lb)
Cruising speed:	785km/h (488mph) at 10,670m (35,000ft)
Service ceiling:	10,670m (35,000ft)
Range:	2300km (1430 miles)
Passengers + crew:	80 + 4

Aerospatiale Caravelle Series 10B3

The abortive General Electric project had encouraged Sud-Aviation to think about new powerplants for the Caravelle, and the outcome was the Caravelle 10A Horizon, which was powered by two General Electric CJ805 engines. The main production version of this so-called 'Super Caravelle', however, was the Caravelle 10B, later known as the 10R, which used the Pratt & Whitney JT8D-7 rather than the General Electric engine. Finnair was a major Caravelle user, with an initial fleet of three Caravelle IIIs. In December 1962, Finnair became launch customer for the Series 10B3 and took delivery of 10 of this new model. The aircraft illustrated is the fourth machine delivered, OHLSD (No 187). Caravelle 10Bs were also operated by Sterling, LTU, Iberia, ALIA (the Jordanian carrier) and the French company JTA, which used them on Pacific routes from Noumea.

Country of origin:	France
Engines:	two Pratt & Whitney JT8D-7 turbojets of 6350kg (14,000lb) thrust each
Wingspan:	34.3m (112ft 6in)
Length:	32.01m (105ft)
Height:	8.69m (28ft 6in)
Weight loaded:	52,000kg (114,640lb)
Cruising speed:	800km/h (497mph) at 10,670m (35,000ft)
Service ceiling:	10,670m (35,000ft)
Range:	2300km (1430 miles)
Passengers + crew:	80 + 4

Aerospatiale Caravelle 11R

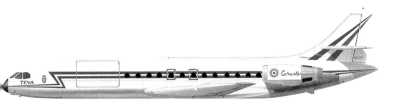

The Caravelle 11R was a mixed passenger/freight version, derived from the 10R and also powered by Pratt & Whitney JT8D-7 turbojets. The length of the front fuselage was increased by 0.93m (36.6in). The floor was strengthened, the number of cargo attachment rails increased from four to seven, and a cargo door provided on the port side of the front fuselage. In an all-passenger configuration, the 11R could be fitted with up to 99 seats. Named Teva, the Caravelle IIR illustrated is airframe No 264, and was originally delivered to Iberia as EC-BRY. It was sold to the Armée de l'Air in October 1976, fitted with the forward cargo door shown here, and entered service with ETOM82 based at Pepeete in French Polynesia. Until recently it operated a freight and passenger service to the French atomic weapons Pacific test centre at Mururoa. Only six Caravelle IIRs were built.

Country of origin:	France
Engines:	two Pratt & Whitney JT8D-7 turbojets of 6350kg (14,000lb) thrust each
Wingspan:	34.3m (112ft 6in)
Length:	32.71m (107ft 4in)
Height:	8.69m (28ft 6in)
Weight loaded:	54,000kg (119,050lb)
Cruising speed:	800km/h (497mph) at 10,670m (35,000ft)
Service ceiling:	10,670m (35,000ft)
Range:	2300km (1430 miles)
Passengers + crew:	99 + 4

Aerospatiale Caravelle 12/58T

The Caravelle 11R and Caravelle 12 were the last variants of this airliner. The Caravelle 12 was a stretched model with two fuselage plugs, behind and in front of the wing, and it was produced to the requirements of Sterling Airways, which then had a need for a dozen examples. In fact, Sterling took delivery of only seven aircraft, and the remainder went on lease to Air Inter. The last of these was airframe No 280, and its first flight on 8 March 1973 brought production of the Caravelle to a close. Caravelles were the mainstay of the Air Inter fleet, and operated to 23 destinations throughout metropolitan France. The aircraft shown here (FBTOA, No 274) is a late-production Caravelle 12/58T, and was fitted with a high-density, 128-seat, economy-class cabin layout. It entered service with Air Inter on 20 October 1972.

Country of origin:	France
Engines:	two Pratt & Whitney JT8D-9 turbojets of 6804kg (15,000lb) thrust each
Wingspan:	34.3m (112ft 6in)
Length:	36.24m (118ft 10in)
Height:	8.69m (28ft 6in)
Weight loaded:	56,000kg (123,460lb)
Cruising speed:	800km/h (497mph) at 10,670m (35,000ft)
Service ceiling:	10,670m (35,000ft)
Range:	1620km (1006 miles)
Passengers + crew:	128 + 4

Airbus A300B4-100

One of the keys to the success of the Airbus programme, following a slow start and poor initial sales, was the launch of the A300B4 for medium-haul routes. Four A300B4s were taken by Eastern Air Lines on a six-month lease, beginning in late 1977. The airline was so impressed by the aircraft, it bought the original four, together with 25 more. It was the beginning of the Airbus success story; by 1978, Airbus had secured orders from other American airlines, and had become second only to Boeing in wide-body sales. Within three years, it had pushed Boeing into second place. The aircraft shown is one of eight A300B4-100s operated by Olympic Airways. Now the Greek national airline, Olympic, was founded in 1957 by Aristotle Onassis, who bought TAE Greek National Airlines, and gained a monopoly of internal routes and national designation for overseas services.

Country of origin:	International
Engines:	two General Electric CF6-50C turbofans of 23,133kg (51,000lb) thrust each
Wingspan:	44.84m (147ft 1in)
Length:	53.75m (176ft 4in)
Height:	16.53m (54ft 3in)
Weight loaded:	157,000kg (346,125lb)
Cruising speed:	917km/h (570mph) at 9145m (30,000ft)
Service ceiling:	10,675m (35,020ft)
Range:	4818km (2993 miles)
Passengers + crew:	269 + 3

Airbus A300B4-200

EgyptAir ordered eight A300B4-200s in 1978–79 and, while awaiting delivery, leased the Series B4-100 SU-AZY from Bavaria-Germanair, from May 1977 to January 1978, by which time the German airline had merged into Hapag-Lloyd. Formed in 1932 as Misr Airwork (later Misrair), EgyptAir became United Arab Airlines in 1969, and adopted its present name in 1971. The A300B4-200 differed only in minor detail from the 100 Series. On 4 March 1982, the A300B family celebrated its millionth accident-free flying hour, a remarkable achievement by any standard. Since its introduction, the A300B had averaged a technical despatch reliability of 98.5 per cent, higher than that of any other wide-body. Figures issued by the US Civil Aeronautics Board showed that the A300B8's direct maintenance costs in the United States were the lowest for all wide-bodies then in service.

Country of origin:	International
Engines:	two General Electric CF6-50C turbofans of 23,133kg (51,000lb) thrust each
Wingspan:	44.84m (147ft 1in)
Length:	53.75m (176ft 4in)
Height:	16.53m (54ft 3in)
Weight loaded:	157,000kg (346,125lb)
Cruising speed:	917km/h (570mph) at 9145m (30,000ft)
Service ceiling:	10,675m (35,020ft)
Range:	4818km (2993 miles)
Passengers + crew:	269 + 3

Airbus A300B-2

The Japanese internal airline Toa Domestic (renamed Japan Air System in April 1988) ordered eight A300B2s in 1979, including JA8466, seen here. TDA's management liked the Airbus 'house colours' so much that they adopted them as the airline's new livery. TDA subsequently bought five used A300s, and later seven A300-600Rs delivered to JAS, which now flies 36 A300 series airliners. By the end of June 1998, Airbus had secured 488 firm orders for the A300 from customers worldwide. The joint A300 and A310 (the medium-/long-haul version) production line was running at about six aircraft per year, having peaked at 45 units per month in 1990. It is now estimated that an Airbus-built airliner takes off somewhere in the world every 20 seconds. The Airbus Industrie programme is one of the biggest success stories of post-war commercial aviation.

Country of origin:	International
Engines:	two General Electric CF6-50C turbofans of 23,133kg (51,000lb) thrust each
Wingspan:	44.84m (147ft 1in)
Length:	53.75m (176ft 4in)
Height:	16.53m (54ft 3in)
Weight loaded:	157,000kg (346,125lb)
Cruising speed:	917km/h (570mph) at 9145m (30,000ft)
Service ceiling:	10,675m (35,020ft)
Range:	4818km (2994 miles)
Passengers + crew:	269 + 3

Airbus A310-204

While the first Airbus model, the A300, introduced the new type into service, and the succeeding A320 heralded the age of the truly high-technology airliner, the A310 in the middle of the range has been somewhat overshadowed. However, this aircraft has achieved superb sales, largely on account of its excellent economy and range performance. These attributes are due to its supercritical wing section, while, at the other end of the speed scale, numerous high lift devices provide good safety factors in operations close to the ground. The A310 is fitted with the best-available, large, fuel-efficient turbofans. Seen here is an A310-204 of Hapag Lloyd, which has four of these aircraft, all fitted with the wingtip fences introduced as standard on later production aircraft. Other German A310 operators are Lufthansa and its charter subsidiary Condor.

Country of origin:	USA
Engines:	two General Electric CF6-80C2A2 high bypass turbofans of 22,650kg (50,000lb) thrust each
Wingspan:	43.86m (143ft 10in)
Length:	46.66m (153ft 1in)
Height:	15.80m (51ft 10in)
Weight loaded:	138,600kg (305,560lb)
Cruising speed:	965km/h (600mph)
Service ceiling:	12,000m (39,370ft)
Range:	9175km (5700 miles)
Passengers + crew:	220 + 2

Airco DH9C

Unlike their counterparts in some other countries, the small British commercial aircraft companies that came into being immediately after 1918 did not have the benefit of state subsidies. Their story was one of continual struggle to make ends meet, and few survived. The first British commercial aircraft company, Aircraft Transport and Travel Ltd (AT&T), was registered in the autumn of 1916. It was founded by George Holt Thomas, head of the Aircraft Manufacturing Co (Airco), which had produced the wartime DH4 and DH9. Both these aircraft were used for commercial transport after World War I. Several DH9 conversions were produced, including the DH9C, a three-seat cabin conversion. Nineteen aircraft were built, 13 sold to operators in the UK, three to Australia and three to Spain. This aircraft, the last to enter service, was operated by Northern Air Lines.

Country of origin:	GB
Engine:	one 420hp Packard Liberty 12 V-12 piston engine.
Wingspan:	14.01m (45ft 11in)
Length:	9.22m (30ft 3in)
Height:	3.45m (11ft 4in)
Weight loaded:	2107kg (4645lb)
Cruising speed:	176km/h (109mph)
Service ceiling:	5105m (16,750ft)
Range:	933km (580 miles)
Passengers + crew:	3 + 1

Antonov An-2

One of the areas in which the versatile An-2 came into its own was the Arctic, a region from which Russia still derives much of its natural resources. The aircraft here was probably used by Aeroflot's Northern or Arctic Directorate, although it does not carry Aeroflot insignia. The bright red upper surfaces were designed to show up against a snow backdrop in case of accident or emergency landing, making the aircraft readily visible to rescuers. For Arctic operations, skis could be quickly fitted to all An-2 variants, although conversion to floats, as in the An-2V version, was not possible outside a factory. In 1966, fire-fighting units in Karelia, and other heavily forested regions where lakes were abundant, were issued with An-2PP floatplanes, whose floats were fitted with special scoops capable of uplifting 630 litres (138.6 gallons) of water per float.

Country of origin:	USSR
Engine:	one 1000hp Shvetsov Ash-621R 9-cylinder radial
Wingspan:	18.18m (59ft 8in)
Length:	12.4m (40ft 8in)
Height:	4.13m (13ft 6in)
Weight loaded:	5500kg (12,125lb)
Cruising speed:	190km/h (118mph)
Service ceiling:	4500m (14,764ft)
Range:	845km (525 miles)
Passengers + crew:	12 + 2

Antonov An-2M

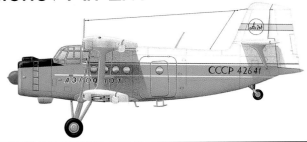

The An-2M was developed by Antonov's Kiev-based design bureau, and was an attempt to improve operating economics. It can be operated by a pilot only, dispensing with a flight engineer, and it has a glass-fibre hopper of increased capacity (1960 litres/431 gallons). The most noticeable changes involve modifications to the engine cowling and the vertical tail surfaces, the aircraft being fitted with a 'squared-off' fin. The basic An-2 design has also been used for experimental purposes; one, which was undesignated, was used to test soft-field landing gear, and another, the An2ZA (Zondirovanyi Atmosferii, or air sampling) was used as a flying laboratory to monitor radiation, among other things. Another 'one-off' aircraft, the An-2NRK, was designed for night observation and artillery fire control, and was fitted with a slender tail boom mounting twin fins.

Country of origin:	USSR
Engine:	one 1000hp Shvetsov Ash-621R 9-cylinder radial
Wingspan:	18.18m (59ft 8in)
Length:	12.4m (40ft 8in)
Height:	4.13m (13ft 6in)
Weight loaded:	5500kg (12,125lb)
Cruising speed:	190km/h (118mph)
Service ceiling:	4500m (14,764ft)
Range:	845km (525 miles)
Passengers + crew:	12 + 2

Antonov An-2T Antek

One of the principal users of the An-2 outside the USSR was Poland, which built the type under licence at the WSK-Mielec factory from 1959. The first 10 Polish-built An-2s were completed in 1960, and the Mielec factory subsequently produced in the region of 10,000 aircraft in its various versions, most of which went to the Soviet Union. In 1968, series production began at Mielec of the An-2P, a feeder-liner version developed in Poland, and equivalent to the AN-2P built in the USSR. The Polish version featured a redesigned and more attractive passenger cabin that incorporated glass-wool soundproofing. There were 12 upholstered forward-facing seats for passengers, plus two folding seats for children in the centre aisle and an infant's cradle. Other modifications included a new propeller and spinner. The illustration shows a Polish-built An-2T.

Country of origin:	Poland
Engine:	one 1000hp Shvetsov Ash-621R 9-cylinder radial
Wingspan:	18.18m (59ft 8in)
Length:	12.4m (40ft 8in)
Height:	4.13m (13ft 6in)
Weight loaded:	5500kg (12,125lb)
Cruising speed:	190km/h (118mph)
Service ceiling:	4500m (14,764ft)
Range:	845km (525 miles)
Passengers + crew:	12 + 2

Antonov An-2TD

In the years following World War II, the Soviet state airline, Aeroflot, went through a period of such rapid expansion, and faced such a diversity of tasks, that it found itself with a requirement for utility aircraft to supplement its growing fleet of freight and passenger types. Thousands of light aircraft were used for countless different purposes. The most outstanding was the Antonov An-2, a rugged and versatile biplane that first appeared in 1947, and which is still in widespread use in many parts of the world. The aircraft pictured is the Antonov An-2TD variant, used for air-experience flying, parachute and navigation training by DOSAAF, the former Soviet Air Force's 'voluntary' basic training organization. This example was delivered in 1956, and operated from Tushino Air Base near Moscow, taking part in many demonstrations at the USSR's annual air day.

Country of origin:	USSR
Engine:	one 1000hp Shvetsov Ash-621R 9-cylinder radial
Wingspan:	18.18m (59ft 8in)
Length:	12.4m (40ft 8in)
Height:	4.13m (13ft 6in)
Weight loaded:	5500kg (12,125lb)
Cruising speed:	190km/h (118mph)
Service ceiling:	4500m (14,764ft)
Range:	845km (525 miles)
Passengers + crew:	12 + 2

Antonov An-3

The An-3 was a natural development of the basic agricultural An-2, re-engined with a turboprop in place of the well-tried Shvetsov radial. Flight trials took place in 1981. After further trials in 1982–83, a pre-production batch followed, the aircraft being fitted with a chemical tank of 2200 litres (580 gallons), and a TVD-20 turboprop in a longer nose. Although the aircraft was produced in limited numbers, no full-scale production or conversion of existing aircraft ensued. Seen here is SSSR-37901, one of the first production An-3s, with a 1450shp Glushenkov TVD-20 turboprop installed. The airframe was almost identical to that of the An-2. Given the track record of the An-2, it seems strange that the development of the turboprop-powered version was not pursued, as all-round performance was greatly improved, especially in terms of manoeuvrability and time-to-height.

Country of origin:	USSR
Engine:	one 1450hp Glushenkov TVD-20 turboprop
Wingspan:	18.18m (59ft 8in)
Length:	12.4m (40ft 8in)
Height:	4.13m (13ft 6in)
Weight loaded:	5800kg (12,787lb)
Cruising speed:	178km/h (111mph)
Service ceiling:	5490m (18,000ft)
Range:	1000km (621 miles)
Passengers + crew:	12 + 2

Antonov An-12

Faced with the problem of providing an efficient logistics service for its huge army, over distances extending from eastern Europe to Kamchatka on the Pacific coast, the Soviet government placed very heavy demands on designers and manufacturers to provide large numbers of heavy freighters. One designer in particular, Oleg Antonov, specialized in this type of aircraft, and his solution was to develop a cargo version of his An-10A turboprop passenger design. Most examples of the new aircraft, the An-12 (NATO reporting name Cub) were for military use, but a number were used by Aeroflot. The specialized civil variant was designated An-12B, and started regular cargo flights between Moscow and Paris on 3 February 1966. Military An-12s were exported to 'friendly foreign' countries; shown here is an aircraft in the markings of the Algerian Air Force.

Country of origin:	USSR
Engines:	four 4000hp Ivchenko AI-20K turboprops
Wingspan:	38m (124ft 8in)
Length:	33.1m (108ft 7in)
Height:	10.53m (34ft 6in)
Weight loaded:	61,000kg (134,482lb)
Cruising speed:	580km/h (360mph)
Service ceiling:	10,200m (33,465ft)
Range:	3400km (2113 miles)
Passengers + crew:	14 + 4

Antonov An-12

Although the An-12 shown here carries the civil registration SU-APA, it is in fact a military aircraft, one of 24 delivered to Egypt in the 1970s. A number of An-12s operating from Egyptian bases were used for gathering electronic intelligence (Elint), but these were Soviet aircraft manned by Soviet crews. Egypt's An-12s were used solely for transport purposes, and were often employed to support major civil construction projects, airlifting heavy engineering plant and construction materials. In the last years of their operational life, the surviving aircraft operated for a period alongside the Egyptian Air Force's fleet of Lockheed C-130H Hercules transports, which eventually replaced them. In many respects, the An-12 is broadly similar to the C-130, although it has a smaller wing, lighter structure, lower gross weight and less powerful engines.

Country of origin:	USSR
Engines:	four 4000hp Ivchenko AI-20K turboprops
Wingspan:	38m (124ft 8in)
Length:	33.1m (108ft 7in)
Height:	10.53m (34ft 6in)
Weight loaded:	61,000kg (134,482lb)
Cruising speed:	580km/h (360mph)
Service ceiling:	10,200m (33,465ft)
Range:	3400km (2113 miles)
Passengers + crew:	14 + 4

Antonov An-12

A total of 41 An-12s were delivered to India, the first eight aircraft in 1961 being followed by further batches of eight and 25 ordered in 1962 and 1963 respectively. As well as fulfilling their primary transport role, Indian Air Force An-12s were used for maritime reconnaissance, search and rescue, and as airborne command- and control-post platforms until they were replaced by Ilyushin Il-76 jet transports. During the 1971 war with Pakistan, they were also used as bombers, the missiles being discharged via the rear loading ramp. In its transport role, the An-12 served the Indian armed forces very well, establishing a reputation for rugged reliability in all climates and conditions. For the first time, it gave the Indian Air Force the means to supply remote Himalayan frontier outposts by air on a regular basis.

Country of origin:	USSR
Engines:	four 4000hp Ivchenko AI-20K turboprops
Wingspan:	38m (124ft 8in)
Length:	33.1m (108ft 7in)
Height:	10.53m (34ft 6in)
Weight loaded:	61,000kg (134,482lb)
Cruising speed:	580km/h (360mph)
Service ceiling:	10,200m (33,465ft)
Range:	3400km (2113 miles)
Passengers + crew:	14 + 4

Antonov An-12

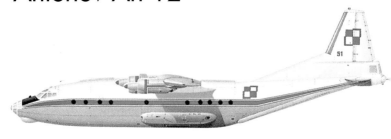

A round 20 An-12 transports were delivered to Poland to serve in military and civilian capacities. Most were used purely as freighters, but some were configured as VIP transports, as shown here. The An-12 also equipped a heavy transport squadron of the former Yugoslav Air Force, being withdrawn from use in November 1990. The An-12B variant, which was intended primarily for use as a passenger aircraft, was used in small numbers by a charter subsidiary of LOT, the Polish state airline. The most obvious difference between this variant and the standard An-12 was that the rear gun turret was removed and replaced by a fairing. A considerable number of An-12s served as test beds for various items of equipment, including sensors for reconnaissance, and for atmospheric research and meteorological forecasting. All such trial aircraft carried civil registrations.

Country of origin:	USSR
Engines:	four 4000hp Ivchenko AI-20K turboprops
Wingspan:	38m (124ft 8in)
Length:	33.1m (108ft 7in)
Height:	10.53m (34ft 6in)
Weight loaded:	61,000kg (134,482lb)
Cruising speed:	580km/h (360mph)
Service ceiling:	10,200m (33,465ft)
Range:	3400km (2113 miles)
Passengers + crew:	14 + 4

Antonov An-12

The An-12 Cub entered production in the People's Republic of China in 1980 under the designation Shaanxi Y-8, having made its first evaluation flights there some six years earlier. It is employed in a wide variety of roles, including that of flight refuelling tanker, airborne early warning (AEW), and drone launcher. A maritime surveillance version, which was designated Y-8X and equipped with a Litton Canada APS-504 search radar in a chin radome, as well as Litton inertial and Omega navigation systems, entered service with the Chinese Navy in 1986. The aircraft illustrated is a standard passenger-freight variant, in the colours of the Chinese Navy, which differs only in minor detail from the parent An-12. To date, two Shaanxi Y-8s have been supplied to the air force of Sri Lanka to carry out a variety of roles.

Country of origin:	China
Engines:	four 4000hp Ivchenko AI-20K turboprops
Wingspan:	38m (124ft 8in)
Length:	33.1m (108ft 7in)
Height:	10.53m (34ft 6in)
Weight loaded:	61,000kg (134,482lb)
Cruising speed:	580km/h (360mph)
Service ceiling:	10,200m (33,465ft)
Range:	3400km (2113 miles)
Passengers + crew:	14 + 4

Antonov An-24

In 1958, Aeroflot produced a requirement for a short-range, turboprop-powered aircraft capable of carrying 32–40 passengers, a figure later raised to 44, and then to 48. The design that emerged was the Antonov An-24 (NATO reporting name Coke), a high-wing monoplane with a low-set fuselage comprising two circular arcs, allowing a spacious high-pressure cabin. The An-24 flew for the first time on 20 December 1959, but development was slow, the aircraft suffering from directional instability. The problem was solved principally by fitting anhedral (negative dihedral) wingtips and tailplane. This resulted in considerable production delays, and certification was not forthcoming until September 1962. The aircraft finally went into service the following year. The example shown serves as a staff transport with the reorganized Czech and Slovakian Air Force.

Country of origin:	USSR
Engines:	two 2550hp Ivchenko AI-24A turboprops
Wingspan:	29.2m (95ft 7in)
Length:	23.5m (77ft 1in)
Height:	8.32m (27 ft 4in)
Weight loaded:	21,000kg (46,300lb)
Cruising speed:	450km/h (280mph) at 3500m (11,500ft)
Service ceiling:	8500m (27,900ft)
Range:	550km (342 miles)
Passengers + crew:	48 + 2–3

Antonov An-24V

Numerically, the most important variants of the An-24 were the An-24V and An-24VT, the latter variant being a freighter. The major customers for the aircraft were Aeroflot and the Soviet Air Force, the Antonov replacing ageing fleets of Ilyushin Il-12 and Il-14 transports in both cases. The An-24 was widely exported abroad, and major overseas customers included Eastern Bloc countries, Cuba, and Soviet-influenced countries in Africa and Asia. Typical of the civil operators of the An-24 was the Polish airline LOT (Polskie Linie Lotnicze), which ordered 14 An-24s to replace the piston-engined Il-14 on its domestic and short-haul international routes. This was the first aircraft delivered, making its first service flight between Warsaw and Wroclaw on 22 March 1966. LOT also acquired a number of ex-Polish Air Force An-24s.

Country of origin:	USSR
Engines:	two 2550hp Ivchenko AI-24A turboprops
Wingspan:	29.2m (95ft 7in)
Length:	23.5m (77ft 1in)
Height:	8.32m (27 ft 4in)
Weight loaded:	21,000kg (46,300lb)
Cruising speed:	450km/h (280mph) at 3500m (11,500ft)
Service ceiling:	8500m (27,900ft)
Range:	550km (342 miles)
Passengers + crew:	48 + 2–3

Antonov An-26

One version of the An-24 was the An-24RT, which was intended for freight or mixed transport, and which had an under-fuselage loading ramp. It was fitted with an RU-19-300 light auxiliary jet engine in the right-hand engine nacelle, producing more power for aircraft operating from airfields at a high elevation and at high temperatures. Antonov used the An-24RT as the basis for the An-26, a more sophisticated transport capable of loading and unloading light, jeep-type vehicles via its under-fuselage ramp, which could be slid forward on railed tracks for direct loading. The aircraft could also be used for air-dropping operations, and could be quickly adapted for passenger, paratroop or transport duties. The An-26 (NATO reporting name Curl) was flight tested in 1968 and deliveries to the first customers began a year later. The type serves with many air arms operators.

Country of origin:	USSR
Engines:	two 2820hp Ivchenko AI-24T turboprops
Wingspan:	29.2m (95ft 7in)
Length:	23.5m (77ft 1in)
Height:	8.32m (27 ft 4in)
Weight loaded:	24,000kg (52,911lb)
Cruising speed:	450km/h (280mph) at 3500m (11,500ft)
Service ceiling:	8500m (27,900ft)
Range:	1300km (808 miles)
Passengers + crew:	50 + 3

Antonov An-26

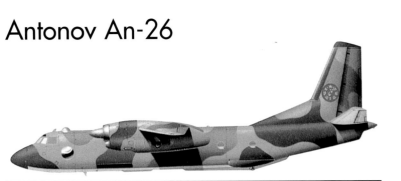

The Soviet-backed Afghan Air Force received at least 40 An-24/26s (the exact split is unknown). One of its An-26s is shown above. Some were destroyed by ground fire and SAMs during the long-running war between the Afghan government and Muslim dissidents, and two An-26s were flown to Pakistan by defecting crews. Before its split with the Soviet Union, China also received 40 examples of both An-24s and An-36s, now largely replaced by XAC Y-7s, which fly with both the air force and the pseudo-military airline CAC. Vietnam's sizeable air force operated three air transport regiments, with some 50 An-26s on strength, while a few aircraft are in joint civil and military use in Mongolia. Many of the An-26s delivered to foreign clients before the collapse of the former Soviet Union fell into disuse through lack of spares and maintenance.

Country of origin:	USSR
Engines:	two 2820hp Ivchenko AI-24T turboprops
Wingspan:	29.2m (95ft 7in)
Length:	23.5m (77ft 1in)
Height:	8.32m (27 ft 4in)
Weight loaded:	24,000kg (52,911lb)
Cruising speed:	450km/h (280mph) at 3500m (11,500ft)
Service ceiling:	8500m (27,900ft)
Range:	1300km (808 miles)
Passengers + crew:	50 + 3

Antonov An-26

One of the biggest customers for the An-26 was Yugoslavia, which at one time had 30 aircraft in service, divided between two squadrons at Zagreb and Belgrade. An example is pictured here. The Polish Air Force's 13th Transport Regiment at Kracow/Balice air base also operated a dozen An-26s. Another major customer for the An-26 was Angola, which received at least 30 aircraft, several of which were used in a quasi-military role, flying for the government or the national airline, TAAG. Some Angolan AN-26s were modified by Antonov to carry bomb racks on the side of the fuselage beneath the wing. Another African customer of the An-26 was Mozambique, which operated about 11 examples from its Maputo air base from 1978. Several were subsequently destroyed. An-26s were purchased for civil and military use by no fewer than 35 countries.

Country of origin:	USSR
Engines:	two 2820hp Ivchenko AI-24T turboprops
Wingspan:	29.2m (95ft 7in)
Length:	23.5m (77ft 2in)
Height:	8.32m (27 ft 4in)
Weight loaded:	24,000kg (52,911lb)
Cruising speed:	450km/h (280mph) at 3500m (11,500ft)
Service ceiling:	8500m (27,900ft)
Range:	1300km (808 miles)
Passengers + crew:	50 + 3

Antonov An-30

SSR-30022, pictured here, was the prototype An-30 photographic and survey aircraft (NATO reporting name Clank). It uses the same basic airframe as the An-24RV, apart from the new forward fuselage, which was redesigned to house a large, glazed nose for the navigator and a darkroom in the main cabin, access between the two being achieved by bodily raising the flight deck. The navigator has special aids to ensure accurate positioning of the aircraft, while the photographic staff have film stores, consoles for controlling the cameras and for processing film. Magnetometers, bolometers or microwave radiometers can be carried to undertake many kinds of geophysical, meteorological or prospecting duties. From an altitude of around 6095m (20,000ft), the An-30 can photograph a continuous swathe of territory 14.4km (9 miles) wide.

Country of origin:	USSR
Engines:	two 2820hp Ivchenko AI-24T turboprops
Wingspan:	29.2m (95ft 7in)
Length:	23.5m (77ft 2in)
Height:	8.32m (27 ft 4in)
Weight loaded:	24,000kg (52,911lb)
Cruising speed:	450km/h (280mph) at 3500m (11,500ft)
Service ceiling:	8500m (27,900ft)
Range:	1300km (808 miles)
Crew:	3

Antonov An-32

Developed from the An-26, this passenger and freight transport was allocated the name Cline under the NATO reporting system. It is easily distinguishable from its predecessor by the much-enlarged ventral fin, and the overwing location of the engines, which are mounted in much deeper nacelles. Tip-up seats along each cabin wall allow the carriage of 39 passengers or 30 paratroops, and low-pressure tyres permit operation from unpaved airstrips. Designed for 'hot-and-high' operations, the An-32 was fitted with various high-lift devices and had more powerful AI-20D engines, similar to those fitted in the An-12 and Il18. India was the first overseas customer to place substantial orders for the type, an initial order for 95 examples being placed in 1979. These equipped five Indian Air Force transport squadrons and the paratroop training school.

Country of origin:	USSR
Engines:	four 4250hp Ivchenko AI-20M turboprops
Wingspan:	29.2m (95ft 7in)
Length:	23.5m (77ft 2in)
Height:	8.32m (27 ft 4in)
Weight loaded:	27,000kg (59,525lb)
Cruising speed:	480km/h (298mph)
Service ceiling:	9500m (31,170ft)
Range:	2200km (1367 miles)
Crew:	5

Antonov An-225 Mriya

Although the concept of a transporter aircraft to carry orbital space vehicles between locations on the ground was pioneered by NASA's Boeing 747/Space Shuttle combination, the idea reached a new peak of development in the former Soviet Union. Following trials with a much-modified Myasishchev Mya-4 Bison bomber (named VM-t Atlant), the massive Antonov An-225 Mriya (Dream) made its appearance in 1988. The trials successfully proved that the 'piggy-back' method of transporting loads was feasible by carrying components of the Energia booster to be used to launch the Russian space shuttle, Buran (Snowstorm). The An-225 was developed specifically with the Russian space programme in mind, and was the first aircraft in the world to be flown at a gross weight of 453,592kg (1,000,000lb). The An-225 is a fully fly-by-wire design, fitted with eight air brakes.

Country of origin:	Russia
Engines:	six Zaporozhye/Lotarev D18T turbofans of 23,370kg (51,522lb) thrust each
Wingspan:	88.40m (290ft)
Length:	84m (275ft 7in)
Height:	18.10m (59ft 5in)
Weight loaded:	600,000kg (1,322,772lb)
Cruising speed:	700–850km/h (435–528mph)
Service ceiling:	n/a
Range:	4500km (2795 miles)
Crew:	3–4

Armstrong Whitworth Argosy I

The three-engined Argosy was Armstrong Whitworth's first venture into the commercial aircraft market, and was built exclusively for Imperial Airways, which had decided, on formation, that its fleet should consist of multi-engined aircraft. Seven Argosies were built for the airline, the second of them, G-EBLO City of Birmingham, beginning a regular service from Croydon to Paris on 5 August 1926. The first Argosy to fly, G-EBLF, was later named City of Glasgow, while the third (G-EBOZ) carried the name City of Wellington (later City of Arundel) in airline service. On 1 May 1927, an Imperial Airways Argosy inaugurated the world's first named air service, 'Silver Wing', in which a steward was carried and a bar installed. Room was made for the latter by the removal of two passenger seats. A later version, the Argosy II, operated on mail routes.

Country of origin:	GB
Engines:	three 385hp Armstrong Siddeley Jaguar IIA 14-cylinder radials
Wingspan:	27.64m (90ft 8in)
Length:	20.07m (65ft 10in)
Height:	6.05m (19ft 10in)
Weight loaded:	8165kg (18,000lb)
Cruising speed:	145km/h (90mph)
Service ceiling:	4000m (13,120ft)
Range:	652km (405 miles)
Passengers + crew:	20 + 2

Armstrong Whitworth AW.650/660 Argosy

The Armstrong Whitworth AW.650 Argosy was the world's first turboprop-powered freighter. The project was initiated in 1956, and the prototype flew on 8 January 1958. Armstrong Whitworth were confident that the aircraft would be a major commercial success, and immediately set up a production line for 10 aircraft. The company's confidence was justified, as an order for four AW.650 Series 100s (later increased to seven) was placed by an American concern, Riddle Airlines. Meanwhile, British European Airways had decided to buy the remaining three aircraft, placing a firm order in April 1961. These three aircraft, known as Series 102s in BEA service, were later traded in for six of the heavier and more powerful Series 200s, the second of which is seen here. The largest order for the Argosy was placed by the RAF, which received 56 AW.660 Argosy C.Mk.1s.

Country of Origin:	GB
Engines:	four 2100hp Rolls-Royce Dart 526 turboprops
Wingspan:	35.05m (115ft)
Length:	26.44m (86ft 9in)
Height:	8.23m (27ft)
Weight loaded:	39,917kg (88,000lb)
Cruising speed:	451km/h (280mph)
Service ceiling:	6100m (20,000ft)
Range:	3218km (2000 miles)
Crew:	2–3

Armstrong Whitworth
AW.27 Ensign

On 24 January 1938, the prototype of one of the most aesthetically pleasing pre-World War II airliner designs made its first flight. This was the Armstrong Whitworth AW.27 Ensign, a landplane ordered by Imperial Airways for service on the Empire Air Mail routes. A cantilever monoplane powered by four Armstrong Siddeley Tiger engines, it had a cruising speed of 274km/h (170mph), and could carry 40 passengers in great comfort over a distance of 1287km (800 miles). Imperial Airways ordered 12 machines off the drawing board in 1935, and began route-proving flights with the type in October 1938. Three were assigned to fly Christmas mail to Australia. However, two of them succumbed to engine trouble, and a third to a landing gear fault. The aircraft were back in service by October 1939. Four of the 12 Ensigns were lost in 1940, two through enemy action.

Country of origin:	GB
Engines:	four 850hp Armstrong Siddeley Tiger IXC radials
Wingspan:	37.49m (123ft)
Length:	33.83m (111ft)
Height:	7.01m (23ft)
Weight loaded:	22,226kg (49,000lb)
Cruising speed:	274km/h (170mph) at 2135m (7000ft)
Service ceiling:	6106m (22,000ft)
Range:	1287km (800 miles)
Passengers + crew:	27–40 + 5

ATR 42

The ATR (Avions de Transport Régional) family of twin-engined airliners is the result of a highly successful collaboration between Aerospatiale of France and Italy's Aeritalia (now Alenia). The prototype ATR 42, F-WEGA, flew from Toulouse on 16 August 1984. The ATR family is highly versatile, and offers various internal configurations, ranging from 42 to 50 seats in the ATR 42, and 64 to 74 in the ATR 72, the 'stretched' version. A dedicated freighter (ATR 42F) has been added to these basic passenger options, in addition to a maritime patrol variant, the Petrel. In service, the aircraft offers excellent economy on the short-range, rapid-turnaround sectors that characterize the regional/feeder carriers. The aircraft are tailored to operate from airports with standard facilities. An ATR 42-300 42-seater of Air Mauritius is shown, which operates on services around the island group.

Country of origin:	International
Engines:	two 1800hp Pratt & Whitney Canada PW120 turboprops
Wingspan:	24.5m (80ft 4in)
Length:	22.6m (74ft 3in)
Height:	7.3m (23ft 11in)
Weight loaded:	18,600kg (41,000lb)
Cruising speed:	560km/h (348mph) at 5500m (18,000ft)
Service ceiling:	7620m (25,000ft)
Range:	1950km (1212 miles)
Passengers + crew:	42–50 + 2

Avia BH-25

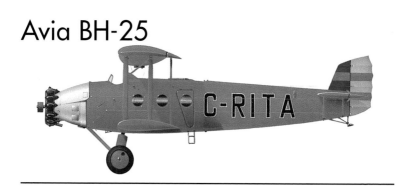

A product of the small and low-key Czechoslovak aircraft industry in the years before the two world wars, the Avia BH-25 prototype flew for the first time in July 1926. An unusual feature of the biplane was that the lower wing was of slightly greater span than the upper wing. The BH-25 is known to have been operated by two airlines. The Czechoslovak airline CLS (Ceskoslovenska Letecka Spolecnost) operated the prototype and four other aircraft on services from Prague to Berlin and Rotterdam. SNNA (Serviciul National de Navigatie Aeriana) of Romania operated four aircraft in the late 1920s; one of which is pictured here. Note that the prefix registration letter C- was changed to YR- in 1939, the Romanian-operated aircraft being re-registered YR-AAA-B, -C, and -D. The Czech aircraft were also re-registered, the prefix letter being changed from L- to OK-.

Country of origin:	Czechoslovakia
Engine:	one 420hp Walter (licence-built) Bristol Jupiter IV 9cylinder radial
Wingspan:	15.3m (50ft 2in)
Length:	12.82m (42ft)
Height:	3.65m (12ft)
Weight loaded:	3100kg (6834lb)
Cruising speed:	160km/h (99mph)
Service ceiling:	4100m (13,450ft)
Range:	600km (373 miles)
Passengers + crew:	6 + 2

Aviation Traders Accountant

The Aviation Traders Accountant was the brainchild of Toby Heal, chief designer of the Hunting Group, who was an advocate of what he termed tension-skin construction, a stressed-skin process by which a sheet of aluminium acquires a strength of its own, and which eliminates the need for a lot of internal framework, thereby saving weight. Taken on by Freddie Laker, Neal was given the go-ahead to design the aircraft, which was to be a 28-seater, and which Laker believed could replace the well-tried DC-3. The prototype, shown above, was built by Aviation Traders at Southend, and flew for the first time on 9 July 1957. It was, however, eclipsed by the Avro (Hawker Siddeley) 748, despite the fact that the Indian government was keen to build it under licence. The Accountant project was cancelled in January 1958, having logged some 200 flying hours.

Country of origin:	GB
Engines:	two 1780hp Rolls-Royce Dart RDa6 Mk 510 turboprops
Wingspan:	25.16m (82ft 6in)
Length:	18.9m (62ft 1in)
Height:	7.7m (25ft 3in)
Weight loaded:	14,496kg (32,000lb)
Cruising speed:	475km/h (295mph) at 7625m (25,000ft)
Service ceiling:	9150m (30,000ft)
Range:	3330km (2070 miles)
Passengers + crew:	28 + 2–3

Avro (Hawker Siddeley) Andover C. Mk I

Following trials in early 1961 to meet a requirement for a multi-purpose transport with STOL capability, able to operate from rough airstrips, desert or even ploughed fields down to 270m (900ft) in length, an order was placed on behalf of RAF Transport Command for 31 military tactical transport variants of the civil Avro 748. They had an extended fuselage incorporating rear loading and paradropping doors, and 'kneeling' main undercarriage legs to facilitate the on and offloading of vehicles. The prototype G-APZV was converted to 748MF (Military Freighter) configuration, flying as G-ARRV on 21 December 1963. RAF aircraft, designated Andover C.Mk.Is, entered service in December 1966 with No 46 Squadron at Abingdon, and served until 1975. Six were modified for radar and navigational air-calibration duties, and others were used for test purposes.

Country of origin:	GB
Engines:	two 2105hp Rolls-Royce Dart Mk 531 turboprops
Wingspan:	30.02m (98ft 5in)
Length:	23.75m (77ft 11inft)
Height:	8.97m (29ft 5in)
Weight loaded:	22,680kg (50,000lb)
Cruising speed:	434km/h (270mph)
Service ceiling:	7470m (24,500ft)
Range:	2300km (1429 miles)
Passengers + crew:	40–52 + 2–3

Avro (Hawker Siddeley) Andover CC. Mk 2

Four Avro 748 Series 2 aircraft with standard fuselages were ordered for VIP transport duties as Andover CC.Mk 2s, entering service with 32 Squadron at Northolt near London, and subsequently with 60 Squadron at RAF Wildenrath, Germany. Their primary task was to carry members of the British government and senior RAF officers on official duty. Two more were assigned to the Queen's Flight at RAF Benson, where they served as transports for the royal family before being replaced by British Aerospace 146s. Other military customers for the HS.748 included the Royal Australian Air Force, which took eight aircraft as VIP transports and a further eight for use as navigation trainers, and the Brazilian Air Force, which ordered six for service on 'shuttle' routes between Brasilia and Rio de Janeiro. The HS.748 Series 2 was also built under licence in India.

Country of origin:	GB
Engines:	two 2105hp Rolls-Royce Dart Mk 531 turboprops
Wingspan:	30.02m (98ft 5in)
Length:	20.42m (67ft)
Height:	7.57m (24ft 10in)
Weight loaded:	17,236kg (38,000lb)
Cruising speed:	434km/h (270mph)
Service ceiling:	7470m (24,500ft)
Range:	1072km (666 miles)
Passengers + crew:	40–52 + 2–3

Avro (Hawker Siddeley) HS.748

Development of the Avro 748, intended to be a replacement for the DC-3 and Vickers Viking, was officially announced on 9 January 1959, when work was already under way at Avro's Chadderton factory on the construction of four prototypes for flight trials and static testing. The final configuration chosen was for a low-wing, twin-turboprop aircraft with a round-section fuselage providing accommodation for up to 44 passengers in a pressurized cabin. G-APZV, the prototype 748, made its first flight on 24 June 1960 and the first production aircraft, one of three ordered by launch customer Skyways Coach Air Ltd, flew on 31 August 1961. Some 600 aircraft were eventually sold to 75 operators worldwide. The 748 shown here is one of two operated by SATENA, an air force-operated airline operating throughout the mountainous nation of Colombia.

Country of origin:	GB
Engines:	two 2105hp Rolls-Royce Dart Mk 531 turboprops
Wingspan:	30.02m (98ft 5in)
Length:	20.42m (67ft)
Height:	7.57m (24ft 10in)
Weight loaded:	17,236kg (38,000lb)
Cruising speed:	434km/h (270mph)
Service ceiling:	7470m (24,500ft)
Range:	1072km (666 miles)
Passengers + crew:	40–52 + 2–3

Avro 504N

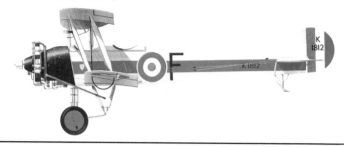

The Avro 504, which first flew at Brooklands in July 1913, was a development of the Type E, which was already on order for the Royal Flying Corps. In a production life spanning well over a decade, more than 10,000 Avro 504s were built, serving as bomber, reconnaissance, fighter and training aircraft during World War I. It is as a trainer that the Avro 504 is best remembered. Thousands of British and Commonwealth pilots learned to fly in it, and after the war, surplus 504s were snapped up, variously being used for joy-riding, 'barnstorming' and for training civilian pilots. The Avro 504N, seen here, was the peacetime production aircraft, converted from the standard Avro 504K RAF trainer, and having a different engine and undercarriage. Series production totalled 598 examples, the last completed in 1932. The Avro 504 was replaced by the Avro Tutor.

Country of origin:	GB
Engine:	one 160hp Armstrong Siddeley Lynx IV rotary
Wingspan:	10.97m (36ft)
Length:	8.69m (28ft 6in)
Height:	3.33m (10ft 11in)
Weight loaded:	1016kg (2240lb)
Cruising speed:	130km/h (81mph)
Service ceiling:	4450m (14,600ft)
Range:	402km (250 miles)
Passengers + crew:	1 + 1

Avro 504N

Denmark was one of the customers for the Avro 504N, which was put to both civil and military training use. The aircraft shown here was originally an Avro 504K, but was converted to 504N standard in 1928, and trained Danish pilots until 1936, when it was sold to Czechoslovakia, where it fell into German hands in 1939. Avro 504s were built in Russia after the revolution under the designation U-1, and were put to a great variety of uses. In 1931, one was used to test solid-fuel rockets, then being developed as auxiliary take-off units, and another was converted as a floatplane with the designation MU-1. The Russian 504s were copies of a White Russian aircraft brought down near Petrosavodsk in 1919. Production began in 1922 and totalled 737. In the training role, it was replaced by the Polikarpov U-2 (Po-2) biplane, which remained in use for many years.

Country of origin:	GB
Engine:	one 160hp Armstrong Siddeley Lynx IV rotary
Wingspan:	10.97m (36ft)
Length:	8.69m (28ft 6in)
Height:	3.33m (10ft 11in)
Weight loaded:	1016kg (2240lb)
Cruising speed:	130km/h (81mph)
Service ceiling:	4450m (14,600ft)
Range:	402km (250 miles)
Passengers + crew:	1 + 1

Avro 536

The years immediately following World War I saw a tremendous surge of enthusiasm for flying. Embryonic flying clubs, often run by pilots who had learned their trade the hard way over the Western Front, sprang up everywhere. At first, the aircraft they used were war-surplus types such as the Avro 504, and in April 1919, Avro produced a four-seat conversion of this well-tried aircraft at its Hamble factory. In all, 25 aircraft were so converted, the last one as a cabin version designated Avro 546. Another, a two-seater with a long-range fuel tank, was used for range flying trials, and another was fitted with floats. The Avro 536 was a complete success and continued in service throughout the 1920s, the last three aircraft, operated by Surrey Flying Services, being withdrawn in 1930. A great many people gained their first taste of air experience flying in the Avro 536.

Country of origin:	GB
Engine:	one 150hp Bentley BR1 rotary
Wingspan:	11.20m (36.9ft)
Length:	9.02m (29ft 5in)
Height:	3.17m (10ft 7in)
Weight loaded:	1010kg (2227lb)
Cruising speed:	130km/h (81mph)
Service ceiling:	3660m (12,000ft)
Range:	322km (200 miles)
Passengers + crew:	4 + 1

Avro 581E Avian

The Avro 581 Avian was a prototype of the Avro 594, and was intended to compete with the de Havilland DH.60 Moth in the two-seat, light-aircraft touring market, but never achieved the Moth's success. Soon after it made its appearance in 1921, the prototype was modified to a single-seat configuration and re-designated 581E. As can be seen from the illustration, it was a very attractive, streamlined machine. In February 1928, fitted with a de Havilland Gipsy II engine in place of the earlier Cirrus, it won the Britannia Trophy for a flight from London to Darwin in 15 days, piloted by Sqn Ldr H. J. L. (Bert) Hinkler. It was the longest flight achieved at that time (18,029km/11,203 miles). The production version of the aircraft was designated Type 594 Avian II. A later production variant, the Type IV, won the SBAC Trophy in June 1931.

Country of origin:	GB
Engine:	one 80hp ADC Cirrus in-line
Wingspan:	9.75m (32ft)
Length:	7.47m (24ft 6in)
Height:	2.59m (8ft 6in)
Weight loaded:	717kg (1580lb)
Cruising speed:	113km/h (70mph)
Service ceiling:	4115m (13,500ft)
Range:	740km (460 miles)
Crew:	1

Avro Canada C-102 Jetliner

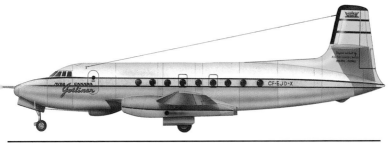

A side from the de Havilland Comet 1, the other pioneer commercial jet aircraft was the Avro Canada C-102 Jetliner. Intended for short-haul operations and of straightforward design, the C-102 flew on 10 August 1949, two weeks after the Comet prototype, and it showed considerable promise. It was designed to be powered by two Rolls-Royce Avon AJ.65 turbojets, but Avro-Canada's Toronto-based team instead adopted four Rolls-Royce Derwent 5s. The C-102 was much smaller than the Comet, and also slower. However, it was still much faster than the piston-engined airliners then in service, and it had a healthy range and rate of climb at sea level. Cargo and baggage were to be carried in two holds aft of the flight deck, and in a further hold in the rear of the aircraft. The project was abandoned due to Avro Canada's commitment to produce the CF-100 fighter.

Country of origin:	Canada
Engines:	four Rolls-Royce Derwent turbojets of 1630kg (3600lb) thrust each
Wingspan:	27.20m (89ft 3in)
Length:	19.86m (65ft 2in)
Height:	5.97m (19ft 7in)
Weight loaded:	29,445kg (64,915lb)
Cruising speed:	737km/h (458mph)
Service ceiling:	10,675m (35,000ft)
Range:	1770km (1100 miles)
Passengers + crew:	50 + 2

Avro Type D

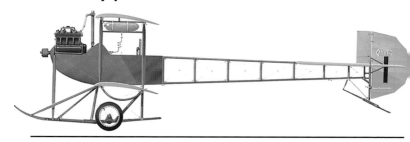

In 1911, Alliott Verdon Roe, the pioneer aviator and founder of the famous Avro company, built and tested the Type D, a biplane version of his earlier Roe IV triplane. Flight trials began at Brooklands early in April 1911, and in July a racing version of the aircraft, with extended-span upper wings, was entered for the Circuit of Britain air race, but was damaged when the extended tips were wrenched off by strong winds. Another Type D, fitted with twin floats and a semi-circular rudder, was tested by naval pilots at Barrow-in-Furness; the first successful British seaplane, it made its first water take-off on 18 November 1911. The Type E, or Avro 500, was a much-refined variant of the Type D, the prototype appearing in 1912 with a more streamlined and fully covered fuselage. Roe always considered this to be his first truly successful aircraft.

Country of origin:	GB
Engine:	one 35hp Green 4-cylinder in-line
Wingspan:	9.45m (31ft)
Length:	8.53m (28ft)
Height:	2.79m (9ft 2in)
Weight loaded:	227kg (500lb)
Maximum speed:	78km/h (49mph)
Ceiling:	not known
Range:	not known
Crew:	1

BAC (Vickers) Model 1151 Super VC10

The BAC Super VC10 was designed to carry larger payloads than the standard VC10 airliner at the cost of a relatively small increase in take-off distance, the fuselage being lengthened by 4.27m (14ft). The Model 1151, 17 of which were operated by BOAC, was the basic passenger transport; the first aircraft, G-ASGA, flew for the first time on 7 May 1964. Five more aircraft, designated Model 1154, were purchased by East African Airways, the only other airline to order the type. These were basically the same as BOAC's Model 1151s, but had a large freight door forward of the wing on the port side and a strengthened floor forward of the wing leading edge to permit mixed passenger/freight operations. The fifth aircraft, delivered in February 1970, was the last of 54 VC10s and Super VC10s built. Some of the latter were converted as flight-refuelling tankers for the RAF.

Country of origin:	GB
Engines:	four Rolls-Royce Conway Mk 550 turbofans of 9905kg (21,800lb) thrust each
Wingspan:	55.6m (182ft)
Length:	52.3m (171ft 7in)
Height:	12m (39ft 4in)
Weight loaded:	152,000kg (335,100lb)
Cruising speed:	935km/h (581mph)
Service ceiling:	11,600m (38,000ft)
Range:	7600km (4725 miles)
Passengers + crew:	139 + 3

BAC-Aerospatiale Concorde

Few aerodynamic engineering achievements can match that of the Anglo-French Concorde, designed to fly at an economical cruising speed of just over Mach 2. The elegantly simple lines of this pioneering supersonic transport tend to disguise the extreme complexity of the aircraft's engineering and aerodynamic systems. For example, the ogival wing has cambered leading edges and creates powerful vortices on which Concorde 'rides' at cruising speed. The four underslung jet engines are fed with carefully controlled air, involving a complex series of intake ramps. With its long nose and high angle of attack, the crew have no forward vision at low speeds, so the nose 'droops' for take-off and landing. Concorde's excellent safety record was blemished on 25 July 2000, when an Air France machine crashed near Charles de Gaulle airport, Paris, killing all on board.

Country of origin:	International
Engines:	four Rolls-Royce/SNECMA Olympus 593 Mk 601 turbojet engines of 17,259kg (38,050lb) thrust each with 15 per cent reheat
Wingspan:	25.55m (83ft 10in)
Length:	62.10m (203ft 9in)
Height:	11.40m (37ft 5in)
Weight loaded:	185,066kg (408,000lb)
Cruising speed:	2179km/h (1354mph – 2.04M) at 15,635m (51,300ft)
Service ceiling:	18,290m (60,000ft)
Range:	6228km (3870 miles) at 2.02M
Passengers + crew:	144 + 3

BAC One-Eleven Series 475

The final British development of the BAC One-Eleven was the Series 475 'hot-and-high' version, which combined the standard fuselage of the Series 400 with the Series 500's extended wings and Spey Mk 512-14DW powerplants, and a strengthened undercarriage to permit operation from poor runway surfaces. The Series 400/500 development aircraft G-ASYD was converted to serve as the prototype, flying in this guise for the first time on 27 August 1970, followed by the first production aircraft, destined for Faucett of Peru, on 5 April 1971. Nine Series 475 aircraft were built. The illustration shows one of three Series 475 aircraft serving with the Sultanate of Oman Air Force's No 4 Squadron; these were fitted with a fuselage-side, upward-hinging cargo door. Executive transport and freighter versions of the BAC One-Eleven were also offered.

Country of origin:	GB
Engines:	two Rolls-Royce Spey Mk 512 turbofans of 5692kg (12,550lb) thrust each
Wingspan:	28.5m (93ft 6in)
Length:	32.61m (107ft)
Height:	7.47m (24ft 6in)
Weight loaded:	47,400kg (104,500lb)
Cruising speed:	871km/h (541mph) at 6400m (21,000ft)
Service ceiling:	10,670m (35,000ft)
Range:	2735km (1700 miles)
Passengers + crew:	84–119 + 2–3

BAC One-Eleven Model 537

Even before the first BAC One-Eleven flew, BAC had considered the possibility of a 'stretched' version of the aircraft, but it was not until British European Airways expressed an interest in the project that work began on the Series 500. BEA ordered 18 'Super One-Elevens' on 27 January 1967, and a week later the Series 400 development prototype was ferried to Hurn Airport for conversion to the aerodynamic prototype for the Series 500. It flew for the first time after conversion on 7 February 1968. UK certification was granted in August, and deliveries to BEA began two weeks later. The various models of the Series 500 proved extremely popular. Cyprus Airways came late to the BAC One-Eleven, its Model 537 aircraft being delivered in 1977–78. They operated to destinations in Europe and the Middle East before being replaced by the Airbus A310 and A320.

Country of origin:	GB
Engines:	two Rolls-Royce Spey Mk 512 turbofans of 5692kg (12,550lb) thrust each
Wingspan:	28.5m (93ft 6in)
Length:	32.61m (107ft)
Height:	7.47m (24ft 6in)
Weight loaded:	47,400kg (104,500lb)
Cruising speed:	871km/h (541mph) at 6400m (21,000ft)
Service ceiling:	10,670m (35,000ft)
Range:	2735km (1700 miles)
Passengers + crew:	84–119 + 2–3

Beagle B.121 Pup

D esign of the Beagle Pup, a fully aerobatic light aircraft with side-by-side seating, was begun in August 1966. Construction of the first prototype (G-AVDF) was started in the following month, and this aircraft flew for the first time on 8 April 1967. The first production Pup 100 (G-AZVM) was flown on 23 February 1968, and deliveries of this version began in April that year. The Pup 150 (B.121 Series 2) was generally similar to the Series 1, but optional seating was provided. To improve aerobatic qualities, including unlimited spinning, a larger rudder was fitted to this version, and was later adopted as standard on both versions. The third prototype Pup (G-AVLN) made its first flight on 17 January 1968 as the prototype Pup 100. The Pup never competed successfully with the American range of light aircraft. Beagle collapsed in January 1970.

Country of origin:	GB
Engines:	one 100hp Rolls-Royce/Continental O-200
Wingspan:	9.45m (31ft)
Length:	6.99m (22ft 11in)
Height:	2.29m (7ft 6in)
Weight loaded:	725kg (1600lb)
Cruising speed:	174km/h (108mph) at 2450m (8000ft)
Service ceiling:	3410m (11,200ft)
Range:	915kim (569 miles)
Passengers + crew:	1 + 1

Beech Model E18S Super 18

The Beech 18 was a small, twin-engined monoplane that originated in 1937 as a civil transport. Thousands were built for military use during World War II, and after the war, the type was continually updated as an executive aircraft. Low operating costs and ready availability made the Beech 18 and its derivatives extremely popular with small airlines running operations on limited budgets. In addition to passenger transport, the type has been heavily used for light cargo work, particularly around the Caribbean and Latin America. Pictured here is a Model E18S Super 18 of Eastern Caribbean Airways. The Super 18 variant, with an improved wing and more powerful engines, first flew on 10 December 1953. A total of 6326 Beech 18s had been built when production ended in 1957, and Super 18 production totalled 762 when that production line closed in 1969.

Country of origin:	USA
Engines:	two 450hp Pratt & Whitney R-985 Wasp Junior radials
Wingspan:	15.17m (49ft 8in)
Length:	10.75m (35ft 3in)
Height:	2.92m (9ft 7in)
Weight loaded:	4128kg (9100lb)
Cruising speed:	346km/h (215mph) at 3050m (10,000ft)
Service ceiling:	5943m (19,500ft)
Range:	2413km (1500 miles)
Passengers + crew:	5–9 + 2

Beech Super King Air B200

In 1969, Beech began work on a new executive turbine transport, the Model 101, later renamed the Super King Air 200. Sharing the same fuselage as the earlier Model 100, this aircraft featured a 'T' tail that raised the tailplane and elevators out of the turbulent downwash of the wings. Two prototypes were built, flying from Wichita on 27 October and 15 December 1972 respectively. FAA certification of the Super King Air 200 was granted on 14 December 1973, and deliveries began two months later. The Super King Air 200 was a benchmark in business aircraft, and hundreds serve in all corners of the world today. The B200 was the final production model, introduced in 1981. Numerous cabin, flight deck, avionics and systems improvements have been incorporated since the first of 831 Model 200 Super King Airs was rolled out. It has also gained substantial military orders.

Country of origin:	USA
Engines:	two 850hp Pratt & Whitney Canada PT6A-42 turboprops
Wingspan:	16.64m (54ft 6in)
Length:	13.38m (43ft 9in)
Height:	4.57m (15ft)
Weight loaded:	5670kg (12,500lb)
Cruising speed:	523km/h (325mph)
Service ceiling:	10,668m (35,000ft)
Range:	3656km (2272 miles)
Passengers + crew:	13 + 2

Bellanca C-27 (Airbus)

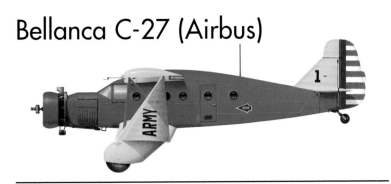

One of the most interesting aspects of civil aviation in North America in the late 1920s and early 1930s was the huge growth in the activity of small airlines throughout the United States. A wide variety of aircraft types were used on these routes; one of them was the Bellanca P-200 Airbus, which came on the market in 1931, but which failed to achieve its deserved success because of the economic depression. Giuseppe Bellanca, an Italian-born American, had begun designing aircraft during World War I, and his concept of a single-engined, high-efficiency load carrier reached its peak in the Airbus design, which could carry a payload comparable with that of many three-engined transports of the time. Only 23 examples of the Airbus and a cargo-carrying equivalent, the Aircruiser, were built, but 14 were produced for the US Army Air Corps as the C-27, pictured here.

Country of origin:	USA
Engine:	one 650hp Pratt & Whitney Hornet S3D-1 radial
Wingspan:	19.81m (65ft)
Length:	13.03m (42ft 9in)
Height:	3.52m (1ft 6in)
Weight loaded:	4613kg (10,170lb)
Cruising speed:	196km/h (122mph)
Service ceiling:	4270m (14,000ft)
Range:	1160km (720 miles)
Passengers + crew:	14 + 1

Bleriot-SPAD S.56-5

In the 1920s, André Herbemont, chief designer of the Bleriot-SPAD company, applied the expertise he had gained in the design of WWI fighter aircraft to the production of a series of light transports that dominated the European market for two decades. The first in the series, the SPAD 33, which made its debut in December 1920, was a small, single-engine biplane that could accommodate five passengers. The type proved successful and 40 were built. In 1921, the next variant, the SPAD 46, appeared, having a greater wingspan and a higher operating ceiling. At least 51 Spad 46s were produced, including 38 delivered to the Franco-Romanian Air Navigation Company, which flew them on routes linking France with eastern European countries. The last variant was the S.56 of 1923. The S.56-5 conversion, pictured here, could carry six passengers.

Country of origin:	France
Engine:	one 380hp Gnome-Rhone Jupiter radial
Wingspan:	13.08m (42ft 11in)
Length:	9.05m (29ft 9in)
Height:	3.2m (10ft 6in)
Weight loaded:	2400kg (5292lb)
Cruising speed:	185km/h (115mph)
Service ceiling:	5050m (16,568ft)
Range:	800km (500 miles)
Passengers + crew:	6 + 1

Boeing 307 Stratoliner

Although only 10 production aircraft were built, with Boeing having to concentrate all its manufacturing effort on the B-17 bomber, the Model 307 Stratoliner was a significant aircraft, being the first four-engined commercial airliner to have a pressurized passenger cabin. The first Stratoliner flew on 31 December 1938, and was followed in 1940 by five production aircraft for TWA, designated SA-307B, and four for Pan American. The 10th, the SB-307B, was bought by the millionaire Howard Hughes, who intended to use it for an attempt on the distance record, but instead turned it into a luxurious executive aircraft. Pan American and TWA withdrew their Stratoliners from service in 1948 and 1951 respectively. The aircraft seen here is one used by TWA for a promotional tour, pending the introduction of the type into full commercial service.

Country of origin:	USA
Engines:	four 900hp Wright GR-1820 Cyclone radials
Wingspan:	32.7m (107ft 3in)
Length:	22.7m (74ft 4in)
Height:	6.3m (20ft 9in)
Weight loaded:	19,050kg (42,000lb)
Cruising speed:	355km/h (220mph)
Service ceiling:	7985m (26,200ft)
Range:	3846km (2390 miles)
Passengers + crew:	33 + 5

Boeing 314A

The Boeing 314 represented a major stride in flying-boat technology, and was one of the first commercial aircraft to undertake regular services across the Atlantic. Pan American Airways ordered six, and on 20 May 1939 one of them, named Yankee Clipper, which was to become Pan Am's celebrated call-sign, inaugurated a mail service between New York and Marseille. On 28 June, a second aircraft, Dixie Clipper, opened a new passenger service between New York and Marseille, and on 8 July, a passenger service was begun between New York and Southampton, England. In all, 12 aircraft were built, the original six being followed by six of the more powerful variant, the Boeing 314A. These aircraft, including three operated by BOAC, flew essential transatlantic services throughout World War II, and the survivors were later sold to charter companies.

Country of origin:	USA
Engines:	four 1600hp Wright GR-2600 Double Cyclone 14-cylinder radials
Wingspan:	46.32m (152ft)
Length:	32.3m (106ft)
Height:	8.4m (27ft 7in)
Weight loaded:	38,100kg (84,000lb)
Cruising speed:	294km/h (183mph)
Service ceiling:	4085m (13,400ft)
Range:	6760km (4200 miles)
Passengers + crew:	40–74 + 10

Boeing 377 Stratocruiser

The Boeing C-97 civil transport had its origins in a requirement issued during World War II by the USAAF for a long-range cargo variant of the B-29 Superfortress. Boeing produced the Model 367, or YC-97, which featured a fully pressurized, two-deck fuselage and which used the same wing, engines, landing gear and tail assembly as the B-29. The military variants were the C-97 Stratofreighter and the KC-97 tanker, nearly 900 of which were produced. The civil version was the Boeing Model 377 Stratocruiser, which first flew on 8 July 1947. The first customer was Pan American, which placed an order for 20. United Air Lines purchased seven. The example seen here, N31225 Mainliner Hawaii, was later operated by BOAC as G-ANTX Cleopatra, and, on 1 March 1958, inaugurated the first London–Nigeria service. She was later used for spare parts.

Country of origin:	USA
Engines:	four 3500hp Pratt & Whitney R-4360 Wasp Major 28-cylinder radials
Wingspan:	43m (141ft)
Length:	33.6m (110ft)
Height:	11.65m (38ft)
Weight loaded:	66,135kg (145,800lb)
Cruising speed:	550km/h (342mph) at 7620m (25,000ft)
Service ceiling:	9755m (32,000ft)
Range:	6760km (4200 miles)
Passengers + crew:	81 + 4

Boeing 377-10-28 Stratocruiser

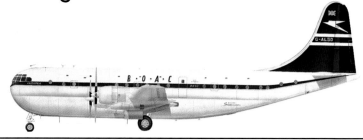

In the immediate post-war years, strong nationalist feelings in the United Kingdom caused an outcry when it was announced that the British Overseas Airways Corporation had purchased a fleet of Boeing Stratocruisers. BOAC bought six Model 37710-32s, configured to the airline's requirements. These were followed by four 377-10-28s that had originally been built for the Scandinavian Airlines System (SAS), but were delivered instead to the UK operator. G-ALSD Cassiopeia, seen here, was the fourth ex-SAS aircraft. All 10 BOAC Stratocruisers carried the same name as the famous pre-war Short S.23 Empire flying boats. In 1954, after the Comet 1 was grounded, Boeing bought seven more Stratocruisers, six from United Airlines and one from Pan American. One aircraft, G-ALSA, was destroyed in a crash on 25 December 1954; the remaining 16 continued in service until 1958–59.

Country of origin:	USA
Engines:	four 3000hp Pratt & Whitney R-4360-TSB-6 Wasp Major 28-cylinder radials
Wingspan:	43.05m (141ft 3in)
Length:	33.63m (110ft 4in)
Height:	11.68m (38ft 3in)
Weight loaded:	67,133kg (148,000lb)
Cruising speed:	547km/h (340mph) at 7620m (25,000ft)
Service ceiling:	9750m (32,000ft)
Range:	6760km (4200 miles)
Passengers + crew:	50–81 + 5

Boeing 707 Dash-338C

The principal series models of the Boeing 707 were the 707-120 (first flight 20 December 1957), and the 707-320 (first flight 11 January 1959). There were many sub-series, designated according to the engines used, and whether the aircraft had main-deck, cargo-carrying capacity. The 707's real success began when turbofan engines were installed, Pratt & Whitney having modified the standard JT3C by replacing the first three stages of the compressor with two stages of enormous blades. Aircraft fitted with turbofans carried the -B or -C suffix. The 707 shown is a Dash-338C used for many years as a mainline vehicle of QANTAS, amassing over 35,000 hours, before being sold in 1979 to the Royal Australian Air Force as its first long-range jet. The RAAF has two such aircraft, both on the strength of No 37 Squadron, based at Richmond, near Sydney, NSW.

Country of origin:	USA
Engines:	four Pratt & Whitney JT3D-7 turbofans of 8620kg (19,000lb) thrust each
Wingspan:	43.33m (142ft 5in)
Length:	46.6m (152ft 11in)
Height:	12.67m (41ft 7in)
Weight loaded:	151,320kg (333,600lb)
Cruising speed:	972km/h (604mph) at 7620m (25,000ft)
Service ceiling:	11,900m (39,000ft)
Range:	9260km (5750 miles)
Passengers + crew:	215 + 4

Boeing 707-358C

In the early 1950s, Boeing took advantage of the expertise it gained in its B-47 and B-52 jet bomber programmes to design what was to become a world-beating jet airliner, the Boeing 707. The prototype, the Boeing Model 36780, known as the 'Dash Eighty', was built in great secrecy, and flew for the first time on 13 July 1954. The US Air Force was quick to recognize the aircraft's potential as a flight-refuelling tanker for its B-52 strategic bomber fleet, and ordered 29 examples as the KC-135. Boeing was soon inundated with civil orders; the first came from Pan American, which ordered 20 in October 1955. The principal series production models were the 707-120 and 707-320. The illustration shows a 707-358C, one of the last to be built. Registered ST-AFA and delivered to Sudan Airways, it operated on the trunk route to London with the individual name Blue Nile.

Country of origin:	USA
Engines:	four Pratt & Whitney JT4A-3 turbojets of 7167kg (15,800lb) thrust each
Wingspan:	43.33m (142ft 5in)
Length:	46.6m (152ft 11in)
Height:	12.67m (41ft 7in)
Weight loaded:	141,520kg (312,000lb)
Cruising speed:	972km/h (604mph) at 7620m (25,000ft)
Service ceiling:	11,340m (37,200ft)
Range:	7450km (4630 miles)
Passengers + crew:	131–89 + 4

Boeing 707-3J9C

Right at the very end of 707 production, in 1976–77, came a batch of 14 extremely well-equipped aircraft for the Imperial Iranian Air Force. They combined special communications for global operation with triple-point, air-to-air refuelling, having both tip-mounted hose and drogue installations, and a Boeing high-speed boom operated from a rear fuselage station. The 707-3J9C was similar in most respects to the USAF's VC-137C, which was equipped with special communications for direct contact with US diplomatic and military centres all over of the world. The VC-137C was used to fly Air Force One missions, with the US president aboard, and one or more of the Iranian 707-3J9Cs served a similar purpose for the Shah of Iran before he was overthrown. The 707-3J9Cs were used as tanker-transports during Iran's long-running war with neighbouring Iraq.

Country of origin:	USA
Engines:	four Pratt & Whitney JT3D-7 turbofans of 8620kg (19,000lb) thrust each
Wingspan:	43.33m (142ft 5in)
Length:	46.6m (152ft 11in)
Height:	12.67m (41ft 7in)
Weight loaded:	151,320kg (333,600lb)
Cruising speed:	972km/h (604mph) at 7620m (25,000ft)
Service ceiling:	11,900m (39,000ft)
Range:	9260km (5750 miles)
Passengers + crew:	215 + 4

Boeing 727-113C

On 22 July 1964, Boeing announced its 727-100C convertible cargo/passenger model. Its sales brochure gave operation from a 1525m (5000ft) runway with carriage of 13,608kg (30,000lb) payloads, over a distance of 3058km (1900 miles), or the carriage of eight pallets (16,670kg/36,750lb) over 2414km (1500 miles). The St Paul, Minneapolis-based Northwest Orient signed for three as the first customer. Almost identical to the Model 727-100, the 727-100C gave operators the option of flying passengers by day and freight by night, thus enhancing utilization. Galleys and seats were quickly removable, and the aircraft could be changed to passenger/cargo or all-passenger configuration within two hours. Seen above is a Boeing 727-113C of Ariana Afghan Airlines, delivered on 15 January 1970 to commence jet services to London and Moscow.

Country of origin:	USA
Engines:	three Pratt & Whitney JT8D-9A turbofans of 6575kg (14,500lb) thrust each
Wingspan:	32.9m (108ft)
Length:	46.7m (153ft 4in)
Height:	10.35m (34ft)
Weight loaded:	95,025kg (209,500lb)
Cruising speed:	920km/h (570mph) at 7620m (25,000ft)
Service ceiling:	11,900m (39,000ft)
Range:	4000km (2485 miles)
Passengers + crew:	189 + 3

Boeing 727-200

Together with excellent field performance, the Boeing 727 had a lively performance and good fuel economy. The upper portion of the fuselage was identical to that of the Model 707/720 series, which saved some $3 million in jig and tool costing, standardized the flight deck layouts, and gave the aircraft intercontinental, six-abreast cabin accommodation for the passengers. Much emphasis was also laid upon independence of operation; the 727 needed nothing on the ground if a stop/go transit were required. It had a Garrett-AirResearch GTC85 auxiliary power unit for electrics, pneumatic starting and cabin conditioning, an airstair on Door 1 Left, and a ventral staircase to the rear. Shown is a Boeing 727-200 of Alaska Airlines, which used them largely for services within Alaska and to Seattle. They had 21 such aircraft, plus four Model 727-100s.

Country of origin:	USA
Engines:	three Pratt & Whitney JT8D-9A turbofans 6575kg (14,500lb) thrust each
Wingspan:	32.9m (108ft)
Length:	46.7m (153ft 2in)
Height:	10.35m (34ft)
Weight loaded:	95,025kg (209,500lb)
Cruising speed:	920km/h (570mph) at 7620m (25,000ft)
Service ceiling:	11,900m (39,000ft)
Range:	4000km (2485 miles)
Passengers + crew:	189 + 3

Boeing 727-212

On 5 December 1960, Boeing announced its intention to produce a short-/
medium-range jet transport, designated Model 727. Design work had been in
progress since June 1959. Eastern and United Air Lines each signed agreements
to purchase the new airliner. The aircraft made its first flight on 9 February 1963,
and Eastern was the first to put the 727 into scheduled service, on 1 February
1964. Later versions of the initial series 727-100 were the -100C and -100QC
(Quick Change) convertible passenger/cargo models. In September 1966,
construction began on the first 727-200, a 6.10m (20ft) longer model with a
standard powerplant of 6575kg (14,500lb) thrust JT8D-9 turbofans, and seating
for up to 189 passengers. The illustration shows a 727-212, which was delivered to
Singapore Airlines on 30 August 1977.

Country of origin:	USA
Engines:	three Pratt & Whitney JT8D-9A turbofans of 6575kg (14,500lb) thrust each
Wingspan:	32.9m (108ft)
Length:	46.7m (153ft 2in)
Height:	10.35m (34ft)
Weight loaded:	95,025kg (209,500lb)
Cruising speed:	920km/h (570mph) at 7620m (25,000ft)
Service ceiling:	11,900m (39,000ft)
Range:	4000km (2485 miles)
Passengers + crew:	189 + 3

Boeing 727-224

Originally intended for Continental Airlines, this Boeing 727-224 (5A-DAH) was delivered to Libyan Arab Airlines on 28 December 1970. Just over two years later, it met with an untimely end. On 21 February 1973, while flying from Benghazi to Cairo, it strayed from its intended track and passed to the south of the Egyptian capital. While approaching the Gulf of Suez, it was detected by Israeli defence radars, and two F-4 Phantom jet fighters were despatched to intercept it. The Israeli pilots, having identified the intruder as it crossed into Sinai, indicated that it was to land. Instead, the 727 turned back towards the west, whereupon the fighter pilots attacked it. The 727 crashed some 15km (10 miles) east of the Suez Canal while attempting a belly landing in the desert. All but five of the 113 persons on board were killed.

Country of origin:	USA
Engines:	three Pratt & Whitney JT8D-9A turbofans of 6575kg (14,500lb) thrust each
Wingspan:	32.9m (108ft)
Length:	46.7m (153ft 2in)
Height:	10.35m (34ft)
Weight loaded:	95,025kg (209,500lb)
Cruising speed:	920km/h (570mph) at 7620m (25,000ft)
Service ceiling:	11,900m (39,000ft)
Range:	4000km (2485 miles)
Passengers + crew:	189 + 3

Boeing 727-243

This Boeing 727-243 of Alitalia was rolled out on 10 September 1976. Named Cita di Siena, the aircraft, and 17 more of the same type, operated throughout Europe and North Africa, as well as on services to Tel Aviv. The entire fleet was replaced by McDonnell Douglas MD-80s, and the 727s were sold to People Express via McDonnell Douglas in late 1983/early 1984. By the late 1970s, Boeing was looking at a new design to continue the sales success of the 727, and this emerged as the Model 757. With deliveries of the new aircraft firmly established, the Model 727 line finally closed. The last of 1832 aircraft, a 727-200F for Federal Express was rolled out on 14 August 1984. Another remarkable success story for Boeing had come to an end, with the 727 becoming the most popular airliner ever. It far outstripped its nearest British rival, the Hawker Siddeley Trident.

Country of origin:	USA
Engines:	three Pratt & Whitney JT8D-9A turbofans of 6575kg (14,500lb) thrust each
Wingspan:	32.9m (108ft)
Length:	46.7m (153ft 2in)
Height:	10.35m (34ft)
Weight loaded:	95,025kg (209,500lb)
Cruising speed:	920km/h (570mph) at 7620m (25,000ft)
Service ceiling:	11,900m (39,000ft)
Range:	4000km (2485 miles)
Passengers + crew:	189 + 3

Boeing 727-2B6

By April 1967, the Boeing 727 was the most widely used commercial jet airliner in service. In that month, SABENA took delivery of the 400th aircraft, while a total of 586 was on order, in comparison with 564 Model 707s. In June 1967, Pan American placed an order for the milestone 600th, and the aircraft was on option or in service with 32 carriers. On 27 July, the first Model 727-200 took off from Renton and, after a flight of 2 hours 10 minutes, landed at Paine Field for FAA inspection. Certification followed on 30 November 1967 after 457 hours of test flying. The Advanced Boeing 727-200 was announced on 12 May 1971. The illustration shows a Boeing 727-2B6 of Royal Air Maroc, which took delivery of this 1236th example on 9 December 1970. Seven more Boeing 727-2B6s were used by the airline to points in North Africa and Europe.

Country of origin:	USA
Engines:	three Pratt & Whitney JT8D-9A turbofans of 6575kg (14,500lb) thrust each
Wingspan:	32.9m (108ft)
Length:	46.7m (153ft 2in)
Height:	10.35m (34ft)
Weight loaded:	95,025kg (209,500lb)
Cruising speed:	920km/h (570mph) at 7620m (25,000ft)
Service ceiling:	11,900m (39,000ft)
Range:	4000km (2485 miles)
Passengers + crew:	163 (two-class) + 3

Boeing 737-200

Although its career has been marred by a number of fatal accidents, the Boeing 737 can be seen as yet another major success story. Development of this famous short-haul jet airliner began in 1964, and within a year, Lufthansa had placed a firm order for 21 aircraft. Production was begun immediately, much time and money being saved by using the same fuselage cross-section as the much larger Boeing 707 and 727. The prototype flew on 9 April 1967. Air Florida, one of whose aircraft is shown, was a successful interstate commercial operator. The 737 was the basis of its fleet, providing services along the length of the US east coast. One of its 737s crashed into the Potomac river, in bleak snow and icy conditions, shortly after taking off from Washington National Airport on 13 January 1982, leading to what became a world-famous accident investigation.

Country of origin:	USA
Engines:	two Pratt & Whitney JTD-9 turbofans of 6575kg (14,500lb) thrust each
Wingspan:	28.35m (93ft)
Length:	30.5m (100ft)
Height:	11.3m (37ft)
Weight loaded:	52,390kg (115,500lb)
Cruising speed:	925km/h (575mph) at 9145m (30,000ft)
Service ceiling:	11,900m (39,000ft)
Range:	3435km (2135 miles)
Passengers + crew:	115 + 3

Boeing 737-298C

Nine months before the delivery deadline for the early-model 737, it was apparent that the design produced far more drag than Boeing had predicted, and that the thrust reversers were not working. New nacelle/wing fairings were designed, and a row of blade-like vortex generators was added to the rear fuselage. The thrust reversers were too near the wings, and the tailpipes of the engines were extended by 102cm (40in) to resolve the problem. Among the many other modifications carried out to the basic design of the Model 737 during its lengthy career is a gravel-field kit, as in this Air Zaire Boeing 737-298C Advanced, to permit operations from low-standard airfields. This modification, consisting of vortex dissipators beneath the engines, and deflector plates on the undercarriage to avoid stone damage, has been adopted by several African nations.

Country of origin:	USA
Engines:	two Pratt & Whitney JT8D-15-17 turbofans of 7030kg (15,500lb) thrust each
Wingspan:	28.35m (93ft)
Length:	30.5m (100ft)
Height:	11.3m (37ft)
Weight loaded:	52,390kg (115,500lb)
Cruising speed:	925km/h (575mph) at 9145m (30,000ft)
Service ceiling:	11,900m (39,000ft)
Range:	4265km (2650 miles)
Passengers + crew:	130 + 3

Boeing 737-2X9 Surveiller

The Boeing Surveiller is a maritime reconnaissance version of the Boeing 737, equipped with Motorola side-looking, airborne, multi-mission radar (SLAMMR) equipment linked to two fairings above the rear fuselage. The radar has a typical range of 185km (115 miles) on each side of the aircraft at a patrol height of 9150m (30,000ft). The aircraft shown is one of three in service with the Indonesian Air Force (Tentara Nasional Indonesia-Angkatan Udara). The USAF also operates a military variant of the Boeing 737. Designated T-43A, it is used as a navigation trainer, and its cabin is equipped with numerous navigator stations. Most are operated by the 323rd Flying Training Wing at Mather Air Force Base in California, although a few are used for transport purposes. Some 737s in the service of a small number of African states are thought to be used in various quasi-military roles.

Country of origin:	USA
Engines:	two Pratt & Whitney JT8D-15-17 turbofans of 7030kg (15,500lb) thrust each
Wingspan:	28.35m (93ft)
Length:	30.5m (100ft)
Height:	11.3m (37ft)
Weight loaded:	52,390kg (115,500lb)
Cruising speed:	925km/h (575mph) at 9145m (30,000ft)
Service ceiling:	11,900m (39,000ft)
Range:	4265km (2650 miles)
Passengers + crew:	130 + 3

Boeing 737-300

S ales of the Boeing 737 were steady, but unspectacular, until 1978, when the market erupted. No fewer than 145 sales were recorded. There were a number of reasons for this. Boeing took two large 'one-off' orders from British Airways and Lufthansa, and the US government abolished the rules that had prevented the small, but efficient, regional airlines from competing on many routes. The regionals purchased Model 737s to hasten their expansion, and three of them (USAir, Southwest and Frontier) became Boeing's biggest 737 customers, aside from United and Lufthansa. The already phenomenal success of the Boeing 737-200, the basic design, achieved renewed vigour with the launch of the -300, -400 and -500 series. The Portuguese airline TAP started 737-200 operations in 1983, and has since added the Series 300, shown here, to its fleet.

Country of origin:	USA
Engines:	two Pratt & Whitney JT8D-15-17 turbofans of 7030kg (15,500lb) thrust each
Wingspan:	28.35m (93ft)
Length:	30.5m (100ft)
Height:	11.3m (37ft)
Weight loaded:	52,390kg (115,500lb)
Cruising speed:	925km/h (575mph) at 9145m (30,000ft)
Service ceiling:	11,900m (39,000ft)
Range:	4265km (2650 miles)
Passengers + crew:	130 + 3

Boeing 737-400

As intended, the advanced model 737 proved attractive to 'Third World' operators, and the airliner became a familiar sight in the Middle and Far East, Africa and Latin America. The aircraft shown above belongs to TACA of El Salvador, which operates 10 737s on services in Central America. In Europe, the holiday charter business had matured to the point where airlines could afford brand-new aircraft; the advanced model 737 proved ideal, with 130 seats and plenty of range. The third important set of customers was the US regional airlines such as Southwest of Dallas and Denver-based Frontier, which also graduated into their first jet equipment. There was also a growing tendency for governments, particularly in the 'Third World', to buy the 737 for VIP use. In 1980, the Boeing 737 overtook the 727 to become the world's best-selling airliner.

Country of origin:	USA
Engines:	two Pratt & Whitney JT8D-15-17 turbofans of 7030kg (15,500lb) thrust each
Wingspan:	28.35m (93ft)
Length:	30.5m (100ft)
Height:	11.3m (37ft)
Weight loaded:	52,390kg (115,500lb)
Cruising speed:	925km/h (575mph) at 9145m (30,000ft)
Service ceiling:	11,900m (39,000ft)
Range:	4265km (2650 miles)
Passengers + crew:	130 + 3

Boeing 747-100

Next to KLM, Avianca of Colombia is the world's oldest established airline. It operated this 747-100 on services mainly to Europe, but eventually replaced it with a 747-200. This aircraft had a lucky escape at Madrid in 1982 when tyres burst on take-off. Another Avianca 747 was not so lucky a year later when it attempted to land at the same airport. It was a Boeing 747283B Combi, a convertible passenger-cargo model with a cargo side door, aft of the wing. It had been cleared to land at Barajas Airport, having taken off from Paris; its ultimate destination was Bogota, Colombia. During an instrument landing system (ILS) approach it crashed into a hill some 12km (7.7 miles) south-east of the airport, killing 181 persons on board, including 19 on-duty and four off-duty crew members. The 11 surviving passengers were seriously injured.

Country of origin:	USA
Engines:	four Pratt & Whitney JT9D-3 turbofans of 19,730kg (43,500lb) thrust each
Wingspan:	59.64m (195ft 8in)
Length:	70.51m (231ft 4in)
Height:	19.33m (63ft 5in)
Weight loaded:	322,050kg (713,000lb)
Cruising speed:	958km/h (595mph) at 9150m (30,000ft)
Service ceiling:	13,715m (45,000ft)
Range:	9138km (5790 miles)
Passengers + crew:	374 + 4

Boeing 747-200

On 11 October 1970, Boeing flew the first Model 747-200, with a greater fuel capacity and increased gross weight. The basic passenger version is the Model 747-200B, while the Model 747-200F is a dedicated cargo version with no windows, a hinged nose for straight-in loading of pallets and containers (up to 20 standard 3.05m/10ft ISO containers, plus 30 lower-lobe containers for up to 112,946kg/249,000lb of cargo), with a loading system that enables tow loaders to load or unload the aircraft in less than 30 minutes. Four 747-200s were bought by the US Air Force to serve as National Emergency Airborne Command Posts. Designated E-4B, these aircraft (one of which is seen here) have an extensive communications suite and in-flight refuelling capability, enabling them to carry the president and his battle staff aloft in the event of a nuclear attack.

Country of origin:	USA
Engines:	four Pratt & Whitney JT9D-7FW turbofans of 22,680kg (50,000lb) thrust each
Wingspan:	59.64m (195ft 8in)
Length:	70.51m (231 ft 4in)
Height:	19.35m (63ft 6in)
Weight loaded:	365,150kg (805,000lb)
Cruising speed:	940km/h (584mph) at 9150m (30,000ft)
Service ceiling:	13,715m (45,000ft)
Range:	9625km (5980 miles)
Passengers + crew:	440 + 3

Boeing 747SP

The 747SP (Special Performance) was not one of Boeing's most successful ventures, with only a small number of this special-performance, short-body, long-range model being built. Introduced in 1975, it featured an enlarged tail fin. Only a handful of airlines had a requirement for the enormous range offered by the model, one of them being China Airlines of Taiwan. Developed from the 747-100, the 747SP represented a major engineering effort and investment. Its fuselage was 14.35m (47ft 1in) shorter than the standard model, which in turn demanded a vertical tail 1.52m (5ft) taller, with double-hinged rudders and a tailplane increased in span by 3.05m (10ft). Among other notable flights, a Pan American 747SP flew around the world in 1 day 22 hours 50 minutes at an average speed of 809km/h (503mph); another traversed the globe by crossing both poles.

Country of origin:	USA
Engines:	four Pratt & Whitney JT9D-3 turbofans of 19,730kg (43,500lb) thrust each
Wingspan:	59.64m (195ft 8in)
Length:	56.16m (184 ft 2in)
Height:	20.86m (68ft 5in)
Weight loaded:	318,427kg (702,000lb)
Cruising speed:	958km/h (595mph) at 9150m (30,000ft)
Service ceiling:	13,715m (45,000ft)
Range:	16,560km (10,290 miles)
Passengers + crew:	289–440 + 4

Boeing 757

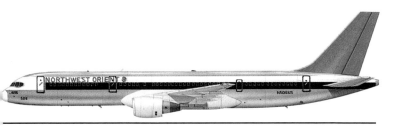

Towards the end of the 1970s, Boeing was faced with a problem: how to keep its highly successful Model 727 at the top of airliner sales. Subsequent improvement studies on the design of the basic airframe resulted in an aircraft that had little in common with its predecessor, but which kept the Boeing sales challenge alive. Designated the 757, the new aircraft eventually began to take its place in ever-growing numbers in the ranks of the world's major airlines, despite disappointing initial sales. No new customers appeared until three aircraft were ordered by Transbrasil and three by Aloha in April 1980. Sales then rocketed. The US giant Northwest purchased a total of 73 757s to begin the replacement of its domestic 727 fleet, operating the type alongside its European rival, the Airbus A320. The other launch customer for the 757 was Eastern Airlines.

Country of origin:	USA
Engines:	two Pratt & Whitney PW2040 or Rolls-Royce RB211-535E of 18,950kg (41,780lb) and 18,230kg (40,200lb) thrust respectively.
Wingspan:	38m (125ft)
Length:	47.5m (155ft 7in)
Height:	13.6m (44ft 6in)
Weight loaded:	100,000kg (220,462lb)
Cruising speed:	965km/h (600mph) at 9150m (30,000ft)
Service ceiling:	11,900m (39,000ft)
Range:	7315km (4545 miles)
Passengers + crew:	201 + 2

Boeing 757-200

Boeing centred the 757 programme on its Renton plant in Seattle, headquarters of the Boeing Commercial Airplane Company. The first Boeing 757 was rolled out on 13 January 1982, and made its maiden flight on 19 February. Scheduled services began with Eastern Airlines and British Airways. Initially only the 757-200 was offered, with a fuselage length of 46.96m (154ft), a choice of two engine types, and a choice between regular and long-range fuselage capacity. By the end of June 1998, Boeing had orders for 920 aircraft of the 757 family from 63 customers. Seen here is a 757 of the UK company Air 2000, which operates 13 aircraft on routes from Gatwick and Glasgow, and on charter services to the United States, the Caribbean and Africa. Another major customer was Monarch, the large UK tour operator, which flies to destinations in the Mediterranean.

Country of origin:	USA
Engines:	two Pratt & Whitney PW2040 or Rolls-Royce RB211-535E of 18,950kg (41,780lb) and 18,230kg (40,190lb) thrust respectively.
Wingspan:	38m (125ft)
Length:	46.96m (154ft)
Height:	13.6m (44ft 6in)
Weight loaded:	100,000kg (220,462lb)
Cruising speed:	965km/h (600mph) at 9150m (30,000ft)
Service ceiling:	11,900m (39,000ft)
Range:	7315km (4545 miles)
Passengers + crew:	231 + 2

Boeing 757-2M6

Three Boeing 757-2M6s were delivered to Royal Brunei Airlines in 1986. These flew on services linking the Sultanate with other destinations in the Far East, including Australia. The Brunei aircraft are powered by Rolls-Royce RB211-535E-4 engines, and can accommodate 148 persons in three classes. The RB211-535E4 proved to be a superb engine, and its development went far more smoothly than had been predicted. It was notable for introducing an entirely new fan, with very wide blades made from thin, diffusion-bonded, titanium skins on a honeycomb core. It also introduced a new nacelle with a short and simple, integrated rear nozzle. The success of the E-4 effectively put General Electric out of the running as a potentional engine constructor, and their proposed CF6-32 engine was never built. This left Pratt & Whitney, with their PW2040, as the only other contender.

Country of origin:	USA
Engines:	two Rolls-Royce RB211-535E of 18,950kg (41,780lb) thrust each
Wingspan:	38m (125ft)
Length:	47.5m (155ft 8in)
Height:	13.6m (44ft 6in)
Weight loaded:	100,000kg (220,462lb)
Cruising speed:	965km/h (595mph) at 9150m (30,000ft)
Service ceiling:	11,900m (39,000ft)
Range:	7315km (4545 miles)
Passengers + crew:	148 + 2

Boeing C-97

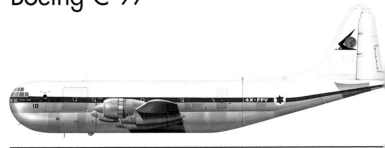

Aircraft X-FPV, seen here, was one of five C-97s purchased by Israeli Aircraft Industries in February 1962, and rebuilt for service in Israel. Other Israeli Stratocruisers were former USAF C-97s, but 4XFPV 'Arbel' was ex-BOAC, and served as a crew trainer and cargo carrier, with side and rear freight doors. Some Israeli C-97 conversions had hinged rear-fuselage sections, a roller-conveyor system being built into the cabin floor of each aircraft for use with freight pallets. These aircraft could operate at a maximum take-off weight of 69,400kg (153,000lb). Israel eventually purchased 15 C-97s from various sources, for use as transports with the Israeli Air Force and for other, more clandestine, roles. One of the aircraft is believed to have operated as an airborne command post during the Six Day War of June 1967, a role subsequently taken over by a modified Boeing 707.

Country of origin:	USA
Engines:	four 3500hp Pratt & Whitney R-4360 Wasp Major 28-cylinder radials
Wingspan:	43m (141ft)
Length:	33.6m (110ft)
Height:	11.65m (38ft 2in)
Weight loaded:	69,400kg (153,000lb)
Cruising speed:	550km/h (340mph) at 7620m (25,000ft)
Service ceiling:	9755m (32,000ft)
Range:	6760km (4200 miles)
Passengers + crew:	100 + 4

Boeing C-97A

The aircraft seen here, USAF serial 48-399, was the third example of the first batch of 50 production C-97A freighters for the USAF, bearing Boeing's designation 367-4-19. Features included extra outer-wing fuel tanks, APS-42 weather radar, and special provision for the rapid air-dropping of stores, usually by parachute, through the open, rear-ramp door. The first of six YC-97s flew on 11 March 1947. During trials, they transformed the Air Transport Command (later MATS) route to Hawaii. In 1948, the first of the YC-97As flew at an average daily utilization of between nine and 12 hours on the Berlin Airlift, relieving fears that the Wasp Major and its new-design General Electric turbochargers would prove unreliable. Boeing had few worries over the viability of the C-97, and was more concerned about whether the commercial version would prove a success.

Country of origin:	USA
Engines:	four 3500hp Pratt & Whitney R-4360 Wasp Major 28-cylinder radials
Wingspan:	43m (141ft)
Length:	33.6m (110ft)
Height:	11.65m (38ft 2in)
Weight loaded:	66,135kg (145,800lb)
Cruising speed:	550km/h (340mph) at 7620m (25,000ft)
Service ceiling:	9755m (32,000ft)
Range:	6760km (4200 miles)
Passengers + crew:	100 + 4

Boeing C-97G

S wiss-registered HB-ILZ was one of three ex-USAF KC-97Gs on wet lease to the International Red Cross in 1969–70 for relief missions to Biafra. Before leaving the United States, these aircraft were gutted of military equipment, including the air-refuelling installation and underwing tank/jet pylons, and refurbished for discharging a full cargo load in as little as 10 minutes. The KC-97G, the major production version with a run of 592 (out of a total of 888 military C/KC-97s), was developed to support Strategic Air Command's B-47 Stratojet strategic bomber force, with 20 tankers assigned to every SAC bomber wing. The KC-97 was gradually replaced by the KC-135A, which in turn was developed to support the Boeing B-52 bomber force. Many of the well-liked KC-97s continued in service in the transport role; some (KC-97L) were fitted with underwing jet booster pods.

Country of origin:	USA
Engines:	four 3500hp Pratt & Whitney R-4360 Wasp Major 28-cylinder radials
Wingspan:	43m (141ft)
Length:	33.6m (110ft)
Height:	11.65m (38ft)
Weight loaded:	66,135kg (145,800lb)
Cruising speed:	550km/h (340mph) at 7620m (25,000ft)
Service ceiling:	9755m (32,000ft)
Range:	6760km (4200 miles)
Passengers + crew:	100 + 4

Boeing KC-97G

KC-97G-120BO serial 52-2632, seen here, was one of the 592 basic G series with full provision for tanking, air refuelling and all forms of troop and cargo transport. Normal interior equipment provided for 96 equipped troops, or 69 stretcher cases, without removing transfer tanks and the boom operator's station. Tests with the 'Flying Boom' fuel-transfer equipment on KC-97As were followed by the production of KC-97E, KC-97F and KC-97G. Typically, the aircraft was developed out of all recognition. Internal fuel capacity was originally a little over 26,498 litres (6991 US gal), but from the KC-97E tanker, the addition of a group tank on the main floor in the fuselage raised the total to a remarkable 56,750 litres (14,974 US gal), almost all of which could be transferred through the 'Flying Boom' worked by an operator lying in the rear fuselage.

Country of origin:	USA
Engines:	four 3500hp Pratt & Whitney R-4360 Wasp Major 28-cylinder radials
Wingspan:	43m (141ft)
Length:	33.6m (110ft)
Height:	11.65m (38ft)
Weight loaded:	66,135kg (145,800lb)
Cruising speed:	550km/h (340mph) at 7620m (25,000ft)
Service ceiling:	9755m (32,000ft)
Range:	6760km (4200 miles)
Passengers + crew:	96 + 5

Boeing KC-97L

With its original serial number prefaced by the letter O (for obsolete), 52-0901 was a USAF KC-97L, originally delivered as a KC-97G-110-BO, rebuilt by Hayes and fitted with J47-GE25A booster jet pods in place of the original long-range underwing tanks. The pods were taken from the KC-97's predecessor in the flying tanker role, the Boeing KB-50, and gave the KC-97L a much-needed speed and altitude boost to operate more effectively with its receiver aircraft, the B-47 Stratojet. The only other C-97s with similar performance were two YC-97Js fitted with 5700hp Pratt & Whitney T34-5 turboprops. All mainstream tankers were designed for rapid conversion to transports, with the removal of the fuselage tanks, boom and operator's station. KC-97L 52-0901 is seen in the insignia of the Illinois Air Guard; some National Air Guard units used the type in Vietnam.

Country of origin:	USA
Engines:	four 3500hp Pratt & Whitney R-4360 Wasp Major 28-cylinder radials, two J47-GE-25A turbojets
Wingspan:	43m (141ft)
Length:	33.6m (110ft)
Height:	11.65m (38ft)
Weight loaded:	66,135kg (145,800lb)
Cruising speed:	550km/h (340mph) at 7620m (25,000ft)
Service ceiling:	9755m (32,000ft)
Range:	6760km (4200 miles)
Passengers + crew:	96 + 5

Boeing VC-137A (707-153)

The Boeing 707 had numerous military applications, not all of them in the transport role. This 707-153, however, was operated as an airborne command post under the designation VC-137A. It was remodelled with a 22-seat VIP interior and carried an extensive communications fit. The forward area of the cabin contained the communications centre, galley, and an eight-seat compartment; the centre portion comprised the Airborne Command HQ, with conference table, swivel chairs, projection screen and two convertible sofa/bunks. The aft cabin contained 14 double reclining passenger seats, two tables, three galleys, two toilets and closets. The first VC137A, 58-6970 shown here, flew for the first time on 7 April 1959, and was delivered to the 89th Military Airlift Wing, with two others; they were later re-engined with JT3D turbofans and designated VC-137Bs.

Country of origin:	USA
Engines:	four Pratt & Whitney JT4A-3 turbojets of 7167kg (15,800lb) thrust each
Wingspan:	43.33m (142ft 2in)
Length:	46.6m (152ft 11in)
Height:	12.67m (41ft 7in)
Weight loaded:	141,520kg (312,000lb)
Cruising speed:	972km/h (604mph) at 7620m (25,000ft)
Service ceiling:	11,340m (37,200ft)
Range:	7450km (4630 miles)
Passengers + crew:	22 + 4

Boulton & Paul P.64 Mailplane

Notable mainly for the design of some exceedingly ugly, but quite successful, bomber types in the years between the two world wars, the British engineering and aircraft manufacturing company Boulton & Paul had been engaged in building Sopwith Camels and 11/2 Strutters during World War I. In 1929, in response to an Imperial Airways requirement for an aircraft capable of carrying a 454kg (1000lb) payload over a range of 1609km (1000 miles), the company developed the P.64 Mailplane, the prototype of which was destroyed in an accident some six months after it first flew. Boulton & Paul then produced a lighter, modified version designated P.71A. Two examples were delivered to Imperial Airways as 13-seat passenger (or seven-seat VIP transport) aircraft. Both aircraft were accidentally destroyed, in October 1935 and September 1936.

Country of origin:	GB
Engines:	two 490hp Armstrong Siddeley Jaguar VIA radials
Wingspan:	16.46m (54ft)
Length:	13.46m (44ft 2in)
Height:	4.62m (15ft 2in)
Weight loaded:	4309kg (9500lb)
Cruising speed:	314km/h (195mph)
Service ceiling:	4575m (15,000ft)
Range:	966km (600 miles)
Passengers + crew:	13 + 2

Breguet 393T

The Breguet 393T three-engined commercial aircraft was a straightforward development of two earlier designs, the 390T of 1931, and the 392T. Only one example of the latter was built, being completed as a freight carrier. The 393T could carry 10 passengers, seated in comfortable armchairs adjacent to large windows. The fuselage was fabric covered. The prototype Breguet 393T flew for the first time in 1933, and deliveries of production aircraft to Air France began in the summer of 1934. Air France's Breguets were operated on the trans-Mediterranean leg of the air route to South America, and on scheduled services to North Africa. F-ANEJ, seen here, was one of the aircraft used on the Toulouse–Casablanca route; it later operated on internal European services. Five Breguets were still in Air France service, in Africa, at the outbreak of World War II.

Country of origin:	France
Engines:	three 350hp Gnome-Rhone 7Kd Titan Major radials
Wingspan:	20.71m (67ft 11in)
Length:	14.76m (48ft 5in)
Height:	not known
Weight loaded:	6000kg (13,228lb)
Cruising speed:	249km/h (155mph)
Service ceiling:	5850m (19,190ft)
Range:	975km (606 miles)
Passengers + crew:	10 + 2

Breguet Bre XIX Super TR

On 1 September 1930, a red biplane piloted by Dieudonné Costes and Maurice Bellonte, took off from Le Bourget, Paris, and set course for New York, with the objective of making an east–west Atlantic crossing. The aircraft, a Breguet XIX Super Bidon called Pointe d'Interrogation (Question Mark), arrived at its destination after a flight of 37 hours 18 minutes, covering a distance of 5950km (3697 miles). In September 1929, the same aircraft had established a new world record by flying from Le Bourget to a destination in Manchuria, a distance of 7905km (4912 miles), in 51 hours 19 minutes. In December 1929, it had beaten the world closed-circuit distance record, flying 8029km (4989 miles) non-stop. The Bre XIX Super TR was derived from the Breguet XIX reconnaissance aircraft. Note the stork insignia of the Escadrille des Cigognes on the fuselage side.

Country of origin:	France
Engine:	one 650hp Hispano-Suiza 12Nb 12-cylinder liquid-cooled V-type
Wingspan:	18.3m (60ft)
Length:	10.41m (34ft 1in)
Height:	4.06m (13ft 3in)
Weight loaded:	6150kg (13,558lb)
Cruising speed:	245km/h (152mph)
Service ceiling:	6700m (22,000ft)
Range:	9000km (5592 miles)
Crew:	2

Bristol 175 Britannia

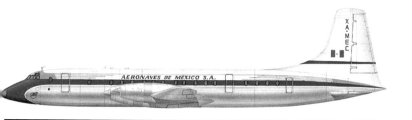

In 1947, BOAC issued a requirement for a Medium Range Empire (MRE) transport aircraft, and the Bristol Aeroplane Company responded with a design envisaging an aircraft powered by four Centaurus piston engines. A contract for 25 aircraft was signed in July 1949, but in the following year, BOAC expressed a preference for the Proteus turboprop, and it was with this powerplant that the prototype Bristol 175 Britannia made its first flight on 16 August 1952. The type entered service on BOAC's London–Johannesburg service on 1 February 1957. Britannias ranged far and wide in their operational life, this example being one of two which were on the Mexican civil register. Originally G-ANCB for BOAC, it was not taken up by the airline and passed to Aeronaves de Mexico SA in 1957, and was eventually withdrawn from operations in 1965.

Country of origin:	GB
Engines:	Four 3780hp Bristol Proteus 705 turboprops
Wingspan:	43.36m (142ft 3in)
Length:	34.75m (114ft)
Height:	11.17m (36ft 8in)
Weight loaded:	70,307kg (155,000lb)
Cruising speed:	582km/h (362mph)
Service ceiling:	7315m (24,000ft)
Range:	7770km (4828 miles)
Passengers + crew:	61–90 + 4

Bristol Britannia Series 312

The Series 312 Britannia carried out a series of route-proving flights over the North Atlantic soon after being delivered to the airline, flying non-stop from London to New York and return. Eighteen Series 312 Britannias were built, many passing to other airlines after being retired from BOAC. Three Britannia 312s were sold to the Israeli airline, El Al, the first delivered in September 1957. They were swiftly put into operation on the Tel Aviv–New York service, flying the 9817km (6100 mile) route in about 15 hours. Six examples of a later variant, the Series 314, were delivered to Canadian Pacific; one set a record time of 11 hours 44 minutes for the 7564km (4,700 mile) Vancouver–Tokyo route on 20 September 1958. Although a fine aircraft, the Britannia had entered the world airliner market too late; operators now had their eyes firmly fixed on all-jet equipment.

Country of origin:	GB
Engines:	Four 4120hp Bristol Proteus 755 turboprops
Wingspan:	43.36m (142ft 3in)
Length:	34.75m (114ft)
Height:	11.17m (36ft 8in)
Weight loaded:	70,307kg (155,000lb)
Cruising speed:	582km/h (362mph)
Service ceiling:	7315m (24,000ft)
Range:	7770km (4828 miles)
Passengers + crew:	93–99 (normal) + 4

Bristol Britannia Series 312

One Series 312 Bristol Britannia that served exclusively with British airlines was G-AOVI. Originally with BOAC, it also saw service with British United and Caledonian Airways. In March 1968, it passed to Monarch Airlines, with whom it served until February 1972, when it was scrapped. One major Britannia user was the Royal Air Force; the aircraft was the first turboprop-powered machine to serve with RAF Transport Command. The first of 20 Britannia C.1s flew on 29 December 1958, and the type entered service with No 99 Squadron in 1959, followed by No 511 Squadron. The aircraft was widely used on long-range strategic missions all over the world, and provided vital support for the Army's United Kingdom Strategic Reserve. Three Britannia C.2s were also delivered; these differed from the C.1 in having a large cargo door.

Country of origin:	GB
Engines:	four 4120hp each Bristol Proteus 755 turboprops
Wingspan:	43.36m (142ft 3in)
Length:	34.75m (114ft)
Height:	11.17m (36ft 8in)
Weight loaded:	70,307kg (155,000lb)
Cruising speed:	582km/h (362mph)
Service ceiling:	7315m (24,000ft)
Range:	7770km (4828 miles)
Passengers + crew:	93–99 (normal) + 4

Bristol Britannia 318

Although it relied mainly on aircraft of Soviet origin, the Cuban National Airline Cubana also used a number of western airliners, one of which was the Britannia Model 318. The example shown here illustrates one of the earlier colour schemes worn by the aircraft. Only 85 Britannias were built, and three of these were involved in major fatal accidents while in airline service, none of which was attributable to any defect in the aircraft. The first occurred on 29 February 1964, when Britannia Series 312 G-AOVO of British Eagle International Airlines crashed near Innsbruck, Austria, with the loss of 83 lives; the second on 1 September 1966, when Britannia 102 of Britannia Airways crashed while attempting to land at Ljubljana, Yugoslavia, killing 98 on board; and the third on 20 April 1967, when a Globe Air Britannia crashed in Cyprus with the loss of 126 lives.

Country of origin:	GB
Engines:	four 4120hp Bristol Proteus 755 turboprops
Wingspan:	43.36m (142ft 3in)
Length:	34.75m (114ft)
Height:	11.17m (36ft 8in)
Weight loaded:	70,307kg (155,000lb)
Cruising speed:	582km/h (362mph)
Service ceiling:	7315m (24,000ft)
Range:	7770km (4828 miles)
Passengers + crew:	93–99 (normal) + 4

Bristol Freighter Mk 21

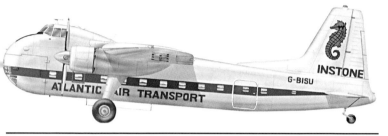

Far from being glamorous, the Bristol 170 was a large, purposeful freight and passenger carrier that gave sterling service all over the world, most notably as a cross-Channel car ferry. The Type 170 was originally intended as a military freighter for the RAF, but that requirement ceased with the end of World War II. Two prototypes were flown, the Type 170 Freighter for passengers or freight (2 December 1945), and the Type 170 Wayfarer, a passenger-only version (30 April 1946). In 1948, the first of 92 Bristol Freighter Mk 21 aircraft appeared; on 14 July, this variant inaugurated the Silver City Airways car ferry service across the English Channel. Production continued with the Mk 31, which had more power and increased all-up weight, followed in 1953 by the Mk 32, which had a redesigned tail unit and a lengthened nose. In all, 214 Bristol 170s were built.

Country of origin:	GB
Engines:	two 1690hp Bristol Hercules 672 radials
Wingspan:	32.9m (108ft)
Length:	22.4m (73ft 4in)
Height:	6.6m (21ft 8in)
Weight loaded:	18,144kg (40,000lb)
Cruising speed:	266km/h (165mph)
Service ceiling:	6400m (21,000ft)
Range:	790km (491 miles)
Passengers + crew:	15–34 + 3

Bristol Type 32 Bullet

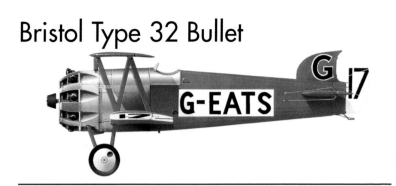

Although designed as a prototype fighter, it was as a racing aircraft that the Bristol Type 32 Bullet achieved a brief moment of fame when it gained second place in the 1921 Aerial Derby at Croydon. The Bristol Aeroplane Company's original intention was to use the sole Type 32, which was married to a Jupiter engine, as a demonstration aircraft, in the hope that it would attract sufficient interest and allow the company to proceed with the development of a fighter version. The combination of Jupiter and Type 32 proved to be a disappointing one, however, despite the fact that Bristol took great pains to streamline the Bullet as much as possible, and overcome the large radial engine mounted in the nose. The Bullet airframe was scrapped in 1924, but the Jupiter engine became one of the success stories of the 1920s.

Country of origin:	GB
Engine:	one 450hp Bristol Jupiter II radial
Wingspan:	9.51m (31ft 2in)
Length:	7.35m (24ft 1in)
Height:	2.95m (9ft 8in)
Weight loaded:	998kg (2200lb)
Maximum speed:	249km/h (155mph)
Service ceiling:	not known
Range:	not known
Crew:	1

Bristol Type 62 Ten-Seater

The Bristol Type 62 was the product of a short-lived era when commercial aviation in the United Kingdom had the benefit of government subsidies. Originally envisaged with a four-wheel undercarriage and accommodation for six passengers, the design was modified to accept nine passengers plus the pilot, who sat in an open cockpit on a level with the upper wing. The first of four aircraft flew in June 1921, and the front set of wheels was removed before the aircraft entered its flight-testing phase, first at Croydon and then at Martlesham Heath. Upon completion of the trials, the aircraft was purchased by the Air Council, who sold it to the Instone Air Line for use on the London–Paris route. Instone also bought the second and fourth Type 62s, and operated them until 1926 as Type 75s; the fourth was later converted into an air ambulance, Type 79.

Country of origin:	GB
Engine:	one 450hp Napier Lion radial
Wingspan:	17.07m (56ft)
Length:	12.34m (40.6ft)
Height:	3.35m (11ft)
Weight loaded:	3064kg (6755lb)
Cruising speed:	177km/h (110mph)
Service ceiling:	2590m (8500ft)
Range:	965km (600 miles)
Passengers + crew:	9 + 1

British Aerospace (Hawker Siddeley) 125-800

HB-VIK

From the mid-1980s, the production version of the British Aerospace 125 was the BAe 125-800, first flown as a prototype on 26 May 1983, and certified on 30 May 1984. The Series 800 is powered by two Garrett turbofans that afford major improvements in take-off, climb and 'hot-and-high' performance, and maximum speed, and provide adequate with-reserves range for non-stop, coast-to-coast operation in the United States, or for transatlantic flights. Many changes were made in developing the Series 800 airframe, including a curved windscreen, redesigned outer wing panels of increased span for reduced drag, greater fuel capacity, enhanced aerodynamic efficiency, and a larger ventral fuel tank. Shown here is one of two Series 800 aircraft that operate with the Swiss Air Ambulance Service, with provision for two stretchers and medical attendants.

Country of origin:	GB
Engines:	two Garrett TFE731-5R turbofans of 1948kg (4300lb) thrust each
Wingspan:	15.66m (51ft 4in)
Length:	15.59m (51ft 2in)
Height:	5.36m (17ft 7in)
Weight loaded:	12,428kg (27,400lb)
Cruising speed:	741km/h (460mph)
Service ceiling:	13,106m (43,000ft)
Range:	8946km (5560 miles)
Passengers + crew:	not known

British Aerospace (Hawker Siddeley) 748 Series 2A

A combination of modern technology and solid design made the HS.748 highly appealing to operators throughout the world who needed an uncomplicated transport aircraft that would function reliably in all kinds of terrain and extremes of climate. The type sold very well in Africa, Asia and South America, and many were still in service at the dawn of a new century, carrying out their daily domestic tasks between major cities and primitive airfields in remote areas. The 48-seat aircraft of Bahamasair, pictured here, are mainly used on services linking the islands in the Bahamas chain and the Turks and Caicos. There were 11 HS.748 variants, culminating in the Andover R.Mk.4, a single C.Mk.1 converted for military photo-reconnaissance duties with No 60 Squadron. This unit was responsible for communications with the then divided city of Berlin.

Country of origin:	GB
Engines:	two Rolls-Royce 2280hp Dart RDa7 Mk535-2 turboprops
Wingspan:	30.02m (98ft 6in)
Length:	20.42m (67ft)
Height:	7.57m (24ft 10in)
Weight loaded:	21,092kg (46,500lb)
Cruising speed:	452km/h (281mph) at 4570m (15,000ft)
Service ceiling:	7620m (25,000ft)
Range:	3132km (1946 miles)
Passengers + crew:	40–58 + 2

British Aerospace (Hawker Siddeley) BAe 125 Series 2

In 1963, the Royal Air Force ordered 20 Hawker Siddeley 125s, de Havilland having been absorbed into the Hawker Siddeley Group. The aircraft were Series 2s, similar to the 1B but with lower-powered Viper 520 engines. Known in RAF service as the Dominie T.Mk.1, the aircraft were used as navigational trainers, and operated by No 6 Flying Training School at RAF Finningley near Doncaster, replacing piston-engined Varsities. From October 1973, Finningley was responsible for all non-pilot aircrew training in the RAF. In December 1976, the Dominies began blind-navigation, low-level training with the use of radar, and in 1977, with the arrival of Dominies from the RAF College, Cranwell, all the training Dominies in the RAF were assembled at Finningley. Training sorties normally involved two students and an instructor.

Country of Origin:	GB
Engines:	two Rolls-Royce Bristol Viper turbojets of 1525kg (3360lb) thrust each
Wingspan:	14.33m (47ft)
Length:	14.45m (47ft 5in)
Height:	5.03m (16ft 6in)
Weight loaded:	10,568kg (23,300lb)
Cruising speed:	724km/h (450mph) at 11,300m (37,000ft)
Service ceiling:	12,500m (41,000ft)
Range:	3120km (1940 miles)
Passengers + crew:	6–12 + 2

British Aerospace (Hawker Siddeley) BAe 125 Series 3B

In February 1961, the de Havilland Aircraft Company announced that it was developing a 'mini' jetliner successor to the DH 104 Dove feederliner and business aircraft. Designated DH 125 Jet Dragon, the aircraft was to seat six or eight passengers in a fully pressurized and air-conditioned executive cabin, powered by two Bristol Siddeley Viper turbojets. The first aircraft, G-ARYA, was rolled out in July 1962 (the name Jet Dragon had been dropped), and flew for the first time on 13 August. Eight DH 125 Series 1 examples were built, including the prototypes; the first customer delivery was made to the West German company Krupp GmbH of Essen on 26 February 1964, a foretaste of the success the aircraft was to enjoy. Shown here is a Series 3B used by the Australian airline QANTAS as a Boeing 707 crew trainer in addition to communications duties.

Country of Origin:	GB
Engines:	two Rolls-Royce Bristol Viper turbojets of 1525kg (3360lb) thrust each
Wingspan:	14.33m (47ft)
Length:	14.45m (47ft 5in)
Height:	5.03m (16ft 6in)
Weight loaded:	10,568kg (23,300lb)
Cruising speed:	724km/h (450mph) at 11,300m (37,000ft)
Service ceiling:	12,500m (41,000ft)
Range:	3120km (1940 miles)
Passengers + crew:	6–12 + 2

British Aerospace (Hawker Siddeley) BAe 125 Series 700

The HS (BAe) 125 admirably fitted the RAF requirement for a fast communications aircraft, and 12 were purchased for use by No 32 (Communications) Squadron, based just outside London at Northolt. Four of the aircraft acquired were CC. Mk.1s (Series 400), two were CC.Mk.2s (Series 600), and six CC.Mk.3s (Series 700), one of which is illustrated here. The Series 700 was first announced in May 1976, and the prototype, converted from a Series 600, made its first flight on 28 June 1976. The Series 700 was the first turbofan-engined BAe 125, powered by two Garrett AirResearch TFE-731-1-3-1Hs, which offered much-improved fuel economy and increased range. Other improvements included the use of countersunk riveting in place of the mushroom-head riveting, the addition of windscreen wiper fairings, and the redesign of the ventral fin.

Country of Origin:	GB
Engines:	two Garret AirResearch TFE731 turbofans of 1676kg (3700lb) thrust each
Wingspan:	14.33m (47ft)
Length:	14.45m (47ft 5in)
Height:	5.03m (16ft 6in)
Weight loaded:	10,568kg (23,300lb)
Cruising speed:	808km/h (502mph) at 8380m (27,500ft)
Service ceiling:	12,500m (41,000ft)
Range:	3929km (2442 miles)
Passengers + crew:	8–10 + 2

British Aerospace BAe 146

The exceptionally quiet, fuel-efficient BAe 146 short-haul four-jet transport flew for the first time in its Series 100 version on 3 September 1981, bearing the apt registration G-SSSH. Type certification followed early in 1983, and Dan-Air, one of whose aircraft is seen here, began scheduled services on 27 May that year. It was an indication of the 146's capability that one of its European destinations in service with Dan-Air was Innsbruck, which had never previously been served by scheduled jet airliners. Production of the 146-100 continued for customers with short-field and noise-reduction requirements, and two aircraft were purchased by the UK government for service with the Queen's Flight. The 146 proved to be at its best in shuttling sizeable numbers of passengers between regional airports and major route centres.

Country of origin:	GB
Engines:	four Avco Lycoming LF502R-3 turbofans of 3093kg (6800lb) thrust each
Wingspan:	26.34m (86ft 5in)
Length:	26.16m (85ft 10in)
Height:	8.61m (28ft 3in)
Weight loaded:	33,838kg (74,600lb)
Cruising speed:	776km/h (482mph) at 7925m (26,000ft)
Service ceiling:	11,280m (37,000ft)
Range:	2180km (1355 miles)
Passengers + crew:	88–109 + 2

British Aerospace BAe 146

Pacific Southwest Airlines, one of whose aircraft is shown here, was a major user of the BAe 146, flying Series 200s along the California–Nevada corridor. The airline merged with USAir in 1989 under the latter's name, which then changed to US Airways in February 1997. Another major customer is the large Ansett concern in Australia, the variant involved being the 146QT. This version performed so well when evaluated by the TNT global package and cargo group that the Australian conglomerate agreed to take five years' production of QTs, a total of 72 aircraft, in stages, for use by TNT Couriers, or for sale and lease by Ansett Worldwide Aviation Services. TNT's 146 fleet, largely confined to Europe, operates a gruelling, night-long schedule involving extremely rapid turnarounds, making use of the fact that the 146 is quiet enough to avoid night-time curfews.

Country of origin:	GB
Engines:	four Avco Lycoming LF502R-3 turbofans of 3093kg (6800lb) thrust each
Wingspan:	26.34m (86ft 5in)
Length:	28.55m (93ft 7in)
Height:	8.61m (28ft 3in)
Weight loaded:	42184kg (93,000lb)
Cruising speed:	776km/h (482mph) at 7925m (26,000ft)
Service ceiling:	11,280m (37,000ft)
Range:	2180km (1355 miles)
Crew:	2

British Aerospace BAe 146 Series 100

The position of the 146's wing on top of the fuselage was dictated by the need to keep the intakes of the four turbofan engines well clear of disturbed air at surface level, and by the fitting of powerful high-lift flaps to enhance short take-off and landing (STOL) performance. This arrangement left an uninterrupted upper surface to provide high lift, and made it possible to put the fuselage close to the ground so that, as a customer option, passengers could board via short airstairs at each end of the cabin, making the aircraft independent of airport jetways or stairways. The high wing led to the main landing gear being mounted in the fuselage. It offers a wider track than that of a C-130 Hercules, giving excellent stability on rough strips or in crosswinds. Illustrated is one of 10 BAe 146 Series 100 aircraft ordered by the Civil Aviation Administration of China.

Country of origin:	GB
Engines:	four Avco Lycoming LF502R-3 turbofans of 3093kg (6800lb) thrust each
Wingspan:	26.34m (86ft 5in)
Length:	26.16m (85ft 10in)
Height:	8.61m (28ft 3in)
Weight loaded:	33,838kg (74,600lb)
Cruising speed:	776km/h (482mph) at 7925m (26,000ft)
Service ceiling:	11,280m (37,000ft)
Range:	2180km (1355 miles)
Passengers + crew:	88–109 + 2

British Aerospace BAe 146 Series 200

It soon became obvious that some operators would trade the 146-100's amazing field capabilities for increased payload. Accordingly, the fuselage was stretched by five frames (a length of 2.39m (7.8ft)) to produce the almost identical 146-200. The first Series 200 was flown on 1 August 1982, and the first scheduled service was flown on 27 June 1983, only a month after the start of Series 100 operations. Almost immediately, the 200 became the baseline standard aircraft, and the launch pad for a cargo version (the 146QT Quiet Trader), a VIP executive version (the Statesman), and four military versions: the STA (Small Tactical Airlifter), the MSL (Military Side Loader), the MT (Military Tanker) and the BAe 146M, a much-modified version with a lowered floor, rear-ramp doors and tandem main-landing gears. Seen here is a BAe 146-200 of Air Wisconsin, the first US customer.

Country of origin:	GB
Engines:	four Avco Lycoming LF502R-3 turbofans of 3093kg (6800lb) thrust each
Wingspan:	26.34m (86ft 5in)
Length:	28.55m (93ft 7in)
Height:	8.61m (28ft 3in)
Weight loaded:	42184kg (93,000lb)
Cruising speed:	776km/h (482mph) at 7925m (26,000ft)
Service ceiling:	11,280m (37,000ft)
Range:	2180km (1355 miles)
Passengers + crew:	111 + 2–3

Britten-Norman BN-2 Islander

One of Britain's greatest civil aviation success stories of the post-war years did not originate with a main manufacturer, but with a small company established at Bembridge Aerodrome on the Isle of Wight by two aeronautical engineers, John Britten and Desmond Norman. Their BN-2 Islander design and its many developments have sold widely around the world, its toughness and dependability having proved ideal for many small operators, both civil and military. Design work on the Britten-Norman BN-2 began in 1963, and the prototype, G-ATCT, flew on 13 June 1965. The production prototype, G-ATWU, made its first flight on 20 August. British launch customers in 1967 were Glos-Air and Loganair. The Islander was superbly suited to conditions in difficult terrain; seen here is an aircraft of Munz Northern Airlines, which flew the type in Alaska.

Country of origin:	GB
Engines:	two 260hp Lycoming O-540-E4C5 6-cylinder air-cooled
Wingspan:	14.94m (49ft)
Length:	10.87m (35ft 8in)
Height:	4.16m (13ft 8in)
Weight loaded:	2857kg (6300lb)
Cruising speed:	257km/h (160mph)
Service ceiling:	6,005m (19,700ft)
Range:	670km (425 miles)
Passengers + crew:	9 + 2

Britten-Norman Trislander

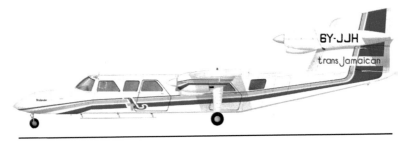

A simple way of extending the Islander design to carry far greater loads was to stretch the fuselage and add a third engine on top of the fin. The result was the Trislander, offering 17 seats in maximum density as opposed to nine in the Islander. The first Trislander was G-ATWU, the converted production prototype of the Islander, which flew on 11 September 1970. The name 'Trislander' was adopted in January 1971, UK certification was granted in May, and the first customer delivery to Aurigny Airlines in the Channel Islands followed on 29 June, only 292 days after the aircraft's maiden flight. Further developments of the Trislander included the BN-2A Mk III-2 with an extended nose, the BN-2 Mk III-3 with an autofeather system, and the BN-2 Mk III-4, which had a stand-by, tail-cone rocket system to provide extra thrust in the event of an engine failure on take-off.

Country of origin:	GB
Engines:	three 260hp Lycoming O-540-E4C5 6-cylinder air-cooled
Wingspan:	16.15m (53ft)
Length:	15.01m (49ft 3in)
Height:	4.32m (14ft 2in)
Weight loaded:	4536kg (10,000lb)
Cruising speed:	241 km/h (150mph)
Service ceiling:	4010m (13,156ft)
Range:	1610km (1,000 miles)
Passengers + crew:	17 + 2

Canadair CC-106 Yukon

In 1954, Canadair took out a licence for the Bristol Britannia as the basis for a maritime patrol aircraft, using only the basic airframe in what became the CL-28 Argus, 33 of which were produced. Canadair's licence extended to a transport version for what was then the RCAF, and this was very competently engineered at Montreal using the Rolls-Royce Tyne engine. Large cargo doors were added to the port side, and there were many other changes, the resulting aircraft flying on 15 November 1959. Designated CL-44-6, it became the CC-106 Yukon in service. Two CC-106 Yukons, one of which is shown here, were used as VIP transports by No 412 Squadron RCAF. Together with the 10 aircraft allocated to No 437 Squadron, they differed from later civil aircraft in having normal cargo doors and no hinged tail. They were replaced by Boeing 707s (designated CC-137) in 1971.

Country of origin:	Canada
Engines:	four 550hp Rolls-Royce Tyne turboprops
Wingspan:	43.35m (142ft 3.6in)
Length:	41.65m (136ft 8in)
Height:	11.76m (38ft 7in)
Weight loaded:	95,250kg (210,000lb
Cruising speed:	463km/h (288mph) at7620m (25,000ft)
Service ceiling:	9144m (30,000ft)
Range:	4625km (2874 miles)
Passengers + crew:	variable + 4

Canadair CL-215

The Canadair CL-215 is the only purpose-built, fire-fighting aircraft in the world, and is designed to scoop up huge volumes of water into built-in tanks as it skims the surface. There are two main water tanks, arranged left and right in the centre of the fuselage, each with a capacity of 2673 litres (705 gallons). They can be pumped full on the ground through a hose, then dumped over the fire through a large drop door, resembling a bomb door, in the planing bottom under each tank. It is then possible to refill the tanks by extending retractable probes under the aircraft, and lowering these into the water as the aircraft flies very low over the surface at 130 km/h (80mph). Using this method, it takes 10 seconds to fill the tanks, compared with two minutes using maximum-pressure hoses on the ground. Illustration shows a CL215 in the colours of the former Yugoslav Air Force.

Country of origin:	Canada
Engines:	two 2100hp Pratt & Whitney Double Wasp radials
Wingspan:	28.6m (93ft 10in)
Length:	19.82m (65ft)
Height:	8.98m (29ft 5in)
Weight loaded:	19,731kg (43,500lb)
Cruising speed:	291 km/h (181 mph)
Service ceiling:	not known
Range:	2095 km (1300 miles)
Passengers + crew:	2 + 2

Canadair CL-215

Piston engines were chosen for the CL-215 because it was designed to operate almost always at very low level, where turboprops would be relatively inefficient. The Pratt & Whitney R-2800 Double Wasp was the obvious choice. The all-metal airframe was designed to withstand harsh use, and as there was no requirement for high speed, the wing was basic and simple, with an extremely deep section and rectangular plan shape, carrying big hydraulically-powered slotted flaps, but manual ailerons. The hull did not have to be especially large, because in the aircraft's primary firefighting role, the load of water occcupies quite a modest volume. The CL-215 carries a normal flight deck crew of two, but for patrol and similar missions, there is provision for a navigator, flight engineer and two observers. Large square doors are fitted front and rear on the port side.

Country of origin:	Canada
Engines:	two 2100hp Pratt & Whitney R-2800 Double Wasp radials
Wingspan:	28.6m (93ft 10in)
Length:	19.82m (65ft)
Height:	8.98m (29ft 5in)
Weight loaded:	19,731kg (43,500lb)
Cruising speed:	291 km/h (181 mph)
Service ceiling:	not known
Range:	2095 km (1300 miles)
Passengers + crew:	2 + 2

Cessna 150

In the mid-1950s, the Cessna Aircraft Company, with its wide experience of producing military trainers and observation aircraft, identified a requirement for a dual-purpose, two-seat, training-and-touring, light aircraft for civil use. The outcome was the Cessna Model 150, which flew for the first time in September 1957, and entered production in August 1958. Cessna's original Model 150 trainer, pictured here, had a square tail and a 100hp Continental O-200A engine. Subsequent models featured a swept-back tail, an all-round vision cockpit (introduced in the Cessna 150D of 1964), and a tubular steel undercarriage; the ultimate Cessna 150L was powered by an 110hp Lycoming engine. The Cessna 150 was produced both at the parent factory, Wichita, and at Reims, France. By the end of 1963, the company had sold over 2200 Cessna 150s.

Country of origin:	USA
Engine:	one 100hp Continental O-200A 4-cylinder air-cooled
Wingspan:	9.97m (32ft 8in)
Length:	7.01m (23ft)
Height:	2.77m (9ft 1in)
Weight loaded:	726kg (1600lb)
Cruising speed:	188km/h (102kt) at 2133m (7000ft)
Service ceiling:	3850m (12,630ft)
Range:	767km (475 miles)
Passengers + crew:	1 + 1

Cessna 172/T-41

The four-seat Cessna 172 was the logical next step after the successful Cessna 150, featuring a 54kg (120lb) baggage space aft of the rear two seats. In July 1964, the USAF ordered 170 early-model 172s under the designation T-41A for delivery between September 1964 and July 1965. USAF student pilots completed about 30 hours of basic training on the T-41A, before passing on to the Cessna T-37B jet primary trainer. T-41As were also ordered by the Ecuadorean and Peruvian Air Forces. In 1965, Cessna began production of a more powerful 172 variant, the R172E; this was ordered by the USAF as the T-41B. The T-41B was later ordered by the air forces of Greece (shown here), Peru, Ecuador, Colombia, Turkey and Honduras. The T-41C and T-41D were fitted with fixed-pitch and constant-speed propellers respectively. The specification refers to the T-41B.

Country of origin:	USA
Engine:	one 210hp Continental IO-360-D 6-cylinder air-cooled
Wingspan:	10.90m (35ft 9in)
Length:	8.20m (26ft 11in)
Height:	3.02m (9ft 11in)
Weight loaded:	1135kg (2500lb)
Cruising speed:	233km/h (145mph) at sea level
Service ceiling:	5335m (17,503ft)
Range:	1285km (800 miles) at 3050m (10,000ft)
Passengers + crew:	4

Cessna 185 Skywagon

The Cessna 172 was followed on the Wichita production line by the Cessna 177 (the deluxe version of which was called the Cardinal), and the Model 180 Skywagon, which had a tailwheel configuration. The success of the Model 180 resulted in a demand for a higher-powered version, and Cessna produced the Model 185 Skywagon, powered by a 260hp engine. It had seats for five passengers, and could be made even more productive by the fitting of the optional under-fuselage cargo pannier illustrated. The prototype Cessna 185 flew for the first time in July 1960, and the first production model was completed in March 1961. The aircraft could be fitted with floats or skis. The Cessna 185 was the subject of lucrative USAF contracts, serving as a light transport/liaison aircraft under the designation U-17A/B.

Country of origin:	USA
Engine:	one 300hp Continental IO-520-D 6-cylinder air-cooled
Wingspan:	11.02m (36ft 2in)
Length:	7.85m (25ft 9in)
Height:	2.36m (7ft 9in)
Weight loaded:	1519kg (3350lb)
Cruising speed:	272km/h (169mph) at 2285m (7500ft)
Service ceiling:	5229m (17,150ft)
Range:	1384km (860 miles)
Passengers + crew:	4

Cessna 210 Centurion

The Cessna 210 was the first production high-wing, light aircraft to be fitted with a retractable undercarriage, the main gear legs having a complex twisting action to allow them to fold into the lower fuselage. Later Model 210 Centurions, such as N3754C pictured here, had all-round vision cockpits and full cantilever wings. The development aircraft was a Cessna 182 (N1296), which flew for the first time in 1956 with the retractable wheels, and a 260hp Continental IO-470S engine. A new engine cowling with a large chin fairing was required, and the higher engine power demanded the addition of a large dorsal fin fairing to the vertical tail. Production Model 210, fitted with down-turned wingtips, began rolling off the line in 1960, and by September that year, 542 aircraft had been delivered. Deliveries of the Centurion and the Turbo Centurion exceeded 8500.

Country of origin:	USA
Engine:	one 285hp Continental IO-520-A 6-cylinder air-cooled
Wingspan:	11.20m (36ft 9in)
Length:	8.61m (28ft 3in)
Height:	2.95m (9ft 8in)
Weight loaded:	1723kg (3800lb)
Cruising speed:	303km/h (188mph) at 2285m (7500ft)
Service ceiling:	4724m (15,500ft)
Range:	2011km (1250 miles)
Passengers + crew:	6

Cessna 650 Citation III

The late 1970s and early 1980s were lean times for business aviation. First produced in 1979, and bearing little resemblance to its straight-winged predecessors, the Citations I and II, the Citation III was the first of the Cessna jets to provide a truly intercontinental range but, like its contemporary the Gates 55 Longhorn, sales did not match those of the previous generation. Both aircraft were powered by a pair of Garrett TFE731 engines, and both represented a major new design departure by their parent companies; they were also, aesthetically, very attractive aircraft. In the case of the Citation III, however, a generally poor economic climate brought an end to Cessna's production run after only 189 had left the factory line. The majority of these went to existing Citation customers in the United States, many of whom were trading in their older models.

Country of origin:	USA
Engines:	two Garrett TFE731-3B-100S turbofans of 1653kg (3644lb) thrust each
Wingspan:	16.33m (53ft 7in)
Length:	16.93m (55ft 6in)
Height:	5.16m (16ft 10in)
Weight loaded:	9979kg (22,000lb)
Cruising speed:	541km/h (336mph)
Service ceiling:	15,544m (51,000ft)
Range:	4352km (2704 miles)
Passengers + crew:	10 + 2

Consolidated 16 Commodore

In 1929, a newly formed (and short-lived) commercial aviation company called the New York, Rio and Buenos Aires Line (NYRBA) opened an air route to South America in direct competition with Pan American, using solitary Sikorsky S.38 amphibian, a twin-engined aircraft developed specifically for use on routes to Central America. In February 1930, NYRBA inaugurated a Miami–Buenos Aires service with another flying-boat type, the Consolidated Commodore, a large aircraft that initially could carry 20 passengers over a distance of 1610km (1000 miles). NYRBA had taken delivery of 10 Commodores when the company was taken over by Pan American, which also acquired four aircraft that had yet to be delivered. Pan American operated its Commodores on the longest oversea non-stop route of the time, flying from Jamaica to Panama.

Country of origin:	USA
Engines:	two 575hp Pratt & Whitney Hornet B 9-cylinder radials
Wingspan:	30.48m (100ft)
Length:	18.79m (61ft 8in)
Height:	5.82m (19ft 1in)
Weight loaded:	11,460kg (25,265lb)
Cruising speed:	174km/h (108mph)
Service ceiling:	3050m (10,000ft)
Range:	1610km (1000 miles)
Passengers + crew:	20–32 + 3

Consolidated PBY Catalina

Although the Consolidated Catalina is best remembered for its wartime service as a maritime patrol and anti-submarine warfare aircraft, many found their way into civil aviation in the years after World War II. The prototype Catalina first flew on 21 March 1945, and the main production models were the PBY-1, 2, -3 and -4 in the first series. These were followed by the PBY-5A, the most numerous variant of all; 753 were built out of a total PBY production of 3290, not counting several hundred built in the USSR. Although the Catalina was not a particularly economic type for commercial use, it proved an excellent transport vehicle in such areas as the Amazon basin and the island groups of South-East Asia. The six aircraft owned by Panair do Brasil operated very successfully as 22-passenger transports along the Amazon river until the company was dissolved in 1965.

Country of origin:	USA
Engines:	two 1200hp Pratt & Whitney R-1830-92 Twin Wasp 14-cylinder radials
Wingspan:	31.70m (104ft)
Length:	19.45m (63ft 10in)
Height:	6.14m (20ft 2in)
Weight loaded:	16,066kg (35,420lb)
Cruising speed:	182km/h (113mph)
Service ceiling:	3962m (13,000ft)
Passengers + crew:	22 + 2–4

Convair 340

Pictured here, N3427 was one of 20 Convair 340s purchased by Braniff to replace the Model 240s acquired after a merger with rival Mid-Continent Airlines. Delivered in July 1953, the aircraft served for 14 years on Braniff's mid-west network, amassing 31,000 hours. It was written off after an engine fire on 23 July 1967, and moved to Barstow Daggett Airport, California, where it remained in open storage until late 1988. It was then bought by Century Airlines, the plan being to refurbish it completely and return it to service as a freighter. In addition to the civil Convair 340s, 36 examples were bought for the US Air Force and designated C-131B. They were used as transports for many years, although six were diverted for temporary trials with missile-tracking equipment. The US Navy also bought 340s for transport and air ambulance duties, designated R4Y1.

Country of origin:	USA
Engines:	two 2500hp Pratt & Whitney R-2800-CB16 radials
Wingspan:	32.1m (105ft 4in)
Length:	24.8m (81ft 6in)
Height:	8.6m (28ft 2in)
Weight loaded:	22,500kg (49,600lb)
Cruising speed:	480km/h (298mph) at 7590m (24,900ft)
Service ceiling:	7625m (25,000ft)
Range:	2100km (1300 miles)
Passengers + crew:	44 + 2–3

Convair 880

The Convair 880, announced in the spring of 1956, seated fewer passengers than its two rivals, the Boeing 707 and Douglas DC8, but had the advantage of being faster. The Model 22 became the standard US domestic version, and first flew on 27 January 1959. First delivery of a production 880 was made on 31 January 1960 to Delta Air Lines, which had ordered 10, and which introduced the aircraft into service on 31 May, two weeks after its FAA certificate was granted. A further 30 were ordered by TWA, some being leased by Northeast Airlines, which began services in December 1960, a month earlier than TWA itself. Other customers were Alaska Airlines, Cathay Pacific, the Federal Aviation Administration, Hughes Tool Company, and Japan Air Lines. Most were sold on to smaller companies, including American Indy Air, one of whose aircraft is shown.

Country of origin:	USA
Engines:	four General Electric CJ805-3B turbojets of 5285kg (11,650lb) thrust each
Wingspan:	36.58m (120ft)
Length:	39.42m (129ft 4in)
Height:	11.07m (36ft 4in)
Weight loaded:	87,540kg (193,000lb)
Cruising speed:	990km/h (615mph) at 6860m (22,500ft)
Service ceiling:	12,500m (41,000ft)
Range:	4630km (2880 miles)
Passengers + crew:	84–110 + 3–4

Curtiss AT-32B Condor II

The AT-32 was a developed version of the Condor, featuring supercharged Wright Cyclone engines driving the then new Hamilton Standard variable-pitch, two-position propellers. It was first flown on 17 March 1934. The enhanced performance of this engine/propeller combination, which was housed in full NACA cowlings and streamlined long-chord nacelles, enabled fuel capacity to be increased to 1420 litres (375 US gallons), and maximum take-off weight to increase to 7940kg (17,500lb). Take-off, climb and cruise performance were all improved over the T-32. The AT-32A and AT-32B were passenger-convertible day/night sleeper models. American Airways was the major customer for the second generation' Condor, and took 19 aircraft in total. The company was impressed by the new variant, and uprated all its Condors to this standard.

Country of origin:	USA
Engines:	two 720hp Wright SGR-1820-F2 Cyclone radials
Wingspan:	25.0m (82ft)
Length:	14.8m (48ft 7in)
Height:	4.9m (16ft 4 in)
Weight loaded:	7940kg (17,500lb)
Cruising speed:	270km/h (167mph)
Service ceiling:	7010m (23,000ft)
Range:	1152km (716 miles)
Passengers + crew:	12 + 2

Curtiss C-46 Commando

Although it tended to be overshadowed by the Douglas C-47, the Curtiss C-46 Commando was a highly capable transport aircraft; some 3180 were built for the USAAF in World War II. Many war surplus C-46s were demilitarized for the commercial market after the war, and by 1960, the aircraft was being used in its civilian capacity by over 90 operators worldwide. Post-war plans to build a dedicated civil version of the Commando for Eastern Airlines did not come to fruition. Seen in the colourful markings of the Japanese Air Self-Defence Force (JASDF) in about 1973, this Curtiss Commando was built as C-46D-20-CU 4478495 (c/n 22318), and later became the JASDF's 51-1114. At this late stage in its career, the aircraft was used for general transport and utility duties. The cavernous dimensions of the C-46's double-lobed fuselage are evident in this illustration.

Country of origin:	USA
Engines:	two 2100hp Pratt & Whitney R-2800 Double Wasp radials
Wingspan:	32.92m (108ft)
Length:	23.27m (76ft 4in)
Height:	6.63m (21ft 9in)
Weight loaded:	22,680kg (50,000lb)
Cruising speed:	378km/h (235mph) at 2743m (9000ft)
Service ceiling:	6706m (22,000ft)
Range:	2897km (1800 miles)
Passengers + crew:	24 + 3

Curtiss CR-6

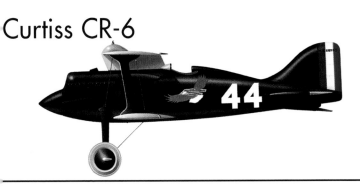

In May 1919, the newspaper owners Ralph Joseph Jr., and Herbert Pulitzer established a trophy to be awarded annually to the aircraft that won a closed-circuit speed competition within the framework of the National Air Races. When the first contest was held in 1920, it attracted no fewer than 65 entries. In the years that followed, it led to the development of high-speed aircraft whose manufacturers had an eye on military orders. One such constructor was Glenn Curtiss, who developed a formidable line of racing aircraft at this time; its precursor was the CR-1, constructed to take part in the 1921 Pulitzer contest, and which it won. Curtiss machines won three more Pulitzer races, in 1922, 1923 and 1935. The latter, also the last, was won by a Curtiss R-6. The aircraft shown is the R-6 flown by Lester Maitland at Selfridge Field, Michigan in the 1922 race.

Country of origin:	USA
Engine:	one 465hp Curtiss D-12 12-cylinder V-type
Wingspan:	5.79m (19ft)
Length:	5.75m (18ft 11in)
Height:	2.41m (7ft 11in)
Weight loaded:	884kg (1950lb)
Maximum speed:	380km/h (236mph)
Service ceiling:	Not established
Range:	455km (283 miles)
Crew:	1

Curtiss JN-4 Jenny

Built in enormous numbers during and after World War I, the Curtiss JN-4 Jenny was one of the most famous training aircraft in aviation history; production totalled 7471 units. Through various production series, the type was subjected to structural modifications in order to improve performance; the JN-4A and JN-4B, for example, were fitted with larger tailplanes to improve stability. The original Jenny, the Curtiss J, was designed by B. Douglas Thomas in 1914, in response to a US Army requirement for a trainer biplane with a tractor propeller. The early versions saw limited action in a reconnaissance role with US forces engaged against Mexican revolutionaries. Numerous Jennies found civilian roles after World War I as mail carriers, advertising banner tugs and, of course, trainers. The aircraft pictured is one of 1260 built by Canadian Aeroplanes.

Country of origin:	USA
Engine:	one 90hp Curtiss OX-5 in-line
Wingspan:	13.3m (43ft 8in)
Length:	8.33m (27ft 4in)
Height:	3.01m (9ft 10in)
Weight loaded:	871kg (1920lb)
Cruising speed:	113km/h (70mph)
Service ceiling:	1980m (6500ft)
Range:	275 miles
Passengers + crew:	1 + 1

Curtiss T-32 Condor II (YC-30)

The Curtiss T-32 Condor was the last civil transport biplane to be built by the American aviation industry. Designed by George Page, the Condor appeared in two versions, the first of which, the Model 18, was a conversion of the Curtiss B-2 biplane bomber of 1929. The Air Corps purchased only 12 machines, and Curtiss turned to the civil market to make up the deficit. Six Model 18s were built, entering service with Eastern Air Transport and Transcontinental Air Transport. The T-32 version flew in January 1930, and nine production aircraft were each delivered to the above companies, two entering service as VIP transports with the Air Corps (one shown above), and one fitted out to support the 1933–35 Byrd Antarctic Expedition. Although almost obsolete, the T-32 was one of the first aircraft to have berths for night flights, and was safe and comfortable.

Country of origin:	USA
Engines:	two Wright Cyclone 9-cylinder radials
Wingspan:	24.99m (82ft)
Length:	14.81m (48ft 7in)
Height:	4.98m (16ft 4in)
Weight loaded:	7938kg (17,500lb)
Cruising speed:	268km/h (167mph)
Ceiling:	7010m (23,000ft)
Range:	1152km (716 miles)
Passengers + crew:	12 + 2

Dassault Falcon 900

I n the hard-fought arena of executive jet sales, the Dassault Falcon series is
unquestionably the best-selling family of business jets, with a pedigree that
stretches back over several decades. The first of the line was the Mystere XX; this
flew on 1 January 1965, and deliveries soon began to the type's American
distributor, Pan American Business Jets. It was initially marketed as the Fan Jet
Falcon, and renamed Falcon 20. Latest in the series is the Falcon 900, the first of
which, named Spirit of Lafayette, flew on 21 September 1984. The second aircraft
set a new distance record for its class when it flew non-stop from Paris to
Dassault's US distribution centre at Little Rock, Arkansas, covering a distance of
7973km (4954 miles) at Mach 0.84. The aircraft shown here is one of four Falcon
900s operated by the Ford Motor Company, and the third off the production line.

Country of origin:	France
Engines:	three Garrett TFE731-5AR-1C turbofans of 2038kg (4500lb) thrust each
Wingspan:	19.35m (63ft 5in)
Length:	20.2m (66ft 7in)
Height:	7.5m (24ft 9in)
Weight loaded:	20,639kg (45,500lb)
Cruising speed:	922km/h (572mph)
Service ceiling:	15,544m (51,000ft)
Range:	7222km (4488 miles)
Passengers + crew:	19 + 2

de Havilland Comet 1

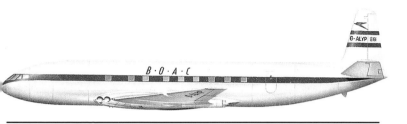

In 1942, at the height of World War II, the British government appointed a group of experts known as the Brabazon Committee to study the feasibility of a jet-propelled transport called the Type IV, primarily for the carriage of transatlantic mail. Numerous designs were produced and rejected, and the requirement was reshaped around a passenger aircraft. The subsequent Ministry of Supply contract went to de Havilland. The first prototype of the DH.106 Comet 1 flew on 27 July 1949. In the meantime, BOAC ordered 14 production Comet 1s, the first of these, G-ALYP shown here, flying on January 1951. On 2 May 1952, BOAC used G-ALYP to inaugurate the first all-jet commercial service, between London and Johannesburg. G-ALYP broke up in mid-air near Elba on 10 January 1954, the latest victim of a then unknown phenomenon – metal fatigue.

Country of origin:	GB
Engines:	four de Havilland Ghost 50 MkI turbojets of 2018kg (4450lb) thrust each
Wingspan:	35.05m (115ft)
Length:	28.38m (93ft 1in)
Height:	8.66m (28ft 4in)
Weight loaded:	47,627kg (105,000lb)
Cruising speed:	788km/h (490mph)
Service ceiling:	12,190m (40,000ft)
Range:	2816km (1750 miles)
Passengers + crew:	36 + 4

de Havilland Comet 1A

The next model to follow the Comet 1 was the 44-seat 1A, fitted with 2268kg (5000lb) Ghost 50 Mk 2 engines with water/methanol injection and increased tankage, which consequently had an increased range at higher, all-up weights. During 1952–53, 10 Comet 1As were delivered to Air France (three), Canadian Pacific (two), UAT (three) and No 412 Transport Squadron of the RCAF (two). F-BGNX, seen here, was the first of Air France's Comet 1As, although the French carrier UAT was actually the first to take delivery of the jet airliner. Air France opened Paris–Rome–Beirut services on 26 August 1953, but never again used Comets after the type's Certificate of Airworthiness was withdrawn in April 1954, following a series of fatal accidents. Despite their misfortunes, the Comet 1s and 1As flew over 30,000 revenue hours in less than two years of service.

Country of origin:	GB
Engines:	four de Havilland Ghost 50 Mk 2 turbojetsof 2268kg (5000lb) thrust each .
Wingspan:	35.05m (115ft)
Length:	28.38m (93ft 1in)
Height:	8.66m ((28ft 4in)
Weight loaded:	47,627kg (105,000lb)
Cruising speed:	788km/h (490mph)
Service ceiling:	12,190m (40,000ft)
Range:	2816km (1750 miles)
Passengers + crew:	44 + 4

de Havilland (Hawker Siddeley) Comet 4B

While the ill-fated Comet 1 was still operational, de Havilland embarked on studies for a 'stretched' version, the Comet 3. Registered G-ANLO, this flew for the first time on 19 July 1954. By the end of 1954, with the full Comet 1 accident findings available, de Havilland combined all of the latest knowledge into a Mk 4 version, and a modified G-ANLO, now fitted with Avon 523 engines, began a flight test programme in February 1957. The first production Comet 4, G-APDA, flew on 27 April 1958, and was the first of 19 ordered by BOAC. On 4 October 1958, BOAC inaugurated the first fare-paying, transatlantic jet service (London–New York), beating Pan American's Boeing 707 by three weeks. The Comet 4A was a still-born version projected for Capital Airlines; from which the Comet 4B was derived. Seen here is G-APYC of Channel Airways.

Country of origin:	GB
Engines:	four Rolls-Royce Avon Mk 542 turbojets of 4763kg (10,500lb) thrust each
Wingspan:	32.87m (107ft 10in)
Length:	35.97m (118ft)
Height:	8.69m (28ft 6in)
Weight loaded:	69,174kg (152,500lb)
Cruising speed:	856km/h (532mph)
Service ceiling:	11,890m (39,000ft)
Range:	3701km (2300 miles)
Passengers + crew:	101–119 + 3–4

de Havilland (Hawker Siddeley) Comet 4C

Hawker Siddeley, into which the old de Havilland firm had been absorbed, ended its Comet 4 programme with the Mk 4C, produced by merging the long body with a large, pinion-tanked wing. The Comet 4C was the most successful model of all, bought initially by Mexicana, Misrair (Eyptair), Aerolineas Argentinas, MEA, Sudan and Kuwait. Altogether, 30 of this series were produced, 23 of them at Hawker Siddeley's Chester factory, bringing total Comet production to 113 machines. The final examples went to King Ibn Saud of Saudi Arabia, the Royal Air Force (five) and the Aeroplane and Armament Experimental Establishment (A&AEE) at Boscombe Down, Wiltshire. The last two went to Hawker Siddeley at Manchester, for conversion to the prototype Nimrod MR.1 maritime patrol aircraft. Pictured is SU-ALC, the first of nine Comet 4Cs for

Country of origin:	GB
Engines:	four Rolls-Royce Avon Mk 545B turbojets of 4763kg (10,500lb) thrust each
Wingspan:	35.0m (114ft 10in)
Length:	35.97m (118ft)
Height:	8.69m (28ft 6in)
Weight loaded:	73,500kg (162,000lb)
Cruising speed:	856km/h (532mph)
Service ceiling:	11,890m (39,000ft)
Range:	4168km (2590 miles)
Passengers + crew:	101–119 + 3–4

de Havilland (Hawker Siddeley) Comet C.Mk.4

The Royal Canadian Air Force and the Royal Air Force were both early recipients, two aircraft being delivered to No 412 Squadron RCAF in 1953, and five Comet C.2s to No 216 Squadron, RAF Transport Command, in June 1956. The Canadian aircraft remained in service until 1964. No 51 Squadron RAF also took delivery of three Comet C.2s, modified for electronic intelligence gathering, and designated Comet Mk.2R, in 1958. Two of these aircraft remained in service until 1974. Meanwhile, in February 1962, No 216 Squadron had added five C.Mk.4s to its strength, and after the withdrawal of the C.2ns in March 1967, it continued to operate these aircraft on Air Support Command's routes around the world, until it disbanded in June 1975. Pictured is Comet C.Mk.4 XR399, which was sold to Dan-Air after being relinquished by the RAF and registered G-BDIX.

Country of origin:	GB
Engines:	four Rolls-Royce Avon Mk 545B turbojets of 4763kg (10,500lb) thrust each
Wingspan:	35.0m (114ft 10in)
Length:	35.97m (118ft)
Height:	8.69m (28ft 6in)
Weight loaded:	73,500kg (162,000lb)
Cruising speed:	856km/h (532mph)
Service ceiling:	11,890m (39,000ft)
Range:	4168km (2590 miles)
Passengers + crew:	101–119 + 3–4

de Havilland Canada DHC-2 Beaver

The DHC-2 Beaver, which first flew in August 1947, was designed in response to bush pilots' need for a modern aeroplane of rugged capability, alternative wheel/float/ski landing gear, and a comparatively large cabin accessed by a wide door on each side. The initial variant was the Beaver Mk 1 with the ruthlessly reliable – and easily maintained and fuelled – Wasp Junior radial. There were 1657 of this major variant, followed by a single Beaver Mk 2 with an Alvis Leonides radial, and by a small number of 10-passenger Turbo-Beaver Mk 3s with the 578shp Pratt & Whitney Canada PT6A-6 or -20 turboprop. In New Zealand, a single Beaver was re-engined with the Garrett TPE-331 turboprop. Seen here is a float-equipped Beaver of Tradewinds Aviation. Red featured in the colour scheme of Canadian-operated Beavers to aid identification against a snow-covered background.

Country of origin:	Canada
Engine:	one 450hp Pratt & Whitney R-985 Wasp Junior
Wingspan:	14.62m (47ft 9in)
Length:	9.24m (30ft 3in)
Height:	2.74m (8ft 9in)
Weight loaded:	2313kg (5100lb)
Cruising speed:	230km/h (145mph) at 1525m (5000ft)
Service ceiling:	5485m (18,000ft)
Range:	1252km (780 miles)
Passengers + crew:	7 + 1

de Havilland Canada DHC-2 Beaver

A classic amongst bush aircraft, the de Havilland Canada Beaver was an ideal vehicle for opening vast tracts of remote land for exploitation. Designed primarily for operations in the hostile environment of the Canadian north, the Beaver was designed from the outset with either a ski or float undercarriage as options. With large areas of remote land under their jurisdiction, the Royal Canadian Mounted Police were natural customers for the type, and used the Beaver for rapid transport and liaison over large distances of hostile terrain. The float undercarriage allowed a landing to be made on any of the lakes covering the Canadian interior. Australia was a major military operator of the Beaver, using its aircraft chiefly to support Antarctic exploration with mixed ski/wheel undercarriage. The latest version is the turboprop-powered Turbo Beaver III.

Country of origin:	Canada
Engine:	one 450hp Pratt & Whitney R-985 Wasp Junior
Wingspan:	14.62m (47ft 9in)
Length:	9.24m (30ft 3in)
Height:	2.74m (8ft 9in)
Weight loaded:	2313kg (5100lb)
Cruising speed:	230km/h (145mph) at 1525m (5000ft)
Service ceiling:	5485m (18,000ft)
Range:	1252km (780 miles)
Passengers + crew:	7 + 1

de Havilland Canada DHC-3 Otter

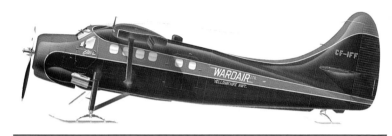

The DHC-2 Beaver convinced all involved that such versatile aircraft were a necessity, not least in the rugged terrain of its Canadian homeland. The heir to the Beaver's throne was the de Havilland Canada Otter, which became king of the 'bush' aircraft. Bigger and faster than the DHC-2, it retained the ability to operate from ice and snow, lakes and river banks; in fact, the ability to deliver people and cargo to wherever they were needed. Among the more colourful Otters was this aircraft operated by Wardair, which began as a local carrier, but which rose to be a major transatlantic operator. In winter, Canadian Otters donned skis to continue services to remote settlements, while in summer, floats were used for landing on the many lakes that dot the Canadian interior. The fuselage side door allowed the admission of sizeable cargo.

Country of origin:	Canada
Engine:	one 600hp Pratt & Whitney S3H1-G Wasp radial
Wingspan:	17.68m (58ft)
Length:	12.75m (41ft 10in)
Height:	3.96m (13ft)
Weight loaded:	3629kg (8100lb)
Cruising speed:	222km/h (138mph)
Service ceiling:	4998m (16,400ft)
Range:	1520km (945 miles)
Pssenger + crew:	9–11 + 1–2

de Havilland Canada DHC-6 Twin Otter

With its Beaver and Otter aircraft, de Havilland Canada established itself as the world's leading manufacturer of aircraft optimized for 'bush flying'. Combining the ruggedness of DHC's Otter design with the reliability and power of two turboprops produced the Twin Otter, which first flew on 20 May 1965. Excellent STOL performance, good load-carrying ability and the capability to land on virtually any surface, including snow and water, quickly established it as the world's standard 'go-anywhere' light transport. The aircraft here is a Series 300 Twin Otter of the Canadian company NorOntair, based at North Bay, Ontario. The bright paint scheme not only catches the eye, but is a critical survival aid if the aircraft needs to make a forced landing in snow, making it readily visible. The motif represents the loon, a well-known bird of eastern Canada.

Country of origin:	Canada
Engines:	two 620hp Pratt & Whitney Canada PT6A-27 turboprops
Wingspan:	19.8m (65ft)
Length:	15.8m (51ft 9in)
Height:	5.9m (19ft 4in)
Weight loaded:	5670kg (12,500lb)
Cruising speed:	337km/h (209mph)
Service ceiling:	8138m (26,700ft)
Range:	1290km (802 miles)
Passengers + crew:	20 + 2

de Havilland DH.16

In 1919, de Havilland converted a number of DH.9A bombers on behalf of several newly formed air transport companies, providing the aircraft with enclosed passenger cabins for two people. The cabin conversion approach was taken a stage further with the DH.16, which was based on the airframe and engine of the DH.9A, but which had the rear fuselage enlarged to accommodate four passengers. Most of the conversions were made for Air Transport & Travel Ltd (AT&T), and on 25 August 1919, a DH.16 flown by Major Cyril Patterson inaugurated the first regular daily air service between London and Paris, leaving London at 12.30pm for Le Bourget with four passengers on board. Nine DH.16s were built; three of AT&T's aircraft had Napier Lion engines instead of the Rolls-Royce Eagle, and one was sold to Compania Rioplatense de Aviacion, Argentina.

Country of origin:	GB
Engine:	one 320hp Rolls-Royce Eagle or 450hp Napier Lion
Wingspan:	14.17m (46ft 6in)
Length:	9.68m (31ft 9in)
Height:	3.45m (11ft 4in)
Weight loaded:	2155kg (4750lb)
Cruising speed:	193km/h (120mph)
Service ceiling:	6400m (21,000ft)
Range:	684km (425 miles)
Passengers + crew:	4 + 1

de Havilland DH.34

The first de Havilland type designed for airline work was the DH.18, which flew early in 1920. The second was the DH.34, which flew for the first time on 26 March 1922. This aircraft, G-EBBQ, was one of two ordered by Daimler Airways, the other being G-EBBS. Delivered to Daimler on 31 March 1922, it flew its first commercial service to Paris two days later. The Air Council also ordered seven DH.34s, later increased to nine; four were loaned to Instone Airline, which opened a service between London and Paris at the same time as Daimler. One Air Council DH.34 was allocated to the Royal Aircraft Establishment, Farnborough. The 12th, and last, DH.34 was delivered to the Soviet airline Dobrolet. In 1924, Daimler and Instone became part of Imperial Airways. By this time, four DH.34s had been lost in crashes; two more were lost, and the rest were scrapped in 1926.

Country of origin:	GB
Engine:	one 450hp Napier Lion
Wingspan:	15.65m (51ft 4in)
Length:	11.89m (39ft)
Height:	3.66m (12ft)
Weight loaded:	3266kg (7200lb)
Cruising speed:	177km/h (110mph)
Service ceiling:	4420m (14,500ft)
Range:	587km (365 miles)
Passengers + crew:	9 + 1

de Havilland DH.37

From the propeller to the trailing edges of the wings, the DH.34 strongly resembled the Airco DH.4 of World War I fame; but it also bore the famous 'de Havilland tailfin' that was to become the hallmark of all de Havilland's light aircraft designs, including the celebrated Tiger Moth trainer. It was designed by Alan Butler, a de Havilland company director and a very experienced pilot; he later went on, in October 1931, to set up a world record by flying from London to Port Darwin in 9 days 2 hours 29 minutes. His DH.37 was delivered in 1922, and after some five years of use, Butler returned it to de Havilland for conversion to single-seat racing configuration, fitted with a 300hp Nimbus in place of its Falcon III. De Havilland built a second DH.37, used by the Comptroller of Civil Aviation in Australia in 1924. It was sold to the Guinea Gold Company in 1927.

Country of origin:	GB
Engine:	one 275hp Rolls-Royce Falcon III in-line
Wingspan:	11.28m (37ft)
Length:	8.53m (28ft)
Height:	3.35m (11ft)
Weight loaded:	1505kg (3318lb)
Cruising speed:	177km/h (110mph)
Service ceiling:	6400m (21,000ft)
Range:	483km (300 miles)
Crew + passengers:	1 + 1

de Havilland DH.50

The relative success of DH.9 conversions as interim short-range commercial transport aircraft encouraged de Havilland to develop a purpose-built successor. This emerged as the DH.50 biplane, the prototype of which (G-EBFN, named Galatea) flew for the first time in August 1923. G-EBFO, shown here, was the second aircraft, and was used on Sir Alan Cobham's route-survey flights, which began with a 27,360km (17,000 mile) journey from England to Rangoon between 20 November 1924 and 18 March 1925. It was refitted with an uncowled Armstrong Siddeley Jaguar III radial engine, before embarking on more long-distance flights from Croydon to Cape Town and Rochester-Melbourne. Cobham returned to London on 1 October 1926 and landed on the Thames opposite the Houses of Parliament, the aircraft having been equipped with floats.

Country of origin:	GB
Engine:	one 385hp Armstrong Siddeley Jaguar radial
Wingspan:	13.03m (42ft 9in)
Length:	9.07m (29ft 9in)
Height:	3.35m (11ft)
Weight loaded:	1769kg (3900lb)
Cruising speed:	180km/h (112mph)
Service ceiling:	4450m (14,600ft)
Range:	612km (380 miles)
Passengers + crew:	4 + 1

de Havilland DH.60 Moth

Named 'Moth' in recognition of Geoffrey de Havilland's renown as a lepidopterist, the first DH.60 was flown by de Havilland himself at Stag Lane on 2 February 1925. That day set a pattern for private flying that was emulated the world over until World War II. By the end of 1925, 20 Cirrus-engined Moths had been completed, including 16 delivered to six government-sponsored flying clubs, and two to private owners. Another 35 were built in 1926, of which 14 were exported, and by the end of 1928 the production total had reached 403. The longest-serving DH.60 Moth, G-EBLV, was the sixth production example, and was one of two Moths supplied to the Lancashire Aero Club on 29 August 1925, the first of the government-sponsored flying clubs initiated by Sir Sefton Brancker. This aircraft was painstakingly restored by de Havilland apprentices in 1951.

Country of origin:	GB
Engine:	one 60hp ADC Cirrus I
Wingspan:	8.84m (29ft)
Length:	7.16m (23ft 6in)
Height:	2.68m (8ft 7in)
Weight loaded:	611kg (1350lb)
Cruising speed:	137km/h (85mph)
Service ceiling:	3965m (13,000ft)
Range:	515km (320 miles)
Passengers + crew:	1 + 1

de Havilland DH.60G Gipsy Moth

T he light aeroplane that made the greatest impact on sporting aviation worldwide in the 1920s was the DH.60 Gipsy Moth; it was flown in almost every country that supported flying facilities. Shown here with Australian registration, the Gipsy Moth was used by flying clubs at Adelaide, Brisbane, Longreach, Melbourne, Perth and Sydney. The Gipsy Moth continued in production until 1943, by which time a total of 595 had been produced in England, in addition to 40 built by Morane-Saulnier in France, 18 by the Moth Aircraft Corporation of Massachusetts, USA, and 32 by the Larkin Aircraft Supply Co Ltd of Melbourne, Australia. A derivative of the wooden Gipsy Moth, the DH.60M, the Metal Moth, was introduced in 1928 to meet overseas demand for a strengthened version. Some of these saw military service in Iraq and elsewhere.

Country of origin:	GB
Engine:	one 100hp de Havilland Gipsy I
Wingspan:	9.15m (30ft)
Length:	7.28m (23ft 11in)
Height:	2.67m (8ft 9in)
Weight loaded:	747kg (1650lb)
Cruising speed:	137km/h (85mph)
Service ceiling:	4422m (14,500ft)
Range:	515km (320 miles)
Passengers + crew:	1 + 1

de Havilland DH.66 Hercules

Like Fokker in the Netherlands and Ford in the USA, de Havilland was attracted to the three-engined, commercial-transport formula, and in 1926 produced the DH.66 Hercules, which had been developed to meet Imperial Airways' requirement for a new generation of comfortable, efficient passenger airliners and to provide postal and freight transport on European and Empire routes. The first DH.66 flew in September 1926, and scheduled services began with Imperial's initial fleet of five aircraft in December 1926, the route extended to Cairo and on to India early in 1927. The debut of the Hercules meant that Imperial Airways could not accept full responsibility for the airmail service to the Far East. On 8 January 1927, the second Hercules, G-EBMX, arrived in Delhi to mark the official hand-over of the service by the RAF. The DH.60 here is G-AARY City of Karachi.

Country of origin:	GB
Engines:	three 420hp Bristol Jupiter VI radials
Wingspan:	24.23m (79ft 6in)
Length:	16.92m (55ft 6in)
Height:	5.56m (18ft 3in)
Weight loaded:	7067kg (15,600lb)
Cruising speed:	177km/h (110mph)
Service ceiling:	3960m (13,000ft)
Range:	845km (525 miles)
Passengers + crew:	8 + 3

de Havilland DH.82A Tiger Moth

Probably the most famous, and one of the most attractive basic training aircraft of all time, the DH.82A Tiger Moth first flew on 26 October 1931, and large-scale production began almost immediately, mostly for the Royal Air Force. This classic aircraft was also licence-built in Canada, New Zealand, Australia, Portugal, Norway and Sweden. The example here was one of 20 produced by AB Svenska Jarnvagsverkstaderna as the Sk 11A for the Royal Swedish Air Force (Flygvapen). No fewer than 8700 Tiger Moths were built. After World War II, they went into the civil market, while others continued to serve in the RAF until replaced by the Percival Prentice and de Havilland Chipmunk. One of the most famous exponents of Tiger Moth flying was the Tiger Club, whose aircraft (The Bishop, The Archbishop, The Deacon and The Canon) became well known for their aerobatic displays.

Country of origin:	GB
Engine:	one 130hp de Havilland Gipsy Major 4-cylinder in-line
Wingspan:	8.94m (29ft 4in)
Length:	7.29m (23ft 11in)
Height:	2.67m (8ft 9in)
Weight loaded:	828kg (1825lb)
Cruising speed:	161km/h (100mph)
Service ceiling:	not known
Range:	483km (300 miles)
Passengers + crew:	1 + 1

de Havilland DH.84 Dragon

Following the success of its single-engined commercial conversions and designs of the 1920s, de Havilland turned its attention to the construction of larger, multi-engined types. In 1932, it produced the DH.84 Dragon, a six-passenger biplane that had been especially ordered by Hillman Airways for use on its planned Romford–Paris route, and also as a light bomber for the Iraqi Air Force. The prototype, later registered G-ACAN, first flew on 24 November 1932, and in April 1933, it inaugurated the Romford–Paris service. The latter proved so popular that Hillman ordered two more Dragons, and had all six aircraft in the fleet converted to eight-seater configuration. The eight military Dragons, which had three machine-gun mountings and could carry up to 16.9kg (20lb) of bombs, were delivered to Iraq in May 1933. De Havilland went on to build 115 Dragons.

Country of origin:	GB
Engines:	two 130hp de Havilland Gipsy Major 4-cylinder in-lines
Wingspan:	14.4m (47ft 4in)
Length:	10.51m (34ft 6in)
Height:	3.07m (10ft 1in)
Weight loaded:	1905kg (4200lb)
Cruising speed:	175km/h (109mph)
Service ceiling:	3810m (12,500ft)
Range:	740km (460 miles)
Passengers + crew:	6–8 + 1

de Havilland DH.85 Leopard Moth

Two famous members of the Moth family were the DH.85 Leopard Moth and the DH.87 Hornet Moth, the former a three-seat, high-wing, cabin aircraft introduced in 1933, and the latter a cabin biplane that made its appearance the following year. Both were ideal 'taxi' aircraft, being operated by such well-known companies as Olley Air Services and Air Taxis Ltd. One Leopard Moth, flown by Jimmie Broadbent, set a new record for the Australia journey, landing at Lympne on 3 May 1937, only 6 days 8 hours and 25 minutes after leaving Darwin. Originally supplied to a wealthy Egyptian in 1934 (as SU-ABM), the DH.85 Leopard Moth in the illustration returned to England in 1946 from Iraq (as YI-ABI); it was then completely rebuilt, given the post-war British civil registration G-AIYS, and used to give pleasure flights at Woburn Abbey by C.M. Roberts of Chrisair.

Country of origin:	GB
Engine:	one 130hp de Havilland Gipsy Major
Wingspan:	11.43m (37ft 6in)
Length:	7.47m (24ft 6in)
Height:	2.66m (8ft 9in)
Weight loaded:	1008kg (2222lb)
Cruising speed:	191km/h (119mph)
Service ceiling:	6557m (21,500ft)
Range:	not known
Passengers + crew:	1 + 2

de Havilland DH.86A

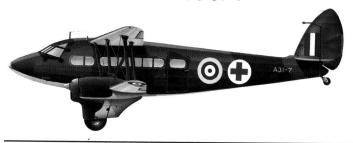

The four-engined DH.86 was designed in response to a joint requirement by the governments of Britain, India and Australia for an aircraft to operate the Singapore–Brisbane sector of a through route between England and Australia, planned to be inaugurated in 1934. The requirement was very demanding, as the proposed route involved flying over long stretches of water, and through often unpredictable tropical weather conditions. The resulting DH.86 resembled a scaled-up DH.34 Dragon, although as well as having four engines, a necessary safety measure given the kind of flying it would have to do, it also had a completely redesigned wing. The prototype made its first flight on 14 January 1934, only four months after design work began. Sixty-two aircraft were eventually delivered. The DH.86A here was used as an air ambulance by the RAAF.

Country of origin:	GB
Engines:	two 200hp de Havilland Gipsy 6 in-lines
Wingspan:	19.66m (64ft 6in)
Length:	14.05m (46ft 1in)
Height:	3.96m (13ft)
Weight loaded:	4649kg (10,250lb)
Cruising speed:	233km/h (145mph)
Service ceiling:	5305m (17,400ft)
Range:	not known
Passengers + crew:	10 + 2

de Havilland DH.87B Hornet Moth

By the late 1920s, flying was out of its infancy. Airframes and engines were becoming ever more reliable, commercial flying was routine, and what passengers and crews alike now demanded was comfort. It was in response to this demand that de Havilland produced the Leopard Moth (described earlier), which was a successor to the very popular Puss Moth, with its three-seat enclosed cabin, and the Hornet Moth, a two-seat cabin monoplane. The aircraft shown here was one of a number of DH.87Bs supplied to Canadian operators flying from lakes in the Northern Territories; fitted in this instance with Fairchild floats, the DH.87B was distinguishable from the earlier 'A' model by its square-cut wingtips. During World War II, Hornet Moths were used by seven RAF squadrons engaged in communications, light transport and radar-calibration duties.

Country of origin:	GB
Engine:	one 130hp de Havilland Gipsy Major I in-line
Wingspan:	8.94m (29ft 4in)
Length:	7.29m (23ft 11in)
Height:	2.69m (8ft 10in)
Weight loaded:	828kg (1825lb)
Cruising speed:	145km/h (90mph)
Service ceiling:	4145m (13,600ft)
Range:	n/a
Passengers + crew:	1 + 1

de Havilland DH.89A Dragon Rapide

Known originally as the Dragon Six because it made use of the then new Gipsy Six engine produced for the DH.86, this updated version of the DH.84 had its name changed to Dragon Rapide in 1935. Soon it was known simply as the Rapide. Its first commercial customer was Hillman's Airways, and by 1939 about 25 other commercial operators were using it in the UK and overseas. By the time production ended on the outbreak of World War II, 205 aircraft had been built at Hatfield. After the 60th aircraft, improvements were incorporated, including the fitting of small split flaps on either side of the engine nacelles to improve the landing characteristics. The aircraft, so modified, became the DH.89A. The aircraft seen here served with the RAF during World War II, and was later sold to Lebanon. In 1964, it returned to England, and was used by the Rothmans Parachute Display Team.

Country of origin:	GB
Engines:	two 200hp de Havilland Gipsy 6 in-lines
Wingspan:	14.63m (48ft)
Length:	10.52m (34ft 6in)
Height:	3.12m (10ft 3in)
Weight loaded:	2495kg (5500lb)
Cruising speed:	214km/h (133mph)
Service ceiling:	5944m (19,500ft)
Range:	930km (578 miles)
Passengers + crew:	6–8 + 1

de Havilland DH.89A Dragon Rapide

The Automobile Association, which early on recognized the value of aircraft to monitor road congestion and provide transport for traffic-accident victims in a serious emergency, employed DH.89A Rapide G-AHKV in the early 1960s. It had previously been used for airborne advertising by Sky Neon, and during World War II it had seen RAF service as a Dominie Mk I. Many DH.89As were impressed for military service with the RAF, RAAF and Air Transport Auxiliary. Production of the military versions, designated Dominie Mk I and Mk II, continued in wartime, with 186 aircraft built by de Havilland and 335 by Brush Coachworks. Wartime Dominies were designated DH.89B, and it was mainly this version that was released on to the civil market in the late 1940s. A number of Rapides are still active on the British civil register, with other examples flying worldwide.

Country of origin:	GB
Engines:	two 200hp de Havilland Gipsy 6 in-lines
Wingspan:	14.63m (48ft)
Length:	10.52m (34ft 6in)
Height:	3.12m (10ft 3in)
Weight loaded:	2495kg (5500lb)
Cruising speed:	214km/h (133mph)
Service ceiling:	5944m (19,500ft)
Range:	930km (578 miles)
Passengers + crew:	6–8 + 1

de Havilland DH.90 Dragonfly

The five-seat DH.90 Dragonfly was a small, luxury development of the Rapide, and constructed with a pre-formed, plywood fuselage. The prototype, G-ADNA, made its first flight at Hatfield on 12 August 1935, and a second aircraft, G-AEBU, flew as the DH.90A demonstrator in February 1936. The new construction methods enabled the Dragonfly to achieve a good performance on low power, but at £2650 the price was high, so initial sales on the British market were restricted to 21. The aircraft's salvation was that it proved highly suitable for commercial operation; it could also be fitted with floats, and had dual controls. Production ended in 1938 after 67 aircraft had been built. One of those built is shown, and originally flew in Mozambique as CR-AAB. It was restored as G-AEDU in 1979 and sold to an owner in Louisville, Kentucky as N190DH in June 1983.

Country of origin:	GB
Engines:	two 130hp de Havilland Gipsy Major in-lines
Wingspan:	13.11m (43ft)
Length:	9.65m (31ft 8in)
Height:	2.79m (9ft 2in)
Weight loaded:	1814kg (4000lb)
Cruising speed:	209km/h (130mph)
Service ceiling:	5515m (18,100ft)
Range:	1006km (625 miles)
Passengers + crew:	4 + 1

de Havilland DH.114 Heron

The immediate success of the DH.104 Dove twin-engined, commuter airliner, the first aircraft to be built by de Havilland after World War II, prompted the company to consider a larger, four-engined version to replace the pre-war DH.86, just as the Dove had replaced the Dragon Rapide. The result was the DH.114 Heron; the prototype, G-ALZL, flew for the first time on 10 May 1950. The first production Heron Series 1 was delivered to Air New Zealand in April 1952. The Heron Series 2, which appeared in December 1952, featured a retractable undercarriage. Refitting with modern engines gave the Heron a new lease of life. This aircraft is a Riley Turbo Skyliner, with Lycoming IO-540 engines, converted from a Heron 2. Sunflower Airlines is based at Suva, Fiji, its operations tailored to tourism. At least three Riley Herons were used, this being the first in service.

Country of origin:	GB
Engines:	four 250hp Gipsy Queen 30 Mk 2
Wingspan:	21.8m (71ft 6in)
Length:	14.8m (48ft 6in)
Height:	4.7m (15ft 7in)
Weight loaded:	5896kg (13,000lb)
Cruising speed:	297km/h (185mph) at 2440m (8,000ft)
Service ceiling:	5638m (18,500ft)
Range:	1475km (915 miles)
Passengers + crew:	14–17 + 2

de Havilland Canada Dash-7

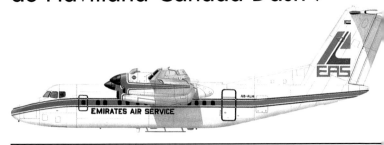

Since the mid-1940s, when the DHC-2 Beaver was introduced, de Havilland Canada has maintained a reputation for building strong, light and reliable utility transports. The Beaver was joined in 1951 by the Otter, and then by the Caribou, Buffalo and Twin Otter. Then came the Dash-7, introducing more sophistication; it became one of the world's leading STOL airliners. Design work on the Dash-7 (DHC-7) began in 1972, the first prototype flying on 27 March 1975. By the time the aircraft received full certification in Canada and the United States, Canadair had already rolled out the first production aircraft. Emirates Air Service was a loyal operator of de Havilland aircraft, and used four Twin Otter 300s in addition to its single passenger version of the Dash-7, seen here. It was based at Abu Dhabi and flew to Dubai, and used on charter services in the general Gulf region.

Country of origin:	Canada
Engines:	four 1120hp Pratt & Whitney PT6A-50 turboprops
Wingspan:	28.35m (93ft)
Length:	24.58m (80ft 8in)
Height:	7.98m (26ft 2in)
Weight loaded:	19.958kg (44,000lb)
Cruising speed:	426km/h (265mph) at 2440m (8000ft)
Service ceiling:	7193m (23,600ft)
Range:	1295km (805 miles)
Passengers + crew:	50 + 2

de Havilland Dash-7

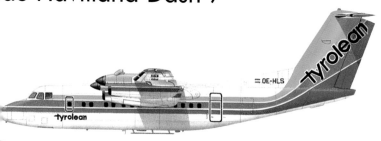

Dash-7 OE-HLS, illustrated here, was one of two aircraft delivered to Tyrolean Airways of Innsbruck. This Austrian airline provides a service between Innsbruck and Vienna three times a day, and also operates on the Innsbruck to Graz route. The Tyrolean fleet has now been increased by the delivery of four of de Havilland's new Dash-8 transports. One of the largest operators of the Dash-7 is Petroleum Air Services, based in Cairo. Five aircraft of this type are on the company's inventory, and operate on support contracts for various North African oil companies. Another Dash-7 operator is the Canadian Armed Forces, which used the type for passenger and freight transport between a number of locations in Europe in support of the Canadian NATO detachment there. In Canadian Armed Forces service, the Dash-7 is designated CC-132.

Country of origin:	Canada
Engines:	four 1120hp Pratt & Whitney PT6A-50 turboprops
Wingspan:	28.35m (93ft)
Length:	24.58m (80ft 8in)
Height:	7.98m (26ft 2in)
Weight loaded:	19.958kg (44,000lb)
Cruising speed:	426km/h (265mph) at 2440m (8000ft)
Service ceiling:	7193m (23,600ft)
Range:	1295km (805 miles)
Passengers + crew:	50 + 2

de Havilland Dash-7

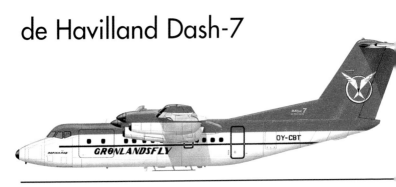

Symbolic of the Dash-7's rugged versatility, OY-CBT, pictured here, is a passenger/freight version of the aircraft, designated Dash-7 Series 101, and equipped with a large forward freight door on the port side of the fuselage. Its owner, Gronlandsfly, operates in the most inhospitable conditions from the capital of Greenland, Godthaab, to Sondrestromfjord, Kulusuk and Narssarssuaq. The aircraft's freight capability is particularly useful for delivery of equipment to the oil industry. The fitting of the cargo door resulted in the repositioning of some of the forward passenger windows, and it is normal for this variant to be fitted with a heavy-duty cargo floor with a roller mat surface. The Series 101 can carry as many as 34 passengers if only one cargo container is uplifted, although a more usual application is a mix of 18 passengers and three containers.

Country of origin:	Canada
Engines:	four 1120hp Pratt & Whitney PT6A-50 turboprops
Wingspan:	28.35m (93ft)
Length:	24.58m (80ft 8in)
Height:	7.98m (26ft 2in)
Weight loaded:	19.958kg (44,000lb)
Cruising speed:	426km/h (265mph) at 2440m (8000ft)
Service ceiling:	7193m (23,600ft)
Range:	1295km (805 miles)
Passengers + crew:	50 + 2

de Havilland Dash-7

Several of the commuter airlines that have bought the Dash-7 have made use of the 'Separate Access Landing System' concept, which has been promoted by de Havilland. This involves the use of limited sections of runways, or 'stub sections', available only due to the unique ability of the aircraft to manoeuvre onto such sections outside the general flow of the airport's traffic. This effectively increases the capacity of any airport, and gives the Dash-7 operator preferential treatment at peak periods. This system has been operated successfully by Ransome Airlines, New York and Washington National, and by Golden West Airways, who have used it in San Francisco. In Europe, Maersk Air has been able to use the same techniques at Copenhagen. One of Maersk's two DHC-7-102 aircraft, OY-MMZ, is shown; they are configured for a single-class, 44-seat layout.

Country of origin:	Canada
Engines:	four 1120hp Pratt & Whitney PT6A-50 turboprops
Wingspan:	28.35m (93ft)
Length:	24.58m (80ft 8in)
Height:	7.98m (26ft 2in)
Weight loaded:	19.958kg (44,000lb)
Cruising speed:	426km/h (265mph) at 2440m (8000ft)
Service ceiling:	7193m (23,600ft)
Range:	1295km (805 miles)
Passengers + crew:	44 + 2

de Havilland Dash 8

At the start of the Dash 8 development programme, a Canadian writer
compared the aircraft with four major rivals, and concluded that the Toronto
product would be 'the benchmark against which the others are measured'.
Although the competition was perhaps tougher than DHC expected, some 567
Dash 8s had been sold by August 1998, and of these 494 had been delivered. The
Franco-German ATR-42/72, the Canadian turboprop's main rival, was only slightly
behind in the market-place with 560 sold, although it started more than a year
later. For the future, the Dash 8 will have to stand up to a whole phalanx of new
similarly sized jet commuters, including the Canadair Regional Jet. The Dash 8
here is part of the regional fleet of DLT, a partner of Lufthansa, one of the
relatively small number of European countries to operate the Canadian product.

Country of origin:	Canada
Engines:	two 2000hp Pratt & Whitney Canada PW120A turboprops
Wingspan:	25.9m (85ft)
Length:	22.5m (74ft)
Height:	7.5m (24ft 6in)
Weight loaded:	15,650kg (34,500lb)
Cruising speed:	500km/h (310mph)
Service ceiling:	7620m (25,000ft)
Range:	2010km (1250 miles)
Passengers + crew:	36 + 2

de Havilland Dash 8

Although the Dash 8 appears to be a fairly basic design, it has many hidden features that enhance its saleability. For example, a movable rear fuselage bulkhead enables mixed passenger/cargo operations to be flown, and the Dash 8 can be operated in the all-cargo mode, in which case the payload is 4268kg (9409lb). Normal fuel capacity is 3160 litres (833 gallons), in integral tanks outboard of the engines. Auxiliary, long-range tanks can be provided, and the Corporate model, marketed in North America by Innotech of Montreal, has centre-section integral tanks that raise fuel capacity sufficient for a range of 3706km (2303 miles). De Havilland Canada's greatest market for the Dash 8 was in North America, where it proved to be a reliable workhorse for feeder carriers. The aircraft shown belonged to Eastern Metro Express, which later collapsed.

Country of origin:	Canada
Engines:	two 2000hp Pratt & Whitney Canada PW120A turboprops
Wingspan:	25.9m (85ft)
Length:	22.5m (74ft)
Height:	7.5m (24ft 6in)
Weight loaded:	15,650kg (34,500lb)
Cruising speed:	500km/h (310mph)
Service ceiling:	7620m (25,000ft)
Range:	2010km (1250 miles)
Passengers + crew:	36 + 2

de Havilland Dash 8-100

During the 1970s, de Havilland Canada continued to study the possibilities and potential for a further product; from the start, it appeared likely that this would be sized to fill the gap between the DHC-6 Twin Otter, typically seating 20, and the big Dash-7. By 1979, these studies had crystallized into the Dash X project, disclosed at the Paris Air Show that year. On 2 April 1980, DHC accepted an order from NorOntair for two aircraft, now designated DHC 8s, or Dash 8s, thereby demonstrating that the design was going ahead. The first of four flight prototypes made its maiden flight on 20 June 1983. Orders came in a healthy stream, reaching 137 by mid-1987, and topping 150 by 1958. Among the customers for the basic Dash 8-100 was Talair, one of the largest carriers in Papua New Guinea. One of its two Dash 8s is illustrated here.

Country of origin:	Canada
Engines:	two 2000hp Pratt & Whitney Canada PW120A turboprops
Wingspan:	25.9m (85ft)
Length:	22.5m (73ft)
Height:	7.5m (24ft 6in)
Weight loaded:	15,650kg (34,500lb)
Cruising speed:	500km/h (310mph)
Service ceiling:	7620m (15,000ft)
Range:	2010km (1250 miles)
Passengers + crew:	36 + 2

de Havilland Dash 8-120

Early in the 1980s, DHC planned a Dash 8 Series 200, with 2200 PW122 turboprops, which could be fitted out as a maritime patrol aircraft. This gave way to the Series 300, a more developed maritime patrol version. Production concentrated on the Series 100 and 300, but in June 1987, DHC, by now a subsidiary of Boeing, disclosed their interest in a further stretched version, the Series 400. This would have additional plugs added to the front and rear fuselage, extending the length by a further 4.67m (15ft 4in) to 29.8m (98ft 7in). Seating capacity would go up into the 66–70 seat region, cruising speed would be increased, as would maximum take-off weight – to around 21,320kg (47,000lb). The Dash 8-400 was launched in June 1995. The major variant remained the 100 Series; seen here is a Dash 8-120s, operated by Air Nova, a subsidiary of Air Canada.

Country of origin:	Canada
Engines:	two 2000hp Pratt & Whitney Canada PW120A turboprops
Wingspan:	25.9m (85ft)
Length:	22.5m (74ft)
Height:	7.5m (24ft 6in)
Weight loaded:	15,650kg (34,500lb)
Cruising speed:	500km/h (310mph)
Service ceiling:	7620m (25,000ft)
Range:	2010km (1250 miles)
Passengers + crew:	36 + 2

Dornier Do 24T

The large, three-engined Dornier Do 24 flying boat was designed in 1935 to fulfil a requirement of the Royal Netherlands Naval Air Service. Three prototypes were begun, and the first flight was made on 3 July 1937 by Do 24V-3 D-ADLR. After acceptance of the type, the Netherlands Navy received 11 Do 24Ks built in Germany, and another 25 aircraft built under licence in Holland. In 1940, invading German forces impressed some of the Dutch-built aircraft for their own use for air-sea rescue duties as Do 24Ns. In 1941, the production of the Do 24T transport and reconnaissance version was resumed. Seen here is D-AEAV, one of a small batch of Fokker-built Do 24T-1 flying boats completed as unarmed civil aeromedical transports operated by the Reichsluftdienst (Air Service). They carried seven stretchers, or a larger number of sitting patients or war casualties.

Country of origin:	Germany
Engines:	three 1000hp BMW-Bramo Fafnir radials (BMW 301R)
Wingspan:	27m (88ft 7in)
Length:	22m (72ft 2in)
Height:	5.75m (18ft 10in)
Weight loaded:	17,800kg (39,249lb)
Cruising speed:	295km/h (183mph)
Service ceiling:	5900m (19,352ft)
Range:	2900km (1801 miles)
Passengers + crew:	variable + 4–5

Dornier Do 24T-2

This Do 24T-2 was one of the later (1943) production series from the Dutch assembly line, the main external difference between this and earlier aircraft being the tall HDL 151 dorsal turret fitted with a Mauser MG 151/20 cannon, instead of the French HS 404 cannon of the Do 24T-1. The aircraft seen here served with the 7 Seenotstaffel (air-sea rescue squadron) SBK XI in the Aegean Sea, where it performed transport as well as ASR duties. As more flying boats were required by the Luftwaffe, the Chantiers Aero-Maritimes de la Seine (CAMS) factory at Sartrouville, France, began production of the Do 24T, and produced around 50 complete and partially complete aircraft up until the liberation. All of the Do 24Ts which had been started were eventually completed, and those that did not go to the Luftwaffe were used by the French Navy until 1953.

Country of origin:	Germany
Engines:	three 1000hp BMW-Bramo Fafnir radials (BMW 301R)
Wingspan:	27m (88ft 7in)
Length:	22m (72ft 2in)
Height:	5.75m (18ft 10in)
Weight loaded:	17,800kg (39,249lb)
Cruising speed:	295km/h (183mph)
Service ceiling:	5900m (19,352ft)
Range:	2900km (1801 miles)
Passengers + crew:	variable + 4–5

Dornier Do 24T-3

In the spring of 1944, Germany persuaded neutral Spain to buy 12 Do 24T-3s to augment the air-sea rescue service in the Mediterranean. The Spanish air-sea rescue group was initially based at Berre flying-boat base, initial training being given on Arado Ar 196 floatplanes. The Spanish Do 24s (later known as HR.5s) rescued pilots of any nationality, and operated at considerable risk, as there was always the significant danger of being attacked by Allied aircraft. None, however, was lost. The Spanish Ejercito del Aire's Do 24T-3s were the last military flying boats in service anywhere in Europe, and they carried out their coastal patrol and rescue duties from Puerto de Pollensa until 1970, serving with the 58th Escuadrilla de Salvamento. Their superb rough-water seaworthiness has never been equalled by any other flying boat of any size.

Country of origin:	Germany
Engines:	three 1000hp BMW-Bramo Fafnir radials (BMW 301R)
Wingspan:	27m (88ft 7in)
Length:	22m (72ft 2in)
Height:	5.75m (18ft 10in)
Weight loaded:	17,800kg (39,249lb)
Cruising speed:	295km/h (183mph)
Service ceiling:	5900m (19,352ft)
Range:	2900km (1801 miles)
Passengers + crew:	variable + 4–5

Dornier Do X

Only three were built, but the Do X remains one of the truly great aircraft of aviation history. Its construction was conventional, and its achievements few and plagued with problems, yet its sheer size made it a breathtaking example of the aircraft constructor's art. Its manufacturer, Dr Claudius Dornier, refused to call it a flying boat, preferring instead the much grander and more appropriate title of Flugsschiff (flying ship). Design of the Do X began in 1916, and the first aircraft, also referred to as the Do-X1, made its first flight on 25 July 1929. On 21 October 1929, it made a one-hour flight with 169 people on board, a crew of 10, 150 passengers and nine stowaways. The aircraft made a worldwide tour in 1930–31. It was destroyed by air attack in Berlin during World War II. The other two Do Xs went to Italy, and were used for experimental flying before being broken up.

Country of origin:	Germany
Engines:	12 525 Britol Jupiter air-cooled (later replaced by 580hp Curtiss Conqueror liquid-cooled)
Wingspan:	48m (157ft 5in)
Length:	40m (131ft 4in)
Height:	10m (32ft 10in)
Weight loaded:	56,000kg (123,460lb)
Cruising speed:	190km/h (118mph)
Service ceiling:	1250m (4100ft)
Range:	1700km (1055 miles)
Passengers + crew:	100 (regular commercial) + 10

Dornier Merkur

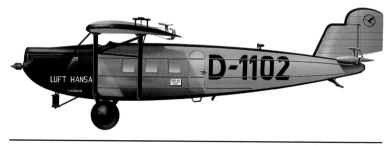

The Dornier Merkur was developed from the Komet series of highwing monoplanes and was outwardly little different from the Komet III; in fact several of the latter were subsequently converted to Merkur standard. The main airframe changes were to be seen in the enlarged vertical tail surfaces, unbraced tailplane, and a cut-out in the centre-section trailing edge of the wings. The largest Merkur operator was Deutsche Lufthansa, which used 22 of the aircraft on its night service between Berlin and Kïnigsberg, and may have had as many as 36, including some converted Komet IIIs. Deruluft, the Russo-German airline, inaugurated a Berlin–Königsberg–Riga–Moscow service with Merkurs on 15 July 1927, and a Tashkent-Kabul service later in the same year. Dornier Merkurs were used on a number of notable proving flights to Asia and southern Africa.

Country of origin:	Germany
Engine:	one 600hp BMW VI 12-cylinder V-type
Wingspan:	19.60m (64ft 4in)
Length:	12.50m (41ft)
Height:	3.45m (11ft 4in)
Weight loaded:	3600kg (7936lb)
Cruising speed:	180km/h (112mph)
Service ceiling:	5200m (17,060ft)
Range:	1050km (650 miles)
Passengers + crew:	10 + 2

Dornier Super Wal

The Dornier Do R Super Wal (Whale) was an enlarged version of the well-tried and very successful Dornier Do J Wal, which was itself a commercial version of a naval flying boat that had been under construction at Lindau at the end of World War I. The prototype Super Wal flew on 30 September 1926, powered by two 650hp Rolls-Royce Condor engines, but the majority of production aircraft had four engines mounted above the wing in two tandem pairs. Sixteen Super Wals were built, of which six went to Deutsche Lufthansa; of these, one had twin Condor engines, one was fitted with four Napier Lions, and four had licence-built Bristol Jupiter engines. Six more Jupiter-engined Super Wals went to the Italian operator SANA, two to Severa GmbH, and two to Stout D & C Airlines, the latter having Pratt & Whitney Hornet radials. The Lion-engined aircraft is shown here.

Country of Origin:	Germany
Engines:	four 485hp Napier Lion VIII W-12 in-lines
Wingspan:	28.60m (93ft 10in)
Length:	24.60m (80ft 8in)
Height:	6.0m (19ft 8in)
Weight loaded:	14,000kg (30,864lb)
Cruising speed:	210km/h (130mph)
Ceiling:	2000m (6500ft)
Range:	2000km (1243 miles)
Passengers + crew:	19 + 3

Douglas C-54 Skymaster

The original C-54s appeared in drab, olive camouflage and were used on load-carrying trips across the Atlantic. Later in the war, they were used to help re-supply Allied forces in the Pacific, where their good range and speed performance made them extremely useful for transporting high-priority material. The aircraft seen here, 41-37274, was a C-54A-DO from the second production batch, which was built solely to military orders; the first batch was being built to fulfil airline orders when it was commandeered on the production lines. A one-off Skymaster conversion was the C-54C, which was used as a VIP transport for US President F.D. Roosevelt and his staff. A small number of C-54s were supplied under Lend-Lease to RAF Transport Command; these were used by Nos 231, 232, and 246 Squadrons on long-range services across the Atlantic and in the Far East.

Country of origin:	USA
Engines:	four 1450hp Pratt & Whitney R-2000 Twin Wasp 14-cylinder radials
Wingspan:	35.81m (117ft 6in)
Length:	28.6m (93ft 10in)
Height:	8.38m (27ft 6in)
Weight loaded:	33,113kg (73,000lb)
Cruising speed:	365km/h (227mph) at 4575m (15,000ft)
Service ceiling:	6795m (22,300ft)
Range:	4025km (2500 miles)
Passengers + crew:	44–86 + 4

Douglas DC-3

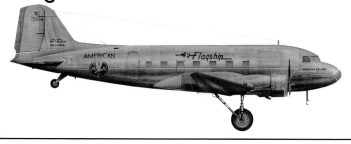

Whereas the Douglas DC-2 was designed to a TWA specification, its successor, the DC-3, began life as the DST (Douglas Sleeper Transport), and was designed for a new carrier, American Airlines. Formed on 11 April 1934, the airline initially used elderly Curtiss Condors leased from the old American Airways, and soon introduced DC-2s. Chairman C. R. Smith then called for an aircraft that would combine the roominess of the Condor with the speed and modernity of the DC-2. He telephoned Donald Douglas and ordered 20 stretched DC-2 sleepers, new aircraft with the designation DST. The order was changed to eight DSTs, the first delivered on 8 June 1936, with 12 21-seat versions, known as the DC-3. The first of these was delivered on 18 August 1936. No one envisaged that, by 1939, the DC-3 would account for 90 per cent of the world's airline trade.

Country of origin:	USA
Engines:	two 1000hp Wright Cyclone SGR-1820 9-cylinder radials
Wingspan:	28.96m (95ft)
Length:	19.65m (64ft 5in)
Height:	4.97m (16ft 3in)
Weight loaded:	10,886kg (24,000lb)
Cruising speed:	298km/h (185mph)
Service ceiling:	7070m (23,200ft)
Range:	2414km (1500 miles)
Passengers + crew:	21 + 2

Douglas DC-3

The German national airline Deutsche Lufthansa first operated the DC-3 during World War II, several aircraft having been seized from KLM when German forces overran Holland in May 1940. These aircraft were operated on German internal routes, and on services to Switzerland and Stockholm. Lufthansa was established as a new company in 1953, and was ready to start operations by mid-1954. Scheduled services began on 31 March 1955, when a Convair 340 took off from Hamburg-Fuhlsbüttel for Düsseldorf-Frankfurt and Munich. The four Convairs in the fleet were operated on short- and medium-haul routes, while four Lockheed Constellations were acquired for long-distance operations. At the same time, three DC-3s, one seen here, were operated on the airline's domestic feeder routes. These aircraft were retired in 1960, after five years' excellent service.

Country of origin:	USA
Engines:	two 1000hp Wright Cyclone SGR-1820 9-cylinder radials
Wingspan:	28.96m (95ft)
Length:	19.65m (64ft 5in)
Height:	4.97m (16ft 3in)
Weight loaded:	10,886kg (24,000lb)
Cruising speed:	298km/h (185mph)
Service ceiling:	7070m (23,200ft)
Range:	2414km (1500 miles)
Passengers + crew:	21 + 2

Douglas DC-3 (Lisunov Li-2)

In the second half of the 1930s, the Soviet Union had no commercial transport aircraft comparable to the Douglas DC-3, and in 1938, the rights to manufacture the latter under licence were acquired by the Soviet government. The first Soviet-built DC-3 was rolled out at Kimkhi plant No 84, near Moscow, towards the end of 1939. Designated PS-84 in Russian service, the DC-3 began operations on Aeroflot's main European and Asian routes from 1940. As the PS-84, the DC-3 underwent a number of modifications to make it better suited to the rigours of operating in the Soviet Union. The airframe was strengthened, and Russian-manufactured engines fitted. In 1941, the DC-3 was redesignated Lisunov Li-2, the designer Lisunov having been responsible for the upgrades. Almost 3000 Li-2s are thought to have been built, adding to an unknown number of Douglas-built DC-3s.

Country of origin:	USA/USSR
Engines:	two 1000hp Ash-621R radials
Wingspan:	28.96m (95ft)
Length:	19.65m (64ft 5in)
Height:	4.97m (16ft 3in)
Weight loaded:	11,280kg (24,872lb)
Cruising speed:	298km/h (185mph)
Service ceiling:	7070m (23,200ft)
Range:	2414km (1500 miles)
Passengers + crew:	21 + 2

Douglas DC-3 Dakota

The name 'Dakota' was bestowed on the DC-3 by the Royal Air Force, which operated some 1200 during and after World War II. The Dakota shown, ZA947, was the last in British service. Despite its military markings, it was technically a civilian aircraft, as it was operated by the Royal Aircraft Establishment, a civilian organisation under government control. Originally a Canadian aircraft, this Dakota was at first allocated the wrong serial, KG661, because traces of the Canadian serial, CAF 661, could still be discerned. The error was picked up, and the ageing aircraft given a new number. It was used by the RAE Transport Flight to ferry personnel and equipment around Ministry of Defence scientific establishments. In RAF service, the Dakota was replaced on short-haul Transport Command routes by the Vickers Valetta, which equipped 14 squadrons.

Country of origin:	USA
Engines:	two 1000hp Wright Cyclone SGR-1820 9-cylinder radials
Wingspan:	28.96m (95ft)
Length:	19.65m (64ft 5in)
Height:	4.97m (16ft 3in)
Weight loaded:	10,886kg (24,000lb)
Cruising speed:	298km/h (185mph)
Service ceiling:	7070m (23,200ft)
Range:	2414km (1500 miles)
Passengers + crew:	21 + 2

Douglas DC-3-216

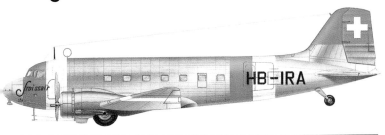

Swissair was an early customer for the revolutionary Douglas DC-2 airliner, and following the success of this aircraft, it was logical that the airline should purchase the DC-3. The first arrived in 1937 and served the airline until 1955; although they operated few services during World War II, they wore neutrality markings in order to avoid any unwanted aggression. During the war, Swissair serviced the half-dozen DC-3s that had been seized by the German airline Lufthansa from KLM, the national Dutch airline. Like many other airlines, Swissair was able to buy ex-military DC-3s very cheaply as the war drew to a close, and began full-scale operations once more on 30 July 1945. Its last DC-3 was withdrawn from service in 1969. Early experiences with the DC-2 and DC-3 cemented a firm bond between Swissair and Douglas, unbroken ever since.

Country of origin:	USA
Engines:	two 1000hp Wright Cyclone SGR-1820 9-cylinder radials
Wingspan:	28.96m (95ft)
Length:	19.65m (64ft 5in)
Height:	4.97m (16ft 3in)
Weight loaded:	10,886kg (24,000lb)
Cruising speed:	298km/h (185mph)
Service ceiling:	7070m (23,200ft)
Range:	2414km (1500 miles)
Passengers + crew:	21 + 2

Douglas DC-4 Carvair

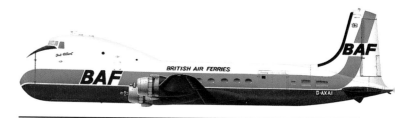

The final variant of the basic DC-4 design was evolved by Aviation Traders in England, who converted existing airframes by adding 2.64m (8ft 8in) to the DC-4 forward fuselage, and adding an hydraulic swing nose to permit direct in-loading of vehicles. Known as the Carvair, an apt contraction of car-via-air, and able to carry five vehicles, this conversion made its first flight at Southend on 21 June 1961. Nineteen Carvairs were operated on cross-Channel ferry flights in the early 1960s, and subsequently used as general transports. Channel Air Bridge was the first operator, followed by British Air Ferries, one of which is shown. Carvairs were also operated by Aer Lingus to carry racehorses and other cargo; Aviaco, which used them on services from Spain to France and the Balearic Islands; Compagnie Air Transport; Ansett/ANA; and Air Cambodge and Dominicana.

Country of origin:	GB
Engines:	four 1450hp Pratt & Whitney R-2000-7M2 Twin Wasp 14-cylinder radials
Wingspan:	35.81m (117ft 6in)
Length:	31.27m (102ft 7in)
Height:	8.38m (27ft 6in)
Weight loaded:	33,475kg (73,800lb)
Cruising speed:	342km/hr (213mph)
Service ceiling:	5700m (18,700ft)
Range:	3700km (2300 miles)
Crew:	3

Douglas DC-4 Skymaster

The evolution of the Douglas DC-4, which was to become one of the most famous civil and military air transports of all time, began in mid-1935 in response to an airline requirement for a medium-range 52-seat airliner. The first DC-4, which featured triple tail fins, flew on 7 June 1938, but was rejected by those airlines looking for smaller capacity. A modified DC-4 flew on 14 February 1942. It was the subject of 61 firm orders from the main US airlines, but with the Unied States at war, all transport aircraft production was devoted to the needs of the US armed forces. It was not until October 1945 that the DC-4 went into service as a civil airliner. By the time production ceased in August 1947, 1084 C-54 Skymasters and 79 civil DC-4s had been built. Many airlines used the DC-4 in the early post-war years, some buying surplus C-54s for conversion.

Country of origin:	USA
Engines:	four 1450hp Pratt & Whitney R-2000 Twin Wasp 14-cylinder radials
Wingspan:	35.81m (117ft 6in)
Length:	28.6m (93ft 10in)
Height:	8.38m (27ft 6in)
Weight loaded:	33,113kg (73,000lb)
Cruising speed:	365km/h (227mph) at 4575m (15,000ft)
Service ceiling:	6795m (22,300ft)
Range:	4025km (2500 miles)
Passengers + crew:	44–86 + 4

Douglas DC-6

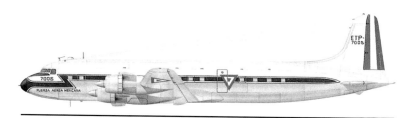

At the end of World War II, the Douglas Aircraft Company found itself seriously behind its main rivals in the long-range air transport market. Although production of the wartime Douglas DC-4 (C-54) transport had topped the 1000 mark, and the type had proven its reliability by making almost 8000 crossings of the Atlantic and Pacific with the loss of only three aircraft, Boeing's Model 307 Stratoliner and Lockheed's Model 749 Constellation were not only larger in freight capacity but were also pressurized to carry passengers in comfort. The USAAF therefore financed Douglas in the building of a larger, pressurized version of the DC-4; this was designated XC-112A, and the prototype first flew on 15 February 1946. Development as a civil airliner continued under the company designation DC-6. Seen here is a DC-6B in the colours of the Mexican Air Force.

Country of Origin:	USA
Engines:	four 2400hp Pratt & Whitney R-2800 Double Wasp 18-cylinder radials
Wingspan:	35.81m (117ft 6in)
Length:	32.18m (105ft 7in)
Height:	8.74m (28ft 8in)
Weight loaded:	48,534kg (107,00lb)
Cruising speed:	507km/h (315mph)
Service ceiling:	7620m (25,000ft)
Range:	4835km (3005 miles)
Passengers + crew:	54–102 + 3

Douglas DC-6

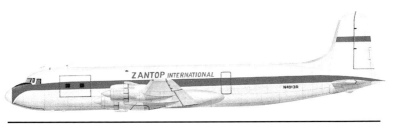

Many different variants of the DC-6 were produced during the aircraft's long career. The original DC-6A freighter was followed by the DC-6B; first flown on 2 February 1951, the DC-6B was a passenger-only version with windows and a lighter structure, and lacking the cargo door. Between 1951 and 1958, 288 were delivered; several were later fitted with a large underbelly tank to fight forest fires. The DC-6C was completed as a quick-change passenger/freight aircraft with windows; a moveable bulkhead could be positioned in any of the four stations for mixed passenger/cargo operations. The DC-6F was a designation applied to DC-6Bs subsequently converted to freighter configuration, often without cabin windows. The example shown here belonged to Zantop, a Detroit-based air freight concern. Some examples were still flying in Latin America in the 1990s.

Country of Origin:	USA
Engines:	four 2400hp Pratt & Whitney R-2800 Double Wasp 8-cylinder radials
Wingspan:	35.81m (117ft 6in)
Length:	32.18m (105ft 7in)
Height:	8.74m (28ft 8in)
Weight loaded:	48,534kg (107,00lb)
Cruising speed:	507km/h (315mph)
Service ceiling:	7620m (25,000ft)
Range:	4835km (3005 miles)
Passengers + crew:	54–102 + 3

Douglas DC-7C Seven Seas

The prototype Douglas DC-7C, the direct successor to the DC6 series, flew on 18 May 1953. It owed its existence to a requirement issued by American Airlines, which wanted an aircraft that was able to compete with the Lockheed Super Constellations ordered by their rival, TWA. Wright Turbo-Compound engines were fitted to 110 DC-7s in the first batch, which retained many features of the DC-6's airframe; these were followed by 112 DC-7Bs, the prototype of which flew in October 1954, for service on transatlantic routes. These two DC-7 variants had a number of faults, not the least of which was excessive engine noise in the passenger cabin. However, these had been eradicated by the time the prototype DC-7C flew in December 1955. This last variant had a restructured wing to allow for the use of extra fuel tanks and a lengthened fuselage.

Country of origin:	USA
Engines:	four 3400hp Wright R-3350-DA3 Turbo-Compound 18-cylinder radials
Wingspan:	38.86m (127ft 6in)
Length:	34.21m (112ft 3in)
Height:	9.7m (31ft 10in)
Weight loaded:	64,864kg (143,000lb)
Cruising speed:	571km/h (355mph)
Service ceiling:	6615m (21,700ft)
Range:	7410km (4605 miles)
Passengers + crew:	60–105 + 4

Douglas DC-8-33

Originally known as the Douglas Model 1881, and conceived as a four-jet domestic airliner, the Douglas DC-8 was announced in June 1955, made its first flight on 30 May 1958, and entered airline service about a year after the Boeing 707. By the time the prototype flew, the order book stood at more than 130 aircraft; the first customer was Pan American, which ordered 25 aircraft. These were to operate alongside the Boeing 707 on the airline's routes to Europe during the 1960s. Seen here is the last DC-8, a Series 33, delivered to Pan American. The Series 30, 40 and 50 were the intercontinental versions, and Series 10 and 20 the domestic models. The Series 10 began operations with United and Delta Airlines on 18 September 1959. On 21 August 1961, a modified DC-8-40 became the first jet airliner to exceed Mach 1, reached in a shallow dive.

Country of Origin:	USA
Engines:	four Pratt & Whitney JT43A turbojets of 7167kg (15,800lb) thrust each
Wingspan:	43.41m (142ft 5in)
Length:	45.87m (150ft 6in)
Height:	13.21m (43ft 4in)
Weight loaded:	125,192kg (276,000lb)
Cruising speed:	964km/h (599mph) at 9144m (30,000ft)
Service ceiling:	13,800m (45,300ft)
Range:	7500km (4660 miles)
Passengers + crew:	105–118 + 4

Douglas DC-8-42

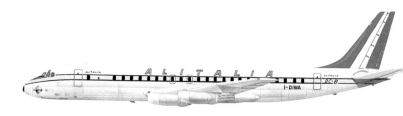

One of the most consistent of European DC-8 operators was the Italian national airline Alitalia, with over 20 years' experience on the type. Seen here is the first aircraft to join the fleet, a DC-8-42, which was delivered on 28 April 1960. This particular machine went on to see 17 years' service with the airline before retirement. The Series 40 DC-8, which first flew on 23 July 1959, was powered by Rolls-Royce Conway RCo 12 by-pass turbojets, and received FAA certification on 24 March 1960. The DC-8 was slightly less expensive than the Boeing 707, and slightly slower, although the speed diference was barely noticeable, even on long trips. After an early flurry of accidents, principally linked to the vastly greater complexity and performance of the jets, they proved to be safe and reliable aircraft. The 707, overall, was somewhat more efficient in service.

Country of origin:	USA
Engines:	four Rolls-Royce Conway RCo12 turbojets of 7620kg (16,800lb) thrust each
Wingspan:	43.41m (142ft 5in)
Length:	45.87m (150ft 6in)
Height:	13.21m (43ft 4in)
Weight loaded:	142,880kg (315,000lb)
Cruising speed:	943km/h (586mph) at 9150m (30,000ft)
Service ceiling:	13,800m (45,300ft)
Range:	9817km (6100 miles)
Passengers + crew:	105–118 + 4

Douglas DC-8-55CF

In January 1963, Douglas delivered the first of a series of freighter and
convertible versions of the DC-8. The basic DC8F Jet Trader, also designated
DC-8-54, was a convertible cargo/passenger version of the Series 50 aircraft, with a
cargo door, a system of rollers, guides and tie-downs built into the floor, and an
increased landing weight. It was superseded by the DC-8-55F, and made available in
the AF (all cargo) or CF (convertible passenger/cargo) configurations. Seen here is a
DC-8-55CF in the colours of Seaboard World Airlines, a major cargo operator which
also undertook charter flights. The DC-8-50 Series, the first of which flew in
December 1960, and which was certificated six months later, were powered by the
Pratt & Whitney JT3D turbofan, enabling them to fly non-stop from the US west
coast to Europe. The series replaced all previous models in production.

Country of origin:	USA
Engines:	four Pratt & Whitney JT3D turbofans of 8172kg (18,000lb) thrust each
Wingspan:	43.41m (142ft 5in)
Length:	45.87m (150ft 6in)
Height:	13.21m (43ft 4in)
Weight loaded:	142,880kg (315,000lb)
Cruising speed:	932km/h (579mph) at 9150m (30,000ft)
Service ceiling:	13,800m (45,300ft)
Range:	9205km (5720 miles)
Passengers + crew:	120–176 + 4

Douglas DC-8-62

In April 1965, Douglas announced three new variants of the DC8. The first was the DC-8 Super 61, a high-capacity transcontinental aircraft with the same wing and engines as the DC-8-50; the second was the Super 62, which was only slightly longer than the standard aircraft, but which was stretched just enough to match the seating capacity of the Boeing 707-320, and which had a completely redesigned engine installation; and the third, the Super 63, which combined the DC-8-61 fuselage with the Super 62 wing and uprated engines. The first Super 61 flew in March 1966, and all three passenger versions were in service by mid-1967, the Super 63CF following in June 1968. The Braniff Airways DC-8-62 seen here was hand-painted by artist Alexander Calder, and made its debut in Paris in 1973. Calder reputedly finished painting the aircraft only hours before it was unveiled.

Country of origin:	USA
Engines:	four Pratt & Whitney JT3D-3B turbofans of 8172kg (18,000lb) thrust each
Wingspan:	45.23m (148ft 5in)
Length:	47.98m (157ft 7in)
Height:	13.11m (43ft)
Weight loaded:	151,950kg (335,000lb)
Cruising speed:	965km/h (600mph) at 9150m (30,000ft)
Service ceiling:	13,800m (45,200ft)
Range:	9640km (6000 miles)
Passengers + crew:	189 + 4

Douglas DF-151

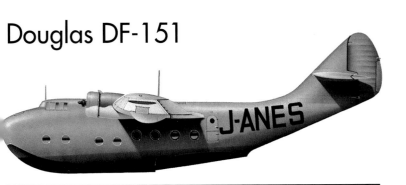

In the early 1930s, in response to the growing market for long-range commercial flying boats, Douglas Aircraft developed a twin-engined aircraft in this class capable of carrying 32 passengers on short flights, and 16 (in sleeping accommodation) on long-haul routes. Although the aircraft clearly had numerous attributes, Douglas failed to find a buyer in the United States, and sold the prototype and first three production aircraft to the Soviet Union. After being subjected to a thorough evaluation, they were assigned to air transport duties, mainly in the Arctic regions. Two Douglas DFs were also acquired by the Japanese government, and tested under the designation Navy Experimental Type D Flying Boat, in common with the then established Japanese practice of purchasing one or two foreign types for use in comparative trials with Japanese-designed aircraft.

Country of origin:	USA
Engines:	two 1000hp Wright SGR-1820-G-2 radials
Wingspan:	28.86m (95ft)
Length:	21.3m (69ft 10in)
Height:	7.47m (24ft 6in)
Weight loaded:	12,927kg (28,500lb)
Cruising speed:	286km/h (178mph)
Service ceiling:	4235m (13,900ft)
Range:	5311km (3300 miles)
Passengers + crew:	16–32 + 4

Douglas M-2

Although early airmail services in the United States were flown by ex-military machines such as the DH4, converted to single-seat configuration and with the front cockpit turned into a cargo compartment, it was not long before demand led to the building of purpose-built aircraft, or the conversion of more modern military types. Douglas approached the problem by converting one of its O-2 observation aircraft, on order for the US Army, into the M-1 mailplane, which was succeeded in turn by the M2. In November 1925, six M-2s were ordered by Western Air Express, which had been awarded a contract to carry mail between Los Angeles and Salt Lake City; operations began on 17 April 1926. The last of the Douglas mail carriers was the M-4, bringing the total production run to 57 aircraft, of which 50 were M3s ordered by the US Post Office.

Country of origin:	USA
Engine:	one 420hp Liberty V-1650-1 V-12 12-cylinder V-type
Wingspan:	13.56m (44ft 6in)
Length:	8.81m (28ft 11in)
Height:	3.07m (10ft 1in)
Weight loaded:	2223kg (4900lb)
Cruising speed:	190km/h (118mph)
Service ceiling:	5030m (16,500ft)
Range:	1127km (700 miles)
Crew:	1

Douglas SC-54D Skymaster

The Skymaster served in the US Navy as the R5D, giving valiant service on long-haul routes around the world. The first US Navy squadron to use the R5D, in May 1943, was Air Transport Squadron VR-1, which operated a regular service from Norfolk, Virginia, to Prestwick in Scotland, via Iceland. In December 1955, two R5Ds of Naval Air Squadron VX-6 forged the first air link with the continent of Antarctica, flying from Christchurch, New Zealand, to the scientific station at McMurdo Sound. The R5Ds' activities were many and varied; in March 1964, for example, they ferried emergency supplies to an earthquake-stricken area of Alaska. Skymasters were also converted to the air-sea rescue role for the USAF as the SC-54D (later HC-54D), seen here. The aircraft pictured, serial 4272566, was the first of 30 machines converted to rescue configuration.

Country of origin:	USA
Engines:	four 1450hp Pratt & Whitney R-2000 Twin Wasp 14-cylinder radials
Wingspan:	35.81m (117ft 6in)
Length:	28.6m (93ft 10in)
Height:	8.38m (27ft 6in)
Weight loaded:	28,125kg (62,600lb)
Cruising speed:	365km/h (227mph) at 4575m (15,000ft)
Service ceiling:	6795m (22,300ft)
Range:	6275km (3900 miles)
Passengers + crew:	30–50 + 6

Douglas World Cruiser

In 1923, the US Army Air Service began to take an interest in making a round-the-world flight, and invited proposals for a suitable aircraft from the various American manufacturers. One company, Douglas, proposed a version of their DT-2 torpedo bomber, then in production for the US Navy. Trials were carried out with a prototype aircraft (serial 23-1210), and four specially modified aircraft were ordered to take part in what had now become a six-nation competition. They were stripped of all non-essential military equipment, fitted with dual controls and direction-finding equipment, and provided with increased fuel tankage for the world flight. Designated DWC (Douglas World Cruiser), the four aircraft were delivered in March 1924. They were numbered 1 to 4 and named, respectively, Seattle, Chicago (pictured here), Boston and New Orleans.

Country of origin:	USA
Engine:	one 120hp Liberty 12A 12-cylinder liquid-cooled V-type
Wingspan:	15.24m (50ft)
Length:	10.82m (35ft 6in)
Height:	4.14m (13ft 7in)
Weight loaded:	3173kg (6995lb)
Cruising speed:	161km/h (100mph)
Service ceiling:	2135m (7000ft)
Range:	2655km (1650 miles)
Crew:	2

Douglas World Cruiser

All four DWCs left Seattle on 6 April 1924, but soon lost Aircraft No 1 (Seattle), which crashed near Port Moller, Alaska, on 30 April. The other three aircraft had almost completed their world tour, flying across the Pacific via the Aleutians to Japan, on across Asia and Europe, and across the Atlantic via Iceland and Greenland, when Aircraft No 3 (Boston, pictured here) was forced to ditch in the North Atlantic on 3 August. The two survivors reached Nova Scotia and were joined by the DWC prototype (23-1210), now named Boston II; the three arrived at Seattle on 28 September 1924 after a flight across the North American continent. The whole round-the-world flight lasted 175 days and covered 45,062km (28,000 miles); no fewer than 29 engine changes in the four aircraft had been necessary. Logistical support was provided by US Navy warships on the ocean routes.

Country of Origin:	USA
Engine:	one 120hp Liberty 12A 12-cylinder liquid-cooled V-type
Wingspan:	15.24m (50ft)
Length:	10.82m (35ft 6in)
Height:	4.14m (13ft 7in)
Weight loaded:	3173kg (6995lb)
Cruising speed:	161km/h (100mph)
Service ceiling:	2135m (7000ft)
Range:	2655km (1650 miles)
Crew:	2

EMBRAER EMB-110B-1

In September 1975, the Uruguayan Air Force (Fuerza Aerea Uruguaya) formed Grupo de Aviacion 6 within Brigada Aerea 1 at Carrasco to operate five EMB-110C civil-standard transports, all of which were delivered the following November, and serialled T580-584. A later arrival, in August 1978, was a single photo-survey transport, T-585. The five original aircraft and the photo-survey machine also undertook tasks on behalf of the country's paramilitary airline TAMU (Transporte Aereo Militar Uruguayo); they were given the parallel civil registrations CX-BJJ, -BJK, -BJB, -BJC, -BJE and -BKF. The illustration shows the first Bandeirante to be delivered. Another country to use the Bandeirante in a dual capacity was Gabon, which received three standard aircraft and a maritime surveillance EMB-111A. One aircraft was assigned to the presidential bodyguard.

Country of origin:	Brazil
Engines:	two 550hp Pratt & Whitney PT6A-20 turboprops
Wingspan:	15.42m (50ft 7in)
Length:	12.74m (41ft 9in)
Height:	5.17m (16ft 11in)
Weight loaded:	4500kg (9920lb)
Cruising speed:	430km/h (267mph) at 2500m (8200ft)
Service ceiling:	9000m (29,500ft)
Range:	1850km (1150 miles)
Passengers + crew:	16 + 2

EMBRAER EMB-110P1A

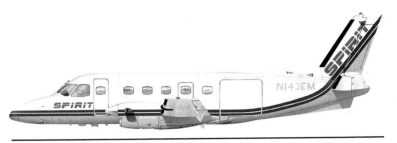

The prime market for the commuter version of the Bandeirante was the United States. In 1978, a distribution agreement was signed between EMBRAER and Aero Industries of Los Angeles, following which the American FAA granted the necessary certification. The Bandeirante continued to face considerable opposition from American air carriers and manufacturers, reflected in charges of predatory pricing through subsidized rates of interest supported by the Brazilian government; this did little to deter many small airlines from buying the type. By May 1978, operators included Wyoming Airlines with three aircraft, Mountain West Airlines with four, and Transmountain Airlines of Denver, Colorado, with three. A later operator was Air Spirit of Dallas, Texas, which ordered six EMB-110P1As, fitted with a large rear freight door; it began operations in April 1984.

Country of origin:	Brazil
Engines:	two 550hp Pratt & Whitney PT6A-20 turboprops
Wingspan:	15.42m (50ft 7in)
Length:	12.74m (41ft 9in)
Height:	5.17m (16ft 11in)
Weight loaded:	4500kg (9920lb)
Cruising speed:	430km/h (267mph) at 2500m (8200ft)
Service ceiling:	9000m (29,500ft)
Range:	1850km (1150 miles)
Passengers + crew:	18 + 2

EMBRAER EMB-110P1K

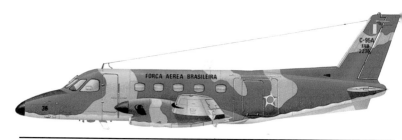

There can be little question that the EMBRAER Bandeirante has been one of the most successful of the modern, light, turboprop commuterliners. By the time production ceased in 1989, over 500 had been sold. In addition to its phenomenal civil success, many were delivered to the military to undertake a variety of roles. Following the first flight of the EMB-110 prototype on 19 August 1972, the Forca Aerea Brasileira (FAB) carried out an official valuation, and confirmed that it was satisfied with the aircraft, allocating it the military designation C-95. The EMB-110P1K used by the FAB has the forward entry door of the stretched Bandeirante models, and is used for freight transport or for carrying up to 19 paratroops. It is fitted with a large rear cargo hatch with an inset sliding door that allows troops to gain clear exit from the rear of the aircraft.

Country of origin:	Brazil
Engines:	two 550hp Pratt & Whitney PT6A-20 turboprops
Wingspan:	15.42m (50ft 7in)
Length:	12.74m (41ft 9in)
Height:	5.17m (16ft 11in)
Weight loaded:	4500kg (9920lb)
Cruising speed:	430km/h (267mph) at 2500m (8200ft)
Service ceiling:	9000m (29,500ft)
Range:	1850km (1150 miles)
Passengers + crew:	18 + 2

EMBRAER EMB-110P2

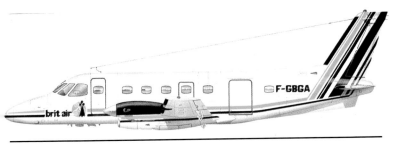

The EMB-110P1 and EMB-110P2 began to gain a foothold in Europe in 1977, when a number of aircraft were sold to French regional carriers. Air Littoral purchased six of the EMB-110P2 model to cover a route network radiating from its home base at Montpellier-Frejorgues to some 29 destinations in southern France, Italy and Spain. Another airline, familiar to users of London Gatwick, is Brit Air, which is based at Morlaix in northwest France, and which used three of the EMB-110P2 model (F-GBGA being pictured here) with the stretched fuselage and forward passenger entry door. This version does not have the large freight door that is fitted to the EMB-110P1A, but it has provision for a toilet in the extreme rear of the aircraft. Brit Air operates a service to Rennes and Quimper every weekday.

aCountry of origin:	Brazil
Engines:	two 550hp Pratt & Whitney PT6A-20 turboprops
Wingspan:	15.42m (50ft 7in)
Length:	12.74m (41ft 9in)
Height:	5.17m (16ft 11in)
Weight loaded:	4500kg (9920lb)
Cruising speed:	430km/h (267mph) at 2500m (8200ft)
Service ceiling:	9000m (29,500ft)
Range:	1850km (1150 miles)
Passengers + crew:	16 + 2

EMBRAER EMB-110P2

The EMB-110P2 variant of the Bandeirante illustrated here (VHMWW, c/n 110194) was built in 1978 and delivered to Masling Commuter Services of Sydney, Australia. This aircraft was taken over by Wings Australia when it bought Masling in 1981, and VHMWW was subsequently leased to East Coast Airlines, which operates local commuter services out of Tamworth and Sydney. The Bandeirante concept was initiated in June 1965 by Max Holste, the French designer who conceived the MH52, the Broussard, widely used by the French armed forces as a communications and observation aircraft, and the Super Broussard, later to become the Nord 262. His design team came under the control of the Brazilian Air Ministry, and was detailed to design a replacement for the ageing fleet of Beech Super 18s then in service with the Brazilian Air Force.

Country of origin:	Brazil
Engines:	two 550hp Pratt & Whitney PT6A-20 turboprops
Wingspan:	15.42m (50ft 7in)
Length:	12.74m (41ft 9in)
Height:	5.17m (16ft 11in)
Weight loaded:	4500kg (9920lb)
Cruising speed:	430km/h (267mph) at 2500m (8200ft)
Service ceiling:	9000m (29,500ft)
Range:	1850km (1150 miles)
Passengers + crew:	16 + 2

EMBRAER 110C(N)

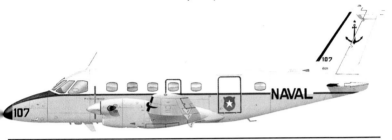

The basic Bandeirante design lent itself very well to light, military transport use. The illustration shows the first of three EMB110C(N)s delivered to the Chilean Navy. It is in use with Transport Squadron VR-2, and is basically a standard commercial aircraft fitted with 16 passenger seats. Chile also operates six of the EMB-111(N) maritime patrol variant, and these are assigned to Patrol Squadron VP-3. The EMB-111 has been produced in only modest numbers, with Brazil the main user. This version of the aircraft carries an APS-128 search radar; it can also be fitted with an optional 50-million candlepower searchlight on the inner starboard wing. Up to eight air-to-surface rockets can also be carried on underwing pylons, and there is provision for bombs and depth charges, giving the aircraft a substantial offensive capability. Data below is for the EMB-110C(N).

Country of origin:	Brazil
Engines:	two 550hp Pratt & Whitney PT6A-20 turboprops
Wingspan:	15.42m (50ft 7in)
Length:	12.74m (41ft 9in)
Height:	5.17m (16ft 11in)
Weight loaded:	4500kg (9920lb)
Cruising speed:	430km/h (267mph) at 2500m (8200ft)
Service ceiling:	9000m (29,500ft)
Range:	1850km (1150 miles)
Passengers + crew:	16 + 2

Fairey (Westland) Rotodyne

The Fairey Rotodyne was a bold attempt to combine the best attributes of a conventional airliner and a large helicopter to produce a hybrid commercial aircraft, having a much higher speed than an ordinary helicopter, while still retaining the latter's V/STOL capability. The Rotodyne prototype (XE521) made its first vertical take-off on 6 November 1957, and trials were under way, when the Rotodyne set a closed-circuit speed record of 307.22km/h (191mph), when Fairey Aviation was taken over by Westland in 1960. The concept showed considerable potential, and seemed suited to both civil and military roles. In 1960, Westland was invited to quote for six Rotodynes for BEA and 12 troop/vehicle transport versions for the RAF. However, no firm orders were forthcoming, the British government withdrew financial backing, and the project was abandoned.

Country of origin:	GB
Engines:	two 3000hp Napier Eland turboprops
Wingspan:	14.17m (46ft 6in). Rotor diameter: 27.43m (90ft)
Length:	17.88m (58ft 8in)
Height:	6.76m (22ft 2in)
Weight loaded:	17,237kg (38,000lb)
Cruising speed:	298km/h (185mph) at 1524m (5000ft)
Service ceiling:	not known
Range:	724km (450 miles)
Passengers + crew:	40 + 3

Farman Goliath

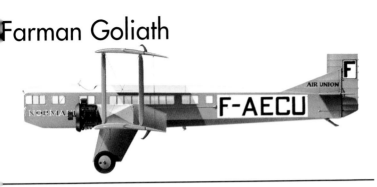

One of the stalwarts of early French airline operation, the Farman Goliath was originally designed as a twin-engined, two-seat night bomber, but World War I ended before it could be brought into operational service. It was converted for commercial use by having a well-lit passenger cabin and an extended nose. The two-man crew were seated side by side, in an elevated open cockpit between the front (four-seat) and rear (eight-seat) passenger compartments. The accommodation for passengers, at first primitive in the extreme, improved considerably later on as airlines tried to attract passengers by providing higher standards of comfort. Some 60 Goliaths were used by operators in France, Belgium, Czechoslovakia, Romania and South America. During its career, the Goliath established several international distance and load-to-altitude records.

Country of origin:	France
Engines:	two 260hp Salmson CM-9 9-cylinder radials
Wingspan:	26.5m (86ft 11in)
Length:	14.33m (47ft)
Height:	4.91m (16ft 1in)
Weight loaded:	4770kg (10,516lb)
Cruising speed:	120km/h (75mph) at 2000m (6500ft)
Service ceiling:	4000m (13,125ft)
Range:	400km (249 miles)
Passengers + crew:	12 + 2

Fokker F.27 Friendship

Among all the short- to medium-range, twin-engined turboprop airliner designs to emerge in the late 1950s, one of the biggest success stories was the Fokker F.27 Friendship. The project was initiated at the beginning of the decade, and progressed rapidly, with the decision to build four prototypes (two flight test aircraft and two static test airframes) taken in 1953. The first of these made a trouble-free maiden flight on 24 November 1955. By this time, the F.27's commercial success was assured, with 30 on the company's order books by the spring of 1956. In April, Fokker entered into a licence agreement with Fairchild in the United States, and production began almost simultaneously in both countries. The aircraft here is a F.27-100, the fifth off the production line; delivered to Aer Lingus in November 1958, it was later sold, serving many years in New Zealand.

Country of origin:	Netherlands
Engines:	two 1670hp Rolls-Royce Dart 511 turboprops
Wingspan:	29m (95ft 2in)
Length:	23.5m (77ft)
Height:	8.4m (27ft 6in)
Weight loaded:	18,370kg (40,500lb)
Cruising speed:	428km (266mph) at 6095m (20,000ft)
Service ceiling:	8840m (29,000ft)
Range:	1250km (777 miles)
Passengers + crew:	40–52 + 2-3

Fokker F.27 Mk 200

Certainly one of the brightest colour schemes to grace the F.27 was that of Hughes Airwest, a regional carrier operating a large network of scheduled services to over 60 destinations in the western United States. This is a Fairchild-built F.27A, one of several that saw service with the airline, offering excellent performance capabilities for services into high-altitude and short-runway airfields. When the airline was taken over by Republic Airlines in 1980, the F.27 fleet was dispersed, although this aircraft had by then been sold to Canadian operator Norcanair. The first recipient of the licence-built Fairchild F.27 was West Coast Airlines, an order that provided an important breakthrough for Fokker into the lucrative US market. As time went by, modification kits were also offered to F.27 operators to enable them to improve the aircraft's performance.

Country of origin:	Netherlands
Engines:	two 2280hp Rolls-Royce Dart Mk 536-7R turboprops
Wingspan:	29m (95ft 2in)
Length:	23.56m (77ft 3in)
Height:	8.5m (27ft 10in)
Weight loaded:	20,412kg (45,000lb)
Cruising speed:	480km/h (298mph) at 6095m (20,000ft)
Service ceiling:	8990m (29,500ft)
Range:	1926km (1197 miles)
Passengers + crew:	40–52 + 2–3

Fokker F.27-500 Friendship

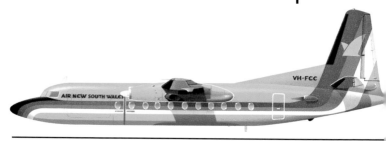

The most important later series F.27 models were the F.27-200 (known as the F.27A in the United States), which had uprated engines, and the F.27-300 and F-27-400 (designated F.27B and F.27C respectively in the United States). These models were more versatile, having a large, freight-loading door in the forward fuselage to permit mixed passenger and freight operations. The next version was the F.27-500, which appeared in November 1967, and resembled the F.27-200 except for a stretched fuselage. The aircraft shown here is an F.27-500 of Air New South Wales, a regional subsidiary of Ansett Airlines, which used the type extensively on services to settlements in the 'Outback'. The F.27-500 was followed in November 1968 by the F.27-600, a development of the Series 200 with a large freight door. Military versions of the Friendship were the Troopship and F.27 Maritime.

Country of origin:	Netherlands
Engines:	two 2255hp Rolls-Royce Dart 532-7R turboprops
Wingspan:	29m (95ft 2in)
Length:	25.04m (82ft 2in)
Height:	8.4m (27ft 6in)
Weight loaded:	20,411kg (45,000lb)
Cruising speed:	428km (266mph) at 6095m (20,000ft)
Service ceiling:	8840m (29,000ft)
Range:	1741km (1082 miles)
Passengers + crew:	36–56 + 2–4

Fokker F.28 Fellowship

Having achieved considerable success with the turboprop-powered F.27, it was logical for Fokker to move into the jet market. Here, the F.28 proved another winner for the Dutch company, offering low-cost, short-range transport from short runways, an aspect that has made it particularly attractive to 'Third World' customers. Sales of the Fokker F.28, the prototype of which flew for the first time on 9 May 1967, have mostly been to European, Asian, African and South American operators, although several US operators adopted the type. One major customer was Garuda of Indonesia, using the type between Jakarta and many centres of population throughout South-East Asia, many of them served by only small airports to which the F.28 was well suited. At one point Garuda had a fleet of 34 Fellowships. The illustration shows an F.28 of the Colombian Air Force.

Country of origin:	Netherlands
Engines:	two Rolls-Royce Spey Mk 555 15 turbofans of 4468kg (9850lb) thrust each
Wingspan:	23.58m (77ft 4in)
Length:	27.40m (89ft 11in)
Height:	8.5m (27ft 10in)
Weight loaded:	29,485kg (65,000lb)
Cruising speed:	843km/h (524mph) at 7000m (23,000ft)
Service ceiling:	10,670m (35,000ft)
Range:	2100km (1305 miles)
Passengers + crew:	85 + 2–3

Fokker F.28 Series 1000

A part from one aircraft for the Argentine Air Force, AeroPeru was the first
South American customer for the Fellowship. Three Series 1000s were
delivered in 1972 and 1973, flying domestic and short-range international
services from Lima. The Mk 1000 was the original version, sized for up to 65
passengers. In 1970, Fokker introduced the Mk 2000. Chronologically, but not
numerically, the next versions were the Mks 5000 and 6000, which flew in 1973,
and which were, respectively, short- and long-fuselage versions of a more
advanced aircraft with slatted wings. Fokker decided that few customers wanted
the slatted wing and two final versions, the Mks 3000 and 4000, were produced
without slats, but with all the other improvements. When the production finished
1986, Fokker had sold 241 Fellowships to 57 operators in 37 countries.

Country of origin:	Netherlands
Engines:	two Rolls-Royce Spey Mk 555 15 turbofans of 4468kg (9850lb) thrust each
Wingspan:	23.58m (77ft 4in)
Length:	27.40m (89ft 11in)
Height:	8.5m (27ft 10in)
Weight loaded:	29,485kg (65,000lb)
Cruising speed:	843km/h (524mph) at 7000m (23,000ft)
Service ceiling:	10,670m (35,000ft)
Range:	2100km (1300 miles)
Passengers + crew:	85 + 2–3

Fokker F.VII-3m 'Southern Cross'

Due to the vast distances involved, the aerial conquest of the Pacific Ocean, unlike that of the Atlantic, got off to a slow start. Prior to 1927, the only trans-Pacific flights had been 'island-hopping' ventures, and it was not until the advent of the Fokker F.VII commercial trimotor, the first aircraft with anything like long-range capability, that long, overwater flights became feasible. The first aircraft to make a crossing of the Pacific, via Honolulu and Fiji, was the famous F.VII-3m 'Southern Cross', which arrived at Brisbane's Eagle Farm Airport on 9 June 1928, after a 11,890km (7390 mile) flight from Oakland, California. The pilot was Charles Kingsford Smith, his second pilot C. T. P. Ulm, his wireless operator James Warner, both Australians, and his navigator, Harry Lyon, an American. The aircraft was a hybrid, built from the components of two other Fokker F.VIIs.

Country of origin:	Netherlands
Engines:	three 240hp Wright Whirlwind radials
Wingspan:	19.31m (63ft 4in)
Length:	14.57m (47ft 10in)
Height:	3.9m (12ft 10in)
Weight loaded:	3986kg (8788lb)
Cruising speed:	170km/h (106mph)
Service ceiling:	4700m (15,420ft)
Range:	2600km (1616 miles) with extra fuel
Crew:	4

Fokker F.VIIA-3m

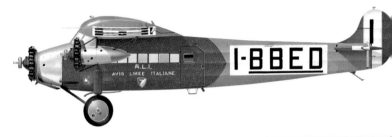

The Italian airline Avioline Italiane received a batch of three F.VIIa-3m aircraft, including I-BBED (c/n 5059) illustrated here. In 1933, this was sold to Societa Aerea Mediterranea and then, in company with other AI aircraft, it was taken on charge by the Ala Littoria company, and is believed to have been scrapped in 1939. The first prototype of the Fokker VII had only a single engine, and flew for the first time on 11 April 1924. The first three-engined aircraft (c/n 4900) was flown in the 1925 Ford Reliability Tour, and was subsequently sold to Edsel Ford. Carrying the name Josephine Ford, it made an historic flight from Spitzbergen to the North Pole on 9 May 1926, under the command of Lt Cdr Richard E Byrd and Floyd Bennett. The F.VIIA-3m was a great favourite with exploration teams because of its reliability and the fact that it could be fitted with floats.

Country of origin:	Netherlands
Engines:	three 240hp Wright Whirlwind radials
Wingspan:	19.31m (63ft 4in)
Length:	14.57m (47ft 7in)
Height:	3.9m (12ft 10in)
Weight loaded:	3986kg (8788lb)
Cruising speed:	170km/h (106mph)
Service ceiling:	4700m (15,420ft)
Range:	2600km (1616 miles) with extra fuel
Passengers + crew:	8 + 2

Fokker F.VIIB-3m

The Fokker F.VIIB-3M, an enlarged version of the F.VIIA-3m, was the world's premier airliner of the 1927–33 period. Fokker and Atlantic built 147, and basically similar machines, with many different types of engine, were built under licence in Belgium, Czechoslovakia, France, Italy, Poland, and the UK. Nine of the licensed sub-types were military, four being bombers. Fokker F.VIIB-3m PH-AFS, illustrated above, was used initially by KLM, who named it Specht (Woodpecker). It was sold in August 1936 to Crilly Airways, but did not see any further airline service because it was then passed on to the Spanish Nationalist Forces, who took it on charge at Burgos, and used it in the fight against the Republican forces. The Czech Avia company built 21 F.VIIB3m aircraft, one a bomber, and followed up with 12 more bombers based on the more powerful Fokker F.IX.

Country of origin:	Netherlands
Engines:	three 300hp Wright J6 Whirlwind 9-cylinder radials
Wingspan:	21.71m (71ft 3in)
Length:	14.57m (47ft 7in)
Height:	3.9m (12ft 10in)
Weight loaded:	5300kg (11,684lb)
Cruising speed:	178km/h (111mph)
Service ceiling:	4400m (14,435ft)
Range:	1200km (746 miles) with extra fuel
Passengers + crew:	8–10 + 2

Fokker F.VIIB-3m

SABENA, the Belgian airline, was a prominent F.VIIB-3m user, and flew aircraft built under licence by the Belgian manufacturing company SABCA. This particular example, OO-AGH, was delivered on 20 September 1932, and flew on European routes until May 1940, when it was taken over by the invading German forces at Haren Airport, near Brussels. Fokker F.VIIs saw a significant level of military service in their lifetime, both as transports during World War II and, earlier, during the Spanish Civil War, where they were used by both sides. For example, three F.VIIB-3ms, originally delivered to Lineas Aereas Potales Españolas (LAPE) in November 1933, were impressed into service as bombers with the Republican Air Force. Makeshift external bomb racks were fitted on spars secured to the window frames.

Country of origin:	Netherlands
Engines:	three 300hp Wright J6 Whirlwind 9-cylinder radials
Wingspan:	21.71m (71ft 3in)
Length:	14.57m (47ft 7in)
Height:	3.9m (12ft 10in)
Weight loaded:	5300kg (11,684lb)
Cruising speed:	178km/h (111mph)
Service ceiling:	4400m (14,435ft)
Range:	1200km (746 miles) with extra fuel
Passengers + crew:	8–10 + 2

Fokker F.VIIB-3m Avro Ten

In 1928, the British aircraft constructor A. V. Roe & Co (Avro) acquired a licence to build the Fokker F.VIIB-3m in Britain. The first to enter production was the Avro Ten (Type 618), seating a crew of two, and eight passengers. This differed only slightly from the standard Dutch-built FVIIB-3ms, and 12 were built betwen 1929 and 1933 for Australian National Airways (seven), Imperial Airways (two, for charter operations), Midland and Scottish Air Ferries (one), and the Egyptian Air Force (two). One of the Egyptian aircraft was sold to Indian National Airways in 1935. The illustration shows G-AASP, named Achilles and delivered to Imperial Airways at its Cairo station in April 1931. It flew pipeline patrols on contract to the Iraq Petroleum Transport Co, later returning to the United Kingdom, where Imperial Airways found charter work for it. It was withdrawn and scrapped in 1939.

Country of origin:	GB
Engines:	three 300hp Wright J6 Whirlwind 9-cylinder radials
Wingspan:	21.71m (71ft 3in)
Length:	14.57m (47ft 7in)
Height:	3.9m (12ft 10in)
Weight loaded:	5300kg (11,684lb)
Cruising speed:	178km/h (111mph)
Service ceiling:	4400m (14,435ft)
Range:	1200km (746 miles) with extra fuel
Passengers + crew:	8 + 2

Ford Model 5-AT-B

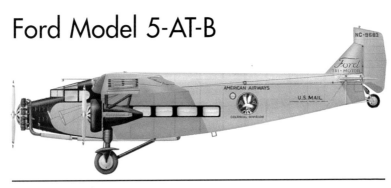

The Ford Trimotor shown here, Model 5-AT-39, had a long and very active life, passing through many minor changes and paint schemes. She is seen in the paintwork she wore when she was four years old in 1933, flying for American Airways. After leaving American, she toiled for operators in many Latin American countries, as well as Alaska and Mexico, before being completely refurbished in 1962 by Aircraft Hydro-Forming, a US company that made prolonged attempts, over a period of 20 years or so, to arouse interest in establishing a production line for an improved and modernised Tri-motor, the Stout Bushmaster 2000. A year later she was bought by American, long since styled Airlines instead of the original Airways, and repainted with her old number for publicity flying. Surving examples of Ford Tri-motors have become valuable collectors' items.

Country of origin:	USA
Engines:	three 420hp Pratt & Whitney Wasp C 9-cylinder radials
Wingspan:	23.72m (77ft 10in)
Length:	15.3m (50ft 3in)
Height:	3.66m (12ft)
Weight loaded:	5738kg (12,650lb)
Cruising speed:	198km/h (123mph)
Ceiling:	5639m (18,500ft)
Range:	885km (550 miles)
Passengers + crew:	15 + 2

Ford Model 6-AT-1

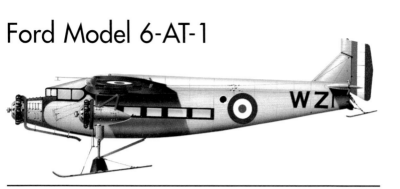

The unique Ford Tri-motor seen here was the Model 6-AT-1, basically a Model 5-AT-C, fitted with low-powered Wright J6 Whirlwind engines, and sold as a sea/skiplane to the Royal Canadian Air Force in 1929. It bore the Canadian civil registration G-CYWZ, the last two letters displayed on the rear fuselage. The Canadian registration prefix was changed to CF- in 1939. Its main duties were forest patrol and spraying, and later it carried out radio research. Another Model 5-AT-C Tri-motor variant was the US Navy's RR-4, with an enlarged wing and three 450hp Wasp engines with Townend ring cowls. The Tri-motor in the US Navy Museum at NAS Pensacola is painted and represented as RR-4 serial A8840, though its true identity is not certain. The US Army used three of these Tri-motors under the designation C-3A, as well as three more powerful 5-AT-Ds (C-4As).

Country of origin:	USA
Engines:	three 350hp Wright J6 Whirlwind 9-cylinder radials
Wingspan:	23.72m (77ft 10in)
Length:	15.3m (50ft 3in)
Height:	3.66m (12ft)
Weight loaded:	5738kg (12,650lb)
Cruising speed:	198km/h (123mph)
Ceiling:	5639m (18,500ft)
Range:	885km (550 miles)
Passengers + crew:	15 + 2

Ford Tri-motor

One of the classic transport aircraft of all time, so much so that surviving examples now change hands at over a million US dollars apiece, the Ford Tri-motor, nicknamed the 'Tin Goose', served with over 100 air transport operators in the United States, Australia, Canada, China, Mexico and Central and South America. The protoype first flew on 11 June 1926, production eventually running to 198. The initial production model, of which 14 were built, was designated 4-AT-A, and was followed in 1927 by the improved 4-AT-B. Other variants, differing mainly from one another in the type of engine installed, were the 4-AT-C, -D, -E and -F, the latter bringing 4-AT production to a close in 1929. However, production continued with the Model 5-AT, an improved version, one of which is pictured here in the livery of Cia Mexicana de Aviacion, an affiliate of Pan American.

Country of origin:	USA
Engines:	three 420hp Pratt & Whitney Wasp C 9-cylinder radials
Wingspan:	23.72m (77ft 10in)
Length:	15.3m (50ft 3in)
Height:	3.66m (12ft)
Weight loaded:	5738kg (12,650lb)
Cruising speed:	198km/h (123mph)
Ceiling:	5639m (18,500ft)
Range:	885km (550 miles)
Passengers + crew:	15 + 2

Ford Tri-motor

Pictured here, N414H is the last Tri-motor in commercial service. Owned by Scenic Airways of Las Vegas, Nevada, it is still in existence and has been used for local pleasure flying, for example, on aerial tours of the Grand Canyon. It is used today for promotional and film work, as well as charter tours. The most famous of all Tri-motors was probably the Model 4-AT-15 donated by Henry and Edsel Ford for the Antarctic expedition of Commander Richard E. Byrd. Pilot Bernt Balchen found that it needed more range, so the span was increased to 22.55m (74ft), fuel tankage was augmented, and a powerful Wright Cyclone engine installed in the nose. It overflew the South Pole. During its career, the Tri-motor inevitably underwent both official and unofficial modification to meet the needs of particular operators, being flown with wheel, float and ski landing gear.

Country of origin:	USA
Engines:	three 420hp Pratt & Whitney Wasp C 9-cylinder radials
Wingspan:	23.72m (77ft 10in)
Length:	15.3m (50ft 3in)
Height:	3.66m (12ft)
Weight loaded:	5738kg (12,650lb)
Cruising speed:	198km/h (123mph)
Ceiling:	5639m (18,500ft)
Range:	885km (550 miles)
Passengers + crew:	15 + 2

Grumman G73 Mallard

The 1930s were years of considerable success for America's flying boat designers. The Grumman G21 Goose was one example of a successful amphibious design during this period. Originally flown in June 1937 as a commercial amphibian aircraft, more than 250 were built for civil and military customers before production ended in September 1945. Two other designs deriving from the Goose were the G44 Widgeon, which first flew in 1940, and the G73 Mallard of 1946. The Mallard, of which a total of 59 were built, featured a shoulder-mounted cantilever wing and an all-metal, double-step, stressed-skin hull. The interior was air conditioned, which made the aircraft popular among users, including King Farouk of Egypt, in hot climates. The aircraft here was operated by Chalk's International, and used regularly between Miami and the Bahamas.

Country of origin:	USA
Engines:	two 600hp Pratt and Whitney R-1340-53H1 Wasp 9-cylinder radials
Wingspan:	20.32m (66ft 8in)
Length:	14.73m (48ft 4in)
Height:	5.72m (18ft 9in)
Weight loaded:	5783kg (12,750lb)
Cruising speed:	346km/h (215mph)
Ceiling:	7010m (23,000ft)
Range:	2221km (1380 miles)
Passengers + crew:	2 + 10

Gulfstream American Gulfstream IV

The original Gulfstream executive aircraft, a product of the Grumman Aircraft Corporation, was powered by twin turboprops, and a jet-powered version was a logical development. The outcome was the Gulfstream II, which was a radical development of the Gulfstream I, and which finally established the company, hitherto famous for its naval combat aircraft, as a supplier to the worldwide corporate elite. The Gulfstream II was succeeded by the III and IV; seen here is the 158th Gulfstream IV off the production line, flying the flag of the American company Navair Incorporated. The most obvious difference between the GIV and preceding aircraft in the Gulfstream series is the former's much larger engine nacelles, which house the 1.2m (47in) Rolls-Royce Tay 610 engines. The Tay enables the GIV to conform to the stringent FAR Pt 36 Stage 3 noise regulations.

Country of origin:	USA
Engines:	two Rolls-Royce Tay Mk 511 8 turbofans of 6260kg (13,800lb) thrust each
Wingspan:	23.27m (76ft 4in)
Length:	26.92m (88ft 4in)
Height:	7.45m (24ft 5in)
Weight loaded:	33,203kg (73,200lb)
Cruising speed:	936km/h (582mph) at 9450m (31,000ft)
Service ceiling:	13,715m (45,000ft)
Range:	6732km (4183 miles)
Passengers + crew:	8 + 3

Handley Page (BAe) Jetstream 31

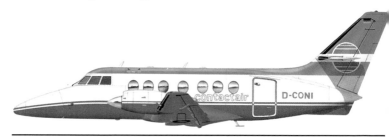

In 1975, the British aviation industry was nationalised, and Scottish Aviation, which had been responsible for Jetstream construction, was combined with BAC and Hawker Siddeley to form British Aerospace. On 5 December 1975, BAe announced plans to produce the Garrett-engined version of the Jetstream, to be built at Prestwick in Scotland, and called the Jetstream 31. The prototype (G-JSSD) flew on 28 March 1980, and production aircraft were offered in airline, executive shuttle, or corporate configurations. Stuttgart-based Contactair joined the Jetstream club in 1982 with the delivery of its first Jetstream 31, pictured here. The airline later took delivery of three more aircraft, becoming Germany's sole Jetstream operator. Contactair's fleet later expanded to accommodate seven DHC-8 Dash-8s, two of its Jetstreams continuing to be used well into the 1990s.

Country of origin:	GB
Engines:	two 900hp Garrett TPE331-10 turboprops
Wingspan:	15.85m (52ft)
Length:	14.35m (47.1ft)
Height:	5.3m (17.5ft)
Weight loaded:	7350kg (16,200lb)
Cruising speed:	490km/h (305mph) at 7620m (25,000ft)
Ceiling:	9630m (31,600ft)
Range:	1250km (780 miles)
Passengers + crew:	18 + 2

Handley Page HP.137 Jetstream

In January 1966, the British aircraft manufacturer Handley Page, then occupied almost exclusively with overhauling RAF Victor tankers , announced a new twin-turboprop executive, feederliner and military transport, the HP.137 Jetstream, together with the news that the first batch of 20 had been ordered by the American International Jetstream Corporation. Initially a prototype, four pre-production Jestreams, and a static test airframe were built, and the prototype (G-ATXH) flew for the first time on 18 August 1967, with temporary Astazou XII turboprop engines. It was followed by the second Mk.I aircraft on 28 December 1967, and the third on 8 March 1968. The excellent airframe design was plagued by the poor performance of the Astazou engines, a problem overcome by the installation of Garrett TPE331 engines in the Jetstream 31, pictured here.

Country of origin:	GB
Engines:	two 900hp Garrett TPE331-10 turboprops
Wingspan:	15.85m (52ft)
Length:	14.35m (47.1ft)
Height:	5.3m (17.5ft)
Weight loaded:	7350kg (16,200lb)
Cruising speed:	490km/h (305mph) at 7620m (25,000ft)
Ceiling:	9630m (31,600ft)
Range:	1250km (780 miles)
Passengers + crew:	18 + 2

Handley Page HP.42W

By far the biggest and most luxurious airliners of the early 1930s were the Handley Page HP.42 Hannibal and Heracles class, four-engined biplanes built for Imperial Airways. Eight HP.42s were completed in 1930–31, built in two versions: the E model for Indian services and African routes, which could cary 24 passengers, and the W for European routes, which could accommodate 38. The HP.42 prototype flew for the first time on 14 November 1930, and began operating on the London–Paris route on 11 June 1931. The aircraft were all named after mythical or historical figures, such as Hannibal, Horsa, Hanno and Hadrian for the HP.42E class, and Heracles, Hengist, Horatius and Helena for the HP.42Ws. These aircraft clocked up a very high mileage, exceeding 16,093,400km (10 million miles) in total, establishing an unrivalled record of safety and reliability.

Country of origin:	GB
Engines:	four 490hp Bristol Jupiter XIF 9-cylinder radials
Wingspan:	39.62m (130ft)
Length:	28.09m (92ft 2in)
Height:	8.23m (27ft)
Weight loaded:	12,701kg (28,000lb)
Cruising speed:	160km/h (100mph)
Ceiling:	4420m (14,500ft)
Range:	805km (500 miles)
Passengers + crew:	38 + 4

Handley Page HPR.7 Dart Herald

The Handley Page Herald mirrored the layout of the Fokker F.27 Friendship, but came nowhere near matching the phenomenal sales achieved by the Dutch design. Certainly, the F.27 was better suited to the requirements of most prospective customers, although it was more expensive, and the Herald suffered considerably from the costly and lengthy design work necessary to re-engine it with turboprops, its customers having refused to accept the original piston-engined aircraft. However, it proved to be a strong and reliable aircraft in service, a fact underlined by its lengthy career, notably with UK domestic operators. Air UK had a sizeable fleet, which, ironically, was replaced by Fokker F.27s. G-APWE, illustrated here, was the first production Handley Page Herald 200, delivered to British Island Airways on 4 January 1962.

Country of origin:	GB
Engines:	two 2105hp Rolls-Royce Dart Mk 527 turboprops
Wingspan:	28.9m (94ft 9in)
Length:	23m (75ft 6in)
Height:	7.34m (24ft 1in)
Weight loaded:	19,505kg (43,000lb)
Cruising speed:	445km/h (277mph) at 4570m (15,000ft)
Service ceiling:	8504m (27,900ft)
Range:	2834km (1761 miles)
Passengers + crew:	36–56 + 2-3

Handley Page O/10

Handley Page was involved in the development of transport aircraft from the very beginning. In 1919, eight of its O/400 bombers, serving with the RAF's No 1 (Communications) Squadron, and suitably converted to carry passengers, flew a regular service between London and Paris during the peace talks, and on 14 June 1919, Handley Page Transport Ltd was formed. The first-ever British Certificates of Airworthiness for civil operation were awarded to four O/400s on 1 May 1919, and HPT's early services, mostly to Paris, Brussels and Amsterdam, were flown with aircraft of this type, with minimal conversion from their original bomber configuration or as fully converted O/7s and O/10s or mixed passenger/cargo O/11s. These converted aircraft were far from suitable for the commercial task, and several were lost. GEATN was one of the last O/400s built.

Country of origin:	GB
Engines:	two 360hp Rolls-Royce Eagle VIII V-12
Wingspan:	30.48m (100ft)
Length:	19.16m (62ft 10in)
Height:	6.7m (22ft)
Weight loaded:	6350kg (14,000lb)
Cruising speed:	177km/h (110mph)
Ceiling:	2590m (8500ft)
Range:	724km (450 miles)
Passengers + crew:	12–16 + 2

Handley Page W.8b

Although Handley Page was quick to enter the commercial air transport field with its converted O/400 bombers after World War I, the need for a tailor-made commercial transport aircraft was apparent, and in 1919, the company built and flew the HP W.8, G-EAPJ model. A W.8a version was proposed but never built, so the next variant was the W.8b, the first of which was G-EBBG Bombay. The aircraft was renamed Princess Mary in May 1922, when HPT took delivery of G-EBBH Prince George and G-EBBI Prince Henry. The trio operated on HPT's Paris and Brussels services until 1 April 1924, when HPT was absorbed into Imperial Airways. G-EBBG crashed in February 1928, while -BH and -BI were scrapped in February 1931 and October 1932 respectively. A fourth W.8b was sold to the Belgian airline Sabena and three more were built in Belgium.

Country of origin:	GB
Engines:	two 350hp Rolls-Royce Eagle VIII 12-cylinder liquid-cooled V-type
Wingspan:	22.86m (75ft)
Length:	18.31m (60ft 1in)
Height:	5.18m (17ft)
Weight loaded:	5443kg (12,000lb)
Cruising speed:	145km/h (90mph)
Ceiling:	3280m (10,700ft)
Range:	805km (500 miles)
Passengers + crew:	12–14 + 2

Hawker Siddeley Trident 1C

The Hawker Siddeley Trident was the British equivalent of Boeing's 727, although it never enjoyed anything like the success of the American airliner. The Trident originated in a BEA requirement, issued in 1957, for a new short-range commercial jet, with an in-service date of 1964. The prototype flew on 9 January 1962, and the first batch of 24 aircraft was destined for BEA, which began regular services with the type on 1 April 1964. In June 1965, a BEA Trident 1 made the first automatic landing during a scheduled passenger service. Shown here is a Trident 1C of Northeast, formerly BKS Air Services, which also operated four Trident 1Es from 1969 on scheduled domestic routes and holiday charters, from Newcastle, Leeds-Bradford and Tees-side Airports. Fifteen Trident 1Es were built, almost all being exported. Later, 117 Tridents were produced in five variants.

Country of origin:	GB
Engines:	three Rolls-Royce Spey 505-5F turbofans of 4462kg (9850lb) thrust each
Wingspan:	27.1m (88ft 10in)
Length:	35.0m (114ft 9in)
Height:	8.2m (27ft)
Weight loaded:	53,207kg (117,300lb)
Cruising speed:	982km/h (610mph)
Service ceiling:	9450m (31,000ft)
Range:	4345m (2700 miles)
Passengers + crew:	139 + 3

Heinkel He 70

The Heinkel He 70 was one of the most aerodynamically refined aircraft of its day, designer Ernst Heinkel combining high streamlining with an elliptical wing to achieve a good high-speed performance, the same formula devised by Reginald Mitchell, designer of the Supermarine Spitfire. Unlike the Spitfire, the He 70 was not particularly manoeuvrable, but the roles of the two aircraft were completely different. In the mid-1930s, Lufthansa used the He 70 mainly on internal routes, carrying high-priority passengers between principal cities; it also operated as a fast mail carrier, ranging as far afield as Seville, Spain on the first leg of the South American route. The Luftwaffe also employed the He 70 as a communications aircraft. Reconnaissance and light bomber versions were also developed, and tested in the Spanish Civil War.

Country of origin:	Germany
Engine:	one 630hp BMW VI V-12
Wingspan:	14.78m (48ft 6in)
Length:	11.48m (37ft 7in)
Height:	3.1m (10ft 2in)
Weight loaded:	3310kg (7300lb)
Cruising speed:	310km/h (193mph)
Service ceiling:	6000m (19,685ft)
Range:	800km (497 miles)
Passengers + crew:	5 + 1

Ilyushin Il-14

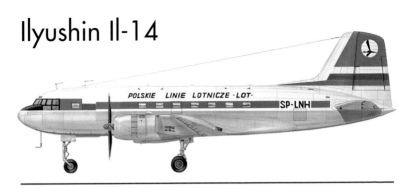

A development of the twin-engined Il-12 transport, the Il-14 represented a determined effort by the Ilyushin Design Bureau to eliminate the snags that had beset the earlier aircraft. The first variant, the Il-14P (Passashirskii, or passenger aircraft) was capable of taking off on one engine, even from elevated airfields, and was fitted with updated, blind-flying equipment. However, the aircraft could carry only 18 passengers, which was not economically viable, and the Il14P was redesigned as the Il-14M (Modifikatsiia), with a longer fuselage and accommodation for 24 passengers. This version made its appearance in 1955. Two other versions, the Il-14F for photographic survey and the Il-14T transport, were also built. Seen here is an Il-14M of the Polish national airline LOT, which also operated Il-12s. The Il-14, NATO reporting name Crate, was widely exported.

Country of origin:	USSR
Engines:	two 1900hp Shvestsov ASh-87T radials
Wingspan:	31.7m (104ft)
Length:	21.3m (69ft 9in)
Height:	7.8m (25ft 5in)
Weight loaded:	17,500kg (38,250lb)
Cruising speed:	320km/h (199mph) at 3000m (10,000ft)
Service ceiling:	7400m (24,280ft)
Range:	1750km (1090 miles)
Passengers + crew:	24-32 + 3

Ilyushin Il-18

Unsophisticated and crude by western standards, the Ilyushin Il-18, branded 'Coot' under the NATO code-name designation system (transport aircraft were allocated names beginning with the letter C), became a mainstay of the Soviet civil aviation scene, and did much to expand the services of Aeroflot, the former Soviet Union's state-run airline. Still in limited service today, the Il-18 also provided an excellent platform for special mission variants, with both civil and military applications, which included electronic intelligence gathering and anti-submarine warfare. The Il-18 shown in the illustration served as a VIP and staff transport with the Democratic and Popular Republic of Algeria. It has since been withdrawn, its role now being filled by a mixture of Gulfstream IIIs, King Air 200s and a Fokker F27.

Country of origin:	USSR
Engines:	four 4000hp Ivchenko A1-20K turboprops
Wingspan:	37.4m (122ft 8in)
Length:	35.9m (117ft 9in)
Height:	10.16m (33ft 4in)
Weight loaded:	61,200kg (134,900lb)
Cruising speed:	650km/h (404mph) at 8000m (26,250ft)
Service ceiling:	10,750m (35,300ft)
Range:	4800km (2980 miles)
Passengers + crew:	84–110 + 5

Ilyushin Il-62M

T he Ilyushin Il-62 (NATO reporting name Classic), which flew for the first time in January 1963, was the first commercial, long-range, four-jet aircraft produced in the Soviet Union. After proving flights by three pre-production aircraft and a second prototype, the Il-62's service with Aeroflot was inaugurated on the Moscow–Khabarovsk and the Moscow–Novosibirsk routes. On 15 September 1967, the type began to replace the Tu-114 on the Moscow—Montreal route, this service continuing on to New York from 15 July 1968. The Il-62M had more powerful engines and extended range, and made its appearance in 1971. The aircraft shown is the second Il-62M delivered to Linhas Aereas de Angola in May 1987, and was used to carry Cuban troops to Angola during the long-running civil war. The Angolan IL-62Ms were still operational in the late 1990s.

Country of origin:	USSR
Engines:	four Soloviev D-30KU turbofans of 10,985kg (24,200lb) thrust each
Wingspan:	43.20m (141ft 9in)
Length:	53.12m (174ft 3in)
Height:	12.35m (40ft 6in)
Weight loaded:	165,000kg (363,762lb)
Cruising speed:	900km/h (560mph)
Service ceiling:	12,800m (42,000ft)
Range:	7800km (4850 miles)
Passengers + crew:	174 + 5

Ilyushin Il-76

The Ilyushin Il-76, NATO reporting name Candid, was the first major project of the Ilyushin Design Bureau in which S.V. Ilyushin himself played no part. The design was directed by G.V. Novozhilov, the work beginning in 1965 to meet an important requirement of both the civil operator Aeroflot and the Soviet military air transport service V-TA for a replacement for the Antonov An-12BP. Among their requirements was the ability to carry a 40-tonne cargo for 5000km (3107 miles) in less than six hours. The aircraft also had to be able to operate from short, unpaved airstrips, maintain reliability in the extreme climatic conditions of the hot southern Steppes and deserts and the Arctic wastes of northern Siberia, and be easy to service. The Il-76 first flew on 25 March 1971. The illustration shows an Il-76MD in the livery of Cubana, the Cuban national carrier.

Country of origin:	USSR
Engines:	four Soloviev D-30KP turbofans of 12,000kg (26,455lb) thrust each
Wingspan:	50.5m (165ft 8in)
Length:	46.59m (152ft 11in)
Height:	14.76m (48ft 5in)
Weight loaded:	170,000kg (374,800lb)
Cruising speed:	800km/h (500mph)
Service ceiling:	15,500m (50,850ft)
Range:	5000km (3100 miles)
Passengers + crew:	variations; up to 130 + 5

Ilyushin Il-76M

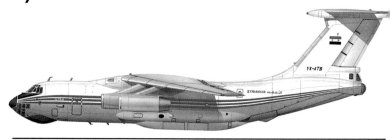

During its operational career, the Il-76 has had a number of applications other than that of transport. A three-point hose-and-drogue tanker variant, the Il-78 (NATO reporting name Midas) became operational in 1987 to replace the Soviet Air Force's ageing Mya-4 Bison tankers, and the type was also converted to the airborne, early-warning role (NATO reporting name Mainstay) to replace the inadequate Tu-126 Moss, which was little more than a stop-gap AEW aircraft at the time. The Il-76M also serves with the Indian Air Force, where it has replaced the Antonov An-12 Cub, as it did in the Soviet Air Force. Another overseas customer was Iraq, which received 19, at least one of which was converted to the AEW role under the name Adnan-1. Two Il-76Ts and two Il-76Ms, one of which is illustrated here, are operated by Syrianair.

Country of origin:	USSR
Engines:	four Soloviev D-30KP turbofans of 12,000kg (26,455lb) thrust each
Wingspan:	50.5m (165ft 8in)
Length:	46.59m (152ft 11in)
Height:	14.76m (48ft 5in)
Weight loaded:	170,000kg (374,800lb)
Cruising speed:	800km/h (500mph)
Service ceiling:	15,500m (50,850ft)
Range:	5000km (3100 miles)
Passengers + crew:	variations up to 130 + 5

Ilyushin Il-76T

It is perhaps no exaggeration to claim that the Soviet Union could not have sustained its unhappy campaign in Afghanistan for as long as it did without the support rendered by its Il76 heavy-lift aircraft, both military and civilian. During the long campaign, Il-76s flew supplies daily into Kabul Airport, making tactical approaches and discharging flares and chaff as a precaution against enemy shoulder-launched SAM. Aeroflot and Soviet Air Force Il-76Ts also undertook many supply and paratroop drops, and all were fitted with a comprehensive infra-red countermeasures suite to deflect heat-seeking missiles. While most Russian aircraft imitate their western counterparts, the Il-76 has no direct equivalent. It is an excellent platform, with its ability to carry large payloads over long distances at high speeds and land on short strips.

Country of origin:	USSR
Engines:	four Soloviev D-30KP turbofans of 12,000kg (26,455lb) thrust each
Wingspan:	50.5m (165ft 8in)
Length:	46.59m (152ft 11in)
Height:	14.76m (48ft 5in)
Weight loaded:	170,000kg (374,800lb)
Cruising speed:	800km/h (500mph)
Service ceiling:	15,500m (50,850ft)
Range:	5000km (3100 miles)
Passengers + crew:	variations up to 140 + 5–7

Ilyushin Il-96

Developed from the earlier Il-86, which suffered from a poor range, the Il-96 turned out to be virtually a new design. Almost the only components left unaltered, or only slightly modified, were major sections of the fuselage (though this was made much shorter), and the four units of the landing gear. The first prototype of the Il-96, SSSR-96000, flew from Khodinka on 28 September 1988, and the type made its international debut at the Paris Air Show in the following June. Aeroflot placed orders for about 100 aircraft for service on its long-range, high-density routes, both at home and overseas. Further developments of the type are the Il-96M with 350 seats for medium-range sectors, and the Il-90 twin-engined version to fill a similar, high-density, short-range role as the Airbus A330. Western engines such as the Trent and PW40 are under consideration for the latter.

Country of origin:	Russia
Engines:	four Soloviev PS-90A turbofans of 14,717kg (32,450lb) thrust each
Wingspan:	57.66m (189ft 2in)
Length:	55.35m (181ft 7in)
Height:	17.57m (57ft 8in)
Weight loaded:	216,000kg (476,200lb)
Cruising speed:	900km/h (559mph)
Service ceiling:	14,600m (47,900ft)
Range:	7500km (4660 miles)
Passengers + crew:	300 + 3

Israel Aircraft Industries Westwind

In 1967, Israel Aircraft Industries acquired all production and marketing rights for the North American Rockwell Corporation (formerly Aero Commander) Jet Commando executive jet transport. Initially, IAI began manufacture of the Jet Commander 1121A almost unchanged, but then developed a much-improved version called the Commodore Jet, which featured a fuselage lengthened to accommodate 10 passengers. The Model 1123 Commodore Jet was first flown on 28 September 1970, and later known as the Westwind Eleven-23. Thirty-six were built before it was superseded by the Model 1124 Westwind, first flown on 21 July 1975. The Westwind was powered by turbofan engines, giving an enhanced performance, and 53 were built. Adding winglets to the tip tanks and redesigning the aerofoil section produced the Westwind 2, illustrated above.

Country of origin:	Israel
Engines:	two Garrett (AlliedSignal) TFE731-3 turbofans of 1680kg (3700lb) thrust each
Wingspan:	13.65m (44ft 10in)
Length:	15.95m (52ft 3in)
Height:	4.8m (15ft 10in)
Weight loaded:	10,600kg (23,500lb)
Cruising speed:	750km/h (465mph) at 9150m (30,000ft)
Service ceiling:	13,715m (45,000ft)
Range:	3985km (2475 miles)
Passengers + crew:	12 + 2

Junkers F13

Immediately after World War I, Professor Hugo Junkers, whose company had produced a number of successful, all-metal, combat aircraft during the conflict, put his design expertise to good use in producing the Junkers F13, the first all-metal cantilever monoplane with an enclosed cabin. The Junkers F13, which first flew on 25 June 1919, was produced in many versions, many with different engines. The largest user was Deutsche Luft Hansa, which was formed in 1926 as the German national airline. Most of its aircraft had previously served with Junkers-Luftverkehr, an airline started in 1921 by the F13's manufacturer. F13s served DLH until 1938, when they were transferred to Luftwaffe flying training schools and pleasure flying companies. More than 320 were built, seeing service with airlines throughout the world. The specification is for the Junkers F13da.

Country of origin:	Germany
Engine:	one 280hp Junkers L2
Wingspan:	17.75m (58ft 3in)
Length:	9.60m (31ft 6in)
Height:	4.1m (13ft 5in)
Weight loaded:	1730kg (3814lb)
Cruising speed:	140km/h (87mph)
Service ceiling:	4000m (31,120ft)
Range:	949km (590 miles)
Passengers + crew:	4 + 2

Junkers Ju 52/3m

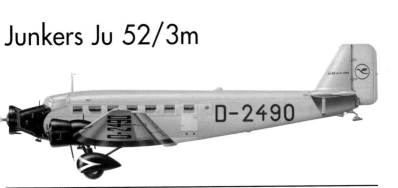

Derived from a single-engined design, the Junkers Ju 52/3m was one of the most important commercial and military transports in the history of aviation. Production of this three-engined aircraft began in 1932, the first two examples being delivered to Lloyd Aereo Boliviano. Understandably, the biggest single commercial operator was Deutsche Lufthansa; by the end of World War II, no fewer than 231 Ju 52/3ms had appeared on the airline's inventory, although most were operated on behalf of the Luftwaffe during the war. The highest known DLH peacetime total was 59, all of which were requisitioned by the Luftwaffe on the outbreak of World War II. The Ju 52/3m was operated by 28 airlines, including British Airways, which had three. Numerous alternative engines were fitted to the Ju 52 airframe during the aircraft's long career. D-2490 was the sixth Ju 52/3m.

Country of origin:	Germany
Engines:	three 660hp BMW 132A-1 radials
Wingspan:	29.25m (95ft 11in)
Length:	18.90m (62ft)
Height:	6.1m (20ft)
Weight loaded:	9200kg (20,282lb)
Cruising speed:	245km/h (152mph)
Service ceiling:	5200m (17,000ft)
Range:	915km (568 miles)
Passengers + crew:	17 + 1

Junkers Ju 52/3m

Junkers Ju 523/3m G-AERX, seen here, was one of three obtained by British Airways in April 1937, having seen service with AB Aerotransport in Sweden. It was named Jupiter in British Airways service, its two sister aircraft bearing the names Juno and Jason. The Ju 52s used by British Airways were powered by three 600hp Pratt & Whitney Wasp radial engines, each driving a Hamilton variable-pitch propeller. Most early civilian Ju 52s were powered by the 525hp Pratt & Hornet, licence-built by BMW, although others had Bristol Pegasus, Hispano Suiza, Junkers Jumo or BMW engines. The Ju 52 was fitted with full-span flaps and high-lift, drooping ailerons, which were said to effectively double the wing area. This gave the Ju 52 an excellent short-field capability, used to good effect in the *Blitzkrieg* of 1940, particularly during the invasion of Holland.

Country of origin:	Germany
Engines:	three 600hp Pratt & Whitney Wasp radials
Wingspan:	29.25m (95ft 11in)
Length:	18.90m (62ft)
Height:	6.1m (20ft)
Weight loaded:	9200kg (20,282lb)
Cruising speed:	245km/h (152mph)
Service ceiling:	5200m (17,000ft)
Range:	915km (568 miles)
Passengers + crew:	17 + 1

Junkers W34

In 1926, Junkers produced developed versions of their F13 single-engined, four-passenger transport, which had made such an impact on German Aviation and air transport in many parts of the world. The new aircraft, the W33 and W34, were mainly intended for cargo-carrying, but had provision for six passengers in their airline versions. Both types were cantilever low-wing monoplanes, with the corrugated metal skin which had become a familiar feature of Junkers designs. The pilot was seated in an open cockpit behind the single engine, but the passenger or cargo compartment was fully enclosed. The types differed solely in that the W33 was normally powered by a liquid-cooled, inline engine, and the W34 by an air-cooled radial. The W34 served widely with airlines and with the German Luftwaffe. The aircraft shown is a float-equipped Canadian Airways W34.

Country of origin:	Germany
Engine:	one 600hp BMW Hornet C 6-cylinder radial
Wingspan:	17.75m (58ft 3in)
Length:	10.27m (33ft 8in)
Height:	3.53m (11ft 7in)
Weight loaded:	2500kg (5511lb)
Cruising speed:	150km/h (93mph)
Ceiling:	4300m (14,100ft)
Range:	1000km (620 miles)
Passengers + crew:	6 + 2

Learjet Longhorn 28

In mid-1977, Gates Learjet announced the development of a new Learjet family. The latest aircraft would represent a clean break with the original design philosophy, featuring a much-enlarged cabin with stand-up headroom. Power would be provided by uprated versions of the TFE731, and lift by a highly modified version of the basic Learjet wing. This was the first on any production aircraft to incorporate the wingtip vertical surfaces known as 'winglets'. Devised by Dr Richard Whitcomb of NASA, winglets are designed to work in the vortex flow that exists at the tip of a wing, turning the flow to provide a small forward thrust, or drag reduction. The new wing, named Longhorn by the company, was tested on a Learjet 25 in August 1977, and a small number of Longhorn 28, illustrated here, and 29 versions of the Learjet were produced.

Country of origin:	USA
Engines:	two Garrett (Allied Signal) TFE731-3A-2B turbofans of 1675kg (3700lb) thrust each
Wingspan:	13.35m (43ft 9in)
Length:	16.8m (55ft 1in)
Height:	4.45m (14ft 6in)
Weight loaded:	9525kg (21,000lb)
Cruising speed:	740km/h (460mph) at 14,235m (47,000ft)
Service ceiling:	15,545m (51,000ft)
Range:	4150km (2580 miles)
Passengers + crew:	10 + 2

Learjet 25C

Learjet claims that its aircraft have appeared in more films and TV programmes than any other aircraft in history, and the Learjet name is one of the few in aviation recognizable enough to find its way into a rock lyric. Behind this popular image, however, is the hard fact that the Learjet has been the world's best-selling business jet since the concept was invented. The Model 25C, shown here, marked Learjet's move into the market for long-range, transcontinental jets; it was based on the original stretched Model 25, but the cabin length was reduced to make room for extra fuel in the centre section. From the start of operations, Learjets were involved in a disturbingly large number of accidents; this was not the fault of the aircraft, but the early models were demanding and ill-suited to inexperienced, under-trained or over-confident pilots.

Country of origin:	USA
Engines:	two General Electric CJ610-6 turbojets of 1340 kg (2950lb) thrust each
Wingspan:	10.84m (35ft 7in)
Length:	13.38m (43ft 3in)
Height:	3.84m (12ft 7in)
Weight loaded:	6123kg (13,500lb)
Cruising speed:	859km/h (534mph) at 13,720m (45,000ft)
Service ceiling:	13,720m (45,000ft)
Range:	3260km (2026 miles)
Passengers + crew:	6 + 2

Learjet 36

A s growing sales brought improved finanacial results, funding became
available for the next stage of Learjet development: the provision of a more
efficient, quieter engine. Garrett AirResearch had started work on such an engine,
designed to replace existing turbojets in this class of aircraft, in the late 1960s, and
in May 1971 the new powerplant, the TFE 7312 turbofan, was flight tested in a
Learjet 25. Both were based on the stretched Learjet 25, with increased wingspan
and a further small fuselage stretch to balance the extra weight of the engines. The
Model 35 was a transcontinental eight-seater, while the Model 36 had an extra
fuselage fuel tank and shorter cabin for transatlantic operations. The Model 36
shown here was used by golfer Arnold Palmer to undertake a round-the-world
flight, marking the 200th anniversary of the founding of the United States.

Country of origin:	USA
Engines:	two Garrett Air Research TF731 turbofans of 1678kg (3700lb) thrust each
Wingspan:	10.84m (35ft 7in)
Length:	13.38m (43ft 9in)
Height:	3.84m (12ft 7in)
Weight loaded:	6123kg (13,500lb)
Cruising speed:	859km/h (534mph) at 13,720m (45,000ft)
Service ceiling:	13,720m (45,000ft)
Range:	4074km (2532 miles)
Passengers + crew:	8 + 2

Lockheed 5B Vega

One of the most famous single-engined aircraft of the late 1920s was the Lockheed Vega, a superbly streamlined, high-wing monoplane designed by John K. Northrop, later to become famous for his flying wing designs. The Vega was built specifically to compete in a trans-Pacific race from California to Hawaii, but it and its crew vanished over water. However, the Vega soon invited orders and 129 were built, used on regular commercial routes and for record-breaking attempts. The most famous Model 5B Vega of all time was undoubtedly NC105-W 'Winne Mae' in which pilot Wiley Post won the National Air Races in 1930. In 1931, he flew around the world in record time with a navigator, and then made a similar flight solo. Post was killed in an air crash in 1935; Winnie Mae survived to become an exhibit at the National Air and Space Museum, Washington.

Country of origin:	USA
Engine:	one 450hp Pratt & Whitney Wasp 9-cylinder radial
Wingspan:	12.5m (41ft)
Length:	8.4m (27ft 7in)
Height:	2.6m (8ft 6in)
Weight loaded:	2155kg (4750lb)
Cruising speed:	265km/h (165mph) at 3050m (10,000ft)
Service ceiling:	5500m (18,000ft)
Range:	885km (550 miles)
Passengers + crew:	7 + 1

Lockheed 14 Super Electra

Left virtually unpainted to save weight, this is the Model 14N Super Electra used by Howard Hughes for his record-breaking, round-the-world flight that began on 10 July 1938. By fitting extra tanks in the cabin (and in so doing blocking out the majority of the windows), fuel capacity was increased by 286 per cent to 6980 litres (1842 gallons). Sophisticated navigation equipment was installed, along with survival gear and flotation bags. In addition to Hughes, the aircraft had a four-man crew comprising co-pilot, navigator, radio operator and flight engineer. The trip covered around 23,611km (14,671 miles) at an average speed of 331.6km/h (206mph), and was completed in 91 hours and 24 minutes. It was a long distance that would stand until April 1947, when a Douglas A-26 Invader flew round the world in 78 hours 56 minutes.

Country of origin:	USA
Engines:	two 900hp Wright SGR-1820-F62 Cyclone radials
Wingspan:	19.96m (65ft 6in)
Length:	13.51m (44ft 4in)
Height:	3.48m (11ft 5in)
Weight loaded:	7938kg (17,500lb)
Cruising speed:	367km/h (228mph)
Service ceiling:	7468m (24,500ft)
Range:	2558km (1590 miles)
Passengers + crew:	10–14 + 2

Lockheed L-1011 Model 385 TriStar

The market requirements that had led to the development of the McDonnell Douglas DC-10 in 1966 also resulted in the Lockheed TriStar high-density jet airliner programme. The project, designated L-1101, was launched in March 1968, by which time 144 orders and options were in place; the first aircraft flew on 16 November 1970. The initial version was the Lockheed L-1011-1, entering regular airline service with Eastern Air Lines on 26 April 1972. The Series 100 TriStars followed, with increased range and power, and further developments took place in later years. Seen here is a Lockheed Model 385 TriStar of All Nippon Airways, Japan's internal operator. Externally, it is impossible to differentiate between the L-1011-1, -50, -100 and -200 models of the TriStar; the main modifications include type of engine, tyre, wheel-rim and oleo strength, and internal fuel tankage.

Country of origin:	USA
Engines:	three Rolls-Royce RB211-524B turbofans of 22,680kg (50,000lb) thrust each
Wingspan:	47.35m (155ft 3in)
Length:	54.35m (178ft 8in)
Height:	16.9m (55ft 3in)
Weight loaded:	225,000kg (496,000lb)
Cruising speed:	975km/h (605mph) at 9150m (30,000ft)
Service ceiling:	12,800m (42,000ft)
Range:	6335km (3950 miles)
Passengers + crew:	400 + 2–4

Lockheed L-1011 Model 385 TriStar

By late 1973, the L-1011-1 TriStar had been delivered, or was pending delivery, to Eastern, TWA, Air Canada, Court Line, Delta Air Lines, All Nippon Airways, and Lufttransport Unternehmen; British Airways had nine with options for nine more. Some 56 were in service, with orders and options for a further 199. It was not enough, because by this time the DC-10 was making inroads into the intercontinental market. Lockheed set about increasing the TriStar's range and payload, starting with the L-1011-100 series. The illustration shows one of Lufttransport Unternehmen's (Air Transport Enterprizes) Model 385 TriStars. LTU operates freight and charter services from Frankfurt, Bremen, Hannover and numerous airports in Germany. Near its peak, LTU's TriStar fleet totalled 11; five L-1011s, one L-1011-100, one L-1011-200 and four extended-range L-1011-500s.

Country of origin:	USA
Engines:	three Rolls-Royce RB211-524B turbofans of 22,680kg (50,000lb) thrust each
Wingspan:	47.35m (155ft 3in)
Length:	54.35m (178ft 8in)
Height:	16.9m (55ft 3in)
Weight loaded:	225,000kg (496,000lb)
Cruising speed:	975km/h (605mph) at 9150m (30,000ft)
Service ceiling:	12,800m (42,000ft)
Range:	6335km (3980 miles)
Passengers + crew:	400 + 2–4

Lockheed L-1011-200

Lockheed's first attempt to increase the TriStar's range and payload resulted in the L-10111-100, powered by RB.211-22B turbofans, which had two fuselage tanks with 8165kg (18,000lb) of extra fuel in addition to the four integral wing tanks: maximum take-off weight was also increased to 211,375kg (466,000lb). Several L-1011-100s were ordered by TWA, Air Canada, Gulf Air, Cathay Pacific, and Saudi Arabian Airlines. Extra power came with the RB.211-524 engine in the Lockheed L-1011200, which received FAA certification on 26 April 1977; this became the most adaptable of the TriStar series, but it failed to match the range and payload capability of the DC-10 Series 30. Operating from Jeddah and Riyadh airports, Saudi Arabian Airlines maintains a powerful fleet of TriStars and Boeing 747s. HZ-AHA is one of 17 L-1011-200 aircraft on the airline's inventory.

Country of origin:	USA
Engines:	three Rolls-Royce RB211-524B turbofans of 22,680kg (50,000lb) thrust each
Wingspan:	47.35m (155ft 3in)
Length:	54.35m (178ft 8in)
Height:	16.9m (55ft 3in)
Weight loaded:	225,000kg (496,000lb)
Cruising speed:	975km/h (605mph) at 9150m (30,000ft)
Service ceiling:	12,800m (42,000ft)
Range:	6335km (3980 miles)
Passengers + crew:	400 + 2–4

Lockheed L-1011-500

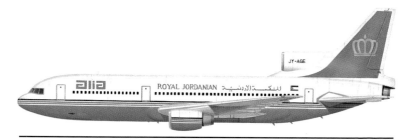

In an attempt to improve radically the TriStar's range, Lockheed introduced the L-1011-500, receiving FAA certification in December 1979. Powered by RB-211-524Bs or B4s, the -500 had a shorter fuselage, six Class A doors, an engine No 2 fairing, and no tail skid. The wingtips were lengthened by 1.37m (4ft 6in), with load relief against gusts and turbulence catered for by the ACS (Active Control System). To guard against excessive accelerations at high Mach numbers, an RSB (Recovery Speed Brake) was fitted, which automatically deployed the speed brakes at 0.85 Mach. Alia, the Royal Jordanian Airline, operated a fleet of Boeing 707, 727 and Airbus A310 aircraft in addition to six Lockheed L-1011-500s on routes from Marka-Amman and the modern airport of Queen Alia, south of Amman. 'Princess Aysha' JY-AGE was the fifth Tristar to be delivered.

Country of origin:	USA
Engines:	three Rolls-Royce RB211-524B turbofans of 22,680kg (50,000lb) thrust each
Wingspan:	47.35m (155ft 3in)
Length:	50m (164ft)
Height:	16.9m (55ft 3in)
Weight loaded:	225,000kg (496,000lb)
Cruising speed:	975km/h (605mph) at 9150m (30,000ft)
Service ceiling:	12,800m (42,000ft)
Range:	9655km (6000 miles)
Passengers + crew:	400 + 2–4

Lockheed L-1011-500

British West Indian Airways International, formed by a consortium of Caribbean states, operates four Lockheed L-1011-500 TriStars, including one that retains a US registration. These fly mainly on routes between the Caribbean and the United States and Europe. Few criticisms can be levelled at the TriStar, which continues to offer much passenger appeal. However, its production run, always threatened by either politics, shortage of funds, or both, came to a halt on 19 August 1983 when the 250th, and last, aircraft was rolled out at Palmdale. Several TriStar Is were later modified to improved standards with RB.211-524B engines, while a few were converted for use by the Royal Air Force as dual-role tanker/transports. The Series 50 was another updated model with increased take-off weight, but which retained the RB.211-22B turbofan.

Country of origin:	USA
Engines:	three Rolls-Royce RB211-524B turbofans of 22,680kg (50,000lb) thrust each
Wingspan:	47.35m (155ft 3in)
Length:	50m (164ft)
Height:	16.9m (55ft 3in)
Weight loaded:	225,000kg (496,000lb)
Cruising speed:	975km/h (605mph) at 9150m (30,000ft)
Service ceiling:	12,800m (42,000ft)
Range:	9655km (6000 miles)
Passengers + crew:	400 + 2–4

Lockheed L-749A Constellation

The first version of the Constellation to be specifically designed for commercial use was the Model 649, which entered service in May 1947, and had improved engines as well as increased load-carrying capacity. This was followed a year later by the Model 749, with increased all-up weight and appropriate modifications to the positioning and capacity of the fuel tanks for overseas operation. This model was joined by a sub-series version, the strengthened Model 749A, which could carry an extra payload of 2200kg (4850lb). These variants won many orders from the large American airlines. Pan American and TWA took delivery of the largest numbers, and they were used successfully on international and internal routes. Total production reached 233 units. Some also found their way to the small operators of South America; shown here is an L-749A of Argo, Dominica.

Country of origin:	USA
Engines:	four 2500hp Wright R-3350-C18-BD1 radials
Wingspan:	37.49m (123ft)
Length:	29m (95ft 2in)
Height:	7.21m (23ft 8in)
Weight loaded:	48,534kg (107,000lb)
Cruising speed:	526km/h (327mph) at 6100m (20,000ft)
Service ceiling:	7620m (25,000ft)
Range:	2830km (1760 miles)
Passengers + crew:	44–81 + 4

Lockheed L-1049C Super Constellation

The L-1049C was the civil version of the Lockheed L-1049B Super Constellation, which had an integrally stiffened floor and two large loading doors. At the request of the US Navy it also had a complex new Wright Turbo-Compound engine derived from the existing R-3350. The 3250hp available from each of the new engines not only promised more speed, but also a jump in gross weight to 60,329kg (133,000lb), representing a further advance in payload/range. Though the Turbo-Compound engine took time to mature, it also removed the slight sluggishness that had crept into the original Model 1049, which cruised at barely 483km/h (300mph). The L1049C was produced for the USAF (C-121C) and the US Navy (R7V-1). A passenger version was used by KLM on the New York–Amsterdam route in August 1953; one of the later L-1049Cs is seen here, fitted with tip tanks.

Country of origin:	USA
Engines:	four 3250hp Wright R3350-C18-DA-1 Turbo Compounds
Wingspan:	37.49m (123ft)
Length:	34.65m (113ft 7in)
Height:	10.25m (33ft 7in)
Weight loaded:	68,100kg (150,000lb)
Cruising speed:	523km/h (325mph) at 6100m (20,000ft)
Service ceiling:	7620m (25,000ft)
Range:	4990km (3100 miles)
Passengers + crew:	109 + 4–5

Lockheed L-1049G
Super Constellation

The L-1049G, the 'Super-G', first flew on 12 December 1954, entering service with Northwest Airlines in early 1955. Many of the earlier Super Constellations were completed as, or converted to, Super-G standard; the total included 38 L-1049Es. Fifty-three more were completed as cargo/passenger L-1049Hs, bringing the total production of the civil variants of the Super Constellation to 254 units. Capacity of the L-1049G was 95 passengers, while the L-1049H could lift 11,021kg (24,297lb) of freight. The L-1049G was the most successful 'Connie' in terms of sales, offering a normal range of 6470km (4020 miles). Lufthansa flew its first intercontinental service with an L-1049G on 8 June 1955, between Hamburg and New York. The Super Constellation represented the ultimate in piston-engined airliner development, its engine and airframe design stretched to their limits.

Country of origin:	USA
Engines:	four 3250hp Wright 972TC-18DA-3 radials
Wingspan:	38.5m (126ft 3in)
Length:	32.15m (105ft 4in)
Height:	10.25m (33ft 7in)
Weight loaded:	65,775kg (145,000lb)
Cruising speed:	570km/h (355mph) at 6890m (22,600ft)
Service ceiling:	7225m (23,700ft)
Range:	8200km (5100 miles)
Passengers + crew:	95 + 4–5

Lockheed L-1049G Super Constellation

When it first took to the air in December 1954, the Lockheed L-1049G Super Constellation was the finest airliner in the world. Structural changes enabled it to carry large wingtip tanks, which combined with the Turbo-Compound engines, gave it the greatest range of any Constellation. One of the main operators of the 99 that were built was TWA, which had sponsored the original Constellation before World War II. With these aircraft, the airline pioneered transatlantic and other long-haul services, including its luxury Ambassador class, which was patronized by businessmen and used private airport suites. The L-1049G brought a new degree of comfort to airline travel, even though its Turbo-Compound engines generated an excessive amount of noise, but its day was brief, for the first-generation jet and turboprop airliners were making their appearance.

Country of origin:	USA
Engines:	four 3250hp Wright 972TC-18DA-3 radials
Wingspan:	38.5m (126ft 3in)
Length:	32.15m (105ft 4in)
Height:	10.25m (33ft 7in)
Weight loaded:	65,775kg (145,000lb)
Cruising speed:	570km/h (355mph) at 6890m (22,600ft)
Service ceiling:	7225m (23,700ft)
Range:	8200km (5100 miles)
Passengers + crew:	95 + 4–5

Lockheed Super Constellation (military variants)

The Super Constellation was an ideal platform for military use, from transport to airborne early warning. The WV-2, for example, served with the US Navy as a high-altitude, reconnaissance and early-warning, radar-intelligence aircraft, and carried some five and a half tons of electronic equipment, while the USAF's EC-121 variant served a similar purpose. Between 1955 and 1965, WV-2s and EC-121s carried out early-warning coverage of the North Atlantic and Pacific, as well as electronic intelligence missions; on 14 April 1969, an EC121 was shot down by North Korean fighters over the Sea of Japan while carrying out one such surveillance mission, with the loss of all 31 crew members. Others were assigned to various air forces once their airline days were over; one such was this Indian Air Force machine, handed over after 10 years of service with Air India.

Country of origin:	USA
Engines:	four 3250hp Wright 972TC-18DA-3 radials
Wingspan:	38.5m (126ft 3in)
Length:	32.15m (105ft 4in)
Height:	10.25m (33ft 7in)
Weight loaded:	65,775kg (145,000lb)
Cruising speed:	570km/h (355mph) at 6890m (22,600ft)
Service ceiling:	7225m (23,700ft)
Range:	8200km (5100 miles)
Passengers + crew:	95 + 4–5

Lockheed L-188A Electra

First flown on 6 December 1957, the Lockheed Electra short-/medium-range airliner was an immediate success, the company having 144 orders on its books by the time the prototype made its maiden flight. Brazilian airline VARIG was perhaps the most faithful Electra operator, and its L-188 services were legendary. Fifteen aircraft were delivered, beginning in the early 1960s, and only one was lost between then and 1991. VARIG's Electras operated the daily air bridge shuttle service between Rio de Janeiro and Sao Paulo. One reason why they continued for so long is that the airport they used in Rio, Santos Dumont, was close to the city centre and was closed to jet traffic. Principal factors, however, were the reliability of the Allison engines and passenger loyalty. The Electra was the first turboprop airliner designed and built in the United States.

Country of origin:	USA
Engines:	four 3750hp Allison 501-D13A turboprops
Wingspan:	30m (99ft)
Length:	32.15m (105ft 4in)
Height:	10.25m (33ft 7in)
Weight loaded:	51,257kg (113,000lb)
Cruising speed:	600km/h (373mph)
Service ceiling:	8656m (28,400ft)
Range:	4458km (2770 miles)
Passengers + crew:	66–98 + 3

Macchi M.67

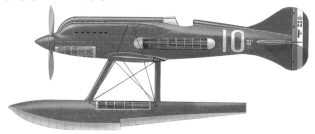

The Macchi M.67 floatplane was designed by Mario Castoldi and built specifically for the 1929 Schneider Trophy contest. It was based on the M.52, and three examples had been entered for the 1927 race, but troubles with the 1030hp Fiat AS3 engine compelled all three to be withdrawn at various stages of the contest. Despite this, the M.52 went on to establish a new seaplane speed record. Its successor, the M.67, was fitted with a big, 18-cylinder engine that generated an enormous amount of heat, so radiators were built into the wing surfaces, the fuselage and the floats. The engine proved temperamental, so the throttle stops had to be adjusted to limit the power output. Two examples took part in the 1929 contest, but both were forced to retire. The next Schneider contest, in 1931, was won outright for Britain by the Supermarine S.6B.

Country of origin:	Italy
Engine:	one 1400hp Isotta-Fraschini Asso 18-cylinder W type
Wingspan:	8.98m (29ft 5in)
Length:	7.62m (25ft)
Height:	not known
Weight loaded:	2180kg (4806lb)
Maximum speed:	584km/h (363mph)
Service ceiling:	not known
Range:	not known
Crew:	1

Martin 4-0-4

First flown on 21 October 1950, the Martin 4-0-4 was a straightforward development of the earlier 2-0-2, the first twin-engined airliner of US post-war design to receive a CAA type operating certificate. Between the autumn of 1951 and the spring of 1953, 101 Martin 4-0-4s were delivered to Eastern (60) and TWA (41). Two more were delivered to the US Coast Guard as RM-1s. Atlanta-based Southern Airways was founded in 1943, but had to wait until the war's end before operating its first passenger service in June 1949. It began operations with DC-3s, and retained these aircraft until the late 1950s. Southern never made the move to turboprops, and by the mid-1960s had a large fleet of Martin 4-0-4s. Many, including the one seen here, were ex-Eastern Aircraft. Southern merged with Frontier in October 1967, but retained its Martin airliners well into the 1970s.

Country of origin:	USA
Engines:	two 2400hp Pratt & Whitney R-2800-CB-16 radials
Wingspan:	28.4m (93ft 3in)
Length:	22.7m (74ft 7in)
Height:	8.6m (28ft 5in)
Weight loaded:	20,366kg (44,900lb)
Cruising speed:	450km/h (280mph)
Service ceiling:	8839m (29,000ft)
Range:	4185km (2600 miles)
Passengers + crew:	40 + 3

Martin M.130 China Clipper

The first M.130 four-engined flying boat for Pan American was commissioned and handed over at Baltimore on 9 October 1935, and a fortnight later the airline was awarded a contract to open an airmail route across the Pacific. On 22 November, the first M.130, serialled NC14716 and named China Clipper, took off from San Francisco Bay, setting course for Honolulu with 832kg (1834lb) of mail. Four days later it reached Manila in the Philippines, after a total flying time of almost 60 hours. Two more, Philippine Clipper and Hawaii Clipper, were delivered to Pan Am. By December, these aircraft were making weekly return mail runs through the islands between San Francisco and the Philippines. In April 1937, the route was extended to Hong Kong. Later, China Clipper and Philippine Clipper were impressed by the US Navy; Hawaii Clipper was lost at sea in 1938.

Country of origin:	USA
Engines:	four 830hp Pratt & Whitney Twin Wasp radials
Wingspan:	39.62m (130ft)
Length:	27.69m (90ft 10in)
Height:	7.49m (24ft 7in)
Weight loaded:	23,700kg (52,252lb)
Cruising speed:	252km/h (157mph)
Service ceiling:	5180m (17,000ft)
Range:	5150km (3200 miles)
Passengers + crew:	15 + 2–3

Martinsyde Type A Mk II

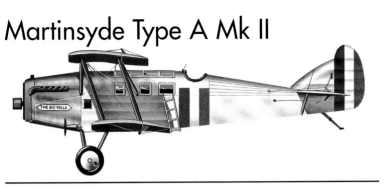

Although the name Martinsyde was eclipsed by those of other British World War I aircraft constructors, such as Sopwith, the company developed a number of successful designs, one of which was the F.4 Buzzard, one of the fastest fighters of its day. Following official trials in June 1918, the Buzzard entered large-scale production for the RAF, and by 31 October 1918, 52 had been delivered, but they came too late to see combat. Production continued for some time, and around 200 were eventually produced. Some surplus Buzzards were purchased for resale by the Aircraft Disposals Co between 1921 and 1930, and sold to various foreign air forces. Martinsyde developed two civil versions before going into liquidation in 1921. One of these was the Type A Mk II four-passenger conversion; the example seen here was the first aircraft to serve with the Irish Air Corps in 1922.

Country of origin:	GB
Engine:	one 300hp Hispano-Suiza 8-cylinder V-type
Wingspan:	10m (32ft 9in)
Length:	7.77m (25ft 6in)
Height:	3.15m (10ft 4in)
Weight loaded:	1038kg (2289lb)
Cruising speed:	233km/h (145mph)
Service ceiling:	7620m (25,000ft)
Range:	579km (360 miles)
Passengers + crew:	4 + 1

McDonnell Douglas C-9B Skytrain II

The versatile DC-9 was an ideal vehicle to meet a medium-range aeromedical evacuation requirement for the US Air Force, which placed an order for a variant designated C-9A Nightingale in August 1967. These aircraft can carry 30 to 40 stretcher patients, and 21 were delivered between 1968 and 1971. Another USAF operator is the Special Air Missions Wing at Andrews AFB, near Washington DC. The US Navy also identified a DC-9 variant as suitable for a fleet logistics-support transport to carry freight to overseas naval bases; it ordered 15 units, designated C-9B Skytrain II. The C-9B has a 3.45m (11ft 4in) x 2.06m (6ft 9in) cargo door in the forward port fuselage, which permits the loading of standard military cargo pallets; eight can be carried in an all-cargo configuration. The Kuwait Air Force also has two examples of this variant, designated C-9K.

Country of origin:	USA
Engines:	two Pratt & Whitney JT8D-9 turbofans of 6575kg (14,500lb) thrust each
Wingspan:	28.47m (93ft 5in)
Length:	31.82m (104ft 5in)
Height:	8.38m (27ft 6in)
Weight loaded:	44,450kg (98,000lb)
Cruising speed:	903km/h (561mph) at 7620m (25,000ft)
Service ceiling:	10,675m (35,000ft)
Range:	2970km (1845 miles)
Cargo + crew:	8 pallets + 2 crew and 5–6 cargo handlers

McDonnell Douglas DC-9 Series 20

If the capacity for development is the hallmark of a great design, the DC-9/MD-80 family deserves a place in that small and exclusive category. The latest model in the family carries very nearly twice as many passengers as the first, and weighs nearly twice as much. The Douglas Aircraft Company, as it originally was, did its utmost to meet any needs a customer might express, and even developed two versions of the DC-9 specifically for one airline, Scandinavian Airlines System. These were the DC-9-40, stretched by two seat rows compared with the DC-9-30 to match the seating capacity of the Boeing Model 737-200, and the DC-9-20, a 'hot-and-high' version retaining the short fuselage of the Series 10, the high-lift wing of the Series 30, and the same high-thrust engine of the DC-9-40. Ten were built. By the end of 1966, Douglas had orders for more than 400 aircraft.

Country of origin:	USA
Engines:	two Pratt & Whitney JT8D-9 turbofans of 6575kg (14,500lb) thrust each
Wingspan:	28.47m (93ft 5in)
Length:	31.82m (104ft 5in)
Height:	8.38m (27ft 6in)
Weight loaded:	44,450kg (98,000lb)
Cruising speed:	903km/h (561mph) at 7620m (25,000ft)
Service ceiling:	10,675m (35,000ft)
Range:	2970km (1845 miles)
Passengers + crew:	90 + 2

McDonnell Douglas DC-9 Series 32

For many years the DC-9 provided the backbone of several European airlines' short-/medium-haul routes. A typical example was Iberia, the Spanish national airline, which operated the Series 32 pictured above. MD-87s were ordered to serve alongside these earlier aircraft, but the order was cancelled. Paradoxically, the very success of the DC-9 brought Douglas to the edge of bankruptcy. The company was still spending money on DC-9 development; at the same time it had sold aircraft at low introductory prices, and the airliner was proving more expensive to build than had been anticipated. Eventually, Douglas was losing money on every DC-9 it delivered; deliveries began to slip behind schedule, and some airline customers launched lawsuits to cover their losses. Facing bankruptcy, Douglas was taken over by the McDonnell company in April 1967.

Country of origin:	USA
Engines:	two Pratt & Whitney JT8D-9 turbofans of 6575kg (14,500lb) thrust each
Wingspan:	28.47m (93ft 5in)
Length:	31.82m (104ft 5in)
Height:	8.38m (27ft 6in)
Weight loaded:	44,450kg (98,000lb)
Cruising speed:	903km/h (561mph) at 7620m (25,000ft)
Service ceiling:	10,675m (35,000ft)
Range:	2970km (1845 miles)
Passengers + crew:	90 + 2

McDonnell Douglas DC-9 Series 40

Douglas, always extremely willing to meet the needs of its customers, developed two versions of the DC-9 specifically for one airline, Scandinavian Airlines System (SAS). These were the DC-9-40, stretched by two seat rows compared with the DC-9-30 to match the seating capacity of the Boeing 737-200, and the DC-9-20, a 'hot-rod' version with the original short fuselage, the high-lift wing of the DC-9-30 and the same high-thrust engine as the DC-9-40. Apart from SAS, the only other customer for the DC-9-40 was Toa Domestic Airways of Japan, one of whose aircraft is seen here. Douglas offered customers a huge variety of other options, such as different fuel capacities, different engine models and different weights, as well as a wide choice of finishes, internal configurations and other features.

Country of origin:	USA
Engines:	two Pratt & Whitney JT8D-9 turbofans of 6575kg (14,500lb) thrust each
Wingspan:	28.47m (93ft 5in)
Length:	38.28m (125ft 7in)
Height:	8.53m (28ft)
Weight loaded:	51,710kg (114,000lb)
Cruising speed:	903km/h (551mph) at 7620m (25,000ft)
Service ceiling:	10,675m (35,000ft)
Range:	1918km (1685 miles)
Passengers + crew:	90 + 2

McDonnell Douglas DC-9 Series 50

Competition in the twin-jet market became very intense in the early 1970s, with the introduction of Boeing's Advanced 737. The DC-9, however, was an inherently easier aircraft to stretch than the 737, and McDonnell Douglas took advantage of this design attribute to launch the 135-seat DC-9-50. The second major stretch of the DC-9, the Series 50 had a fuselage 4.34m (14ft 3in) longer than that of the basic DC-9-30. The DC-9-50 was not intended as a replacement for the Series 30, but to complement it. It had better economics, but was less flexible in terms of range and runway performance. Swissair was the launch customer for the DC-9-50, followed by many others who placed orders for this stretched DC-9-30 development. The aircraft seen here was acquired by Ghana Airways and operated alongside two Fokker F28s and a single DC-10 for long-range work.

Country of origin:	USA
Engines:	two Pratt & Whitney JT8D-9 turbofans of 6575kg (14,500lb) thrust each
Wingspan:	28.47m (93ft 5in)
Length:	36.16m (118ft 7in)
Height:	8.38m (27ft 6in)
Weight loaded:	44,450kg (98,000lb)
Cruising speed:	903km/h (561mph) at 7620m (25,000ft)
Service ceiling:	10,675m (35,000ft)
Range:	2970km (1843 miles)
Passengers + crew:	135 + 2

McDonnell Douglas DC-10 Series 30

The second wide-bodied, high-density aircraft to enter airline service (the first being the Boeing 747), the McDonnell Douglas DC-10 first flew on 29 August 1970; production aircraft entered service on 5 August the following year with American Airlines on the Los Angeles–Chicago route. An extended-range variant, the DC-10-30 flew on 21 June 1972; intended for intercontinental routes, it had more powerful engines, a third main undercarriage unit and increased-span wing; it was followed by several variants, including the more powerful Series 40. The aircraft here, G-AZZC Eastern Belle, was one of six bought at bargain prices by Laker Airways in its heyday to operate the cut-price Skytrain routes, with 345-seat interiors. Freddie Laker made his licence application in 1971, but the United States held up the start of Skytrain until 27 September. The airline failed in 1982.

Country of origin:	USA
Engines:	three General Electric CF6-50A turbofans of 22,226kg (49,000lb) thrust each
Wingspan:	50.39m (165ft 4in)
Length:	55.35m (181ft 7in)
Height:	17.7m (58ft 1in)
Weight loaded:	251,744kg (555,000lb)
Cruising speed:	924km/h (574mph) at 9150m (30,000ft)
Service ceiling:	10,180m (33,400ft)
Range:	7550km (4691 miles)
Passengers + crew:	255–380 + 3–4

McDonnell Douglas MD-11

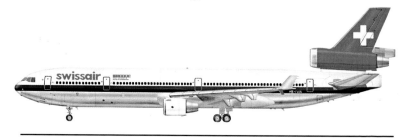

Although the MD-11 clearly owes a great deal in design to the DC-10, there are sufficient changes in the MD-11 to warrant its classification as a totally new aircraft. The fuselage is considerably stretched to provide greater accommodation for both passengers and baggage, while the wings are lengthened and feature winglets. The aerodynamic design is a good deal more advanced than the DC-10's, resulting in greater efficiency, and the tailplane holds a fuel 'trim tank'. For the aircrew, the most obvious difference is the cockpit, where the three-man analog display has been replaced by multi-function CRT displays. One early customer for the MD-11 was Swissair, which began operations on short-range sectors while their crews fully familiarized themselves with the aircraft. Later, the aircraft were assigned to long-range routes, displacing DC-10-30s.

Country of origin:	USA
Engines:	three Pratt & Whitney PW4460 turbofans of 27,360kg (60,300lb) thrust each
Wingspan:	51.66m (169ft 6in)
Length:	61.21m (200ft 10in)
Height:	17.60m (57ft 9in)
Weight loaded:	273,300kg (602,500lb)
Cruising speed:	932km/h (579mph) at 9150m (30,000ft)
Service ceiling:	9935m (32,600ft)
Range:	9270km (5760 miles)
Passengers + crew:	410 + 2

Mitsubishi MU-2

Mitsubishi, which up to the end of World War II had been one of the most prolific of Japanese aircraft manufacturers with more than 80,000 aircraft to its credit (over a quarter of them versions of the famous Zero fighter), resumed manufacturing in 1956 when it began licence construction of the North American F-86F Sabre for the Japanese Air Self Defence Force. The company began design studies for a small twin turboprop utility aircraft in September 1959, aimed at both military and civilian markets; the first of four prototype MU-2s flew on 14 September 1963. The type proved highly successful, achieving excellent sales in the face of stiff competition from long-established American manufacturers such as Beech, Cessna and Piper. Seen here is a MU-2E patrol aircraft, easily identified by its nose radome, of the Air Rescue Wing of the Japan Air Self Defence Force.

Country of origin:	Japan
Engines:	two 705hp AirResearch TPE331-151A turboprops
Wingspan:	11.95m (39ft 2in)
Length:	12.03m (39ft 6in)
Height:	4.17m (13ft 8in)
Weight loaded:	4900kg (10,802lb)
Cruising speed:	482km/h (300mph) at 6100m (20,000ft)
Service ceiling:	8230m (27,000ft)
Range:	2500km (1550 miles)
Passengers + crew:	12 + 2

NAMC YS-11

One of the many designs tailored to replace the Douglas DC-3 on the networks of domestic airlines, Japan's NAMC (Nihon Aircraft Manufacturing Co) YS-11 emerged as very similar in configuration to the Avro 748; but with a capacity for 60 passengers, it was very much larger. The type sold well in the home market, where Toa, JDA (illustrated), and All Nippon were the main customers. It was still in service in the 1990s with Japan Air System, the new name for Toa Domestic Airlines, itself a merger between Toa and JDA. The aircraft seen here, JA8648, was the 14th YS-11 built, and the third for JDA. The Nihon Aircraft Manufacturing Co was created specifically to assume responsibility for the development, flight testing and marketing of the aircraft, which flew for the first time on 30 August 1962, and began domestic services with Toa on 1 April 1965.

Country of origin:	Japan
Engines:	two 3060hp Rolls-Royce Dart Mk 502-10K turboprops
Wingspan:	32m (105ft)
Length:	26.3m (86ft 3in)
Height:	9m (29ft 6in)
Weight loaded:	24,500kg (54,013lb)
Cruising speed:	471km/h (293mph) at 4575m (15,000ft)
Service ceiling:	6980m (22,900ft)
Range:	3218km (2000 miles)
Passengers + crew:	64 + 3

Naval Aircraft Factory N3N

Although designed and widely employed as a US Navy training aircraft, so many N3N-1s were sold off for use by civil operators after World War II that a type merits an entry here. A two-seat biplane for basic training, the N3N was built in two major versions, the N3N-1, powered by a 220hp Wright J-5 engine, and the N3N-3, powered by a 235hp Wright R-760. The XN3N-1 prototype flew for the first time in August 1935, and deliveries to the US Navy started in June 1936, production totalling 179 aircraft. The N3N3 was the major production variant, 816 being delivered from 1938. Both versions could be fitted with wheel or float landing gears, which was one of the reasons why they became so popular in civil use, especially in the island-studded waters off Florida. The aircraft shown in the illustration is an N3N-1, in all-yellow US Navy training colours.

Country of origin:	USA
Engine:	one 220hp Wright J-5/R-760 Whirlwind 7-cylinder radial
Wingspan:	10.36m (34ft)
Length:	7.77m (25ft 6in)
Height:	3.30m (10ft 10in)
Weight loaded:	1266kg (2792lb)
Cruising speed:	290km/h (180mph)
Ceiling:	4635m (15,200ft)
Range:	756km (470 miles)
Passengers + crew:	2

North American (Rockwell) Sabreliner

An important series of twin-jet executive aircraft was developed in the late 1950s by North American (later North American Rockwell and Rockwell International). The main civil versions were the Series 40 and Series 60, derived from the T-39 and CT-39 military training and light transport aircraft produced for the US Air Force. The executive variants were instantly successful, around 150 being sold by the spring of 1969. The Series 75 made its debut in 1977, and was followed by the Sabreliner 75A, with more powerful engines and a larger tailplane. Seen here is the 76th and last production Sabreliner 65 in the colours of the Acopian Technical Company, which they bought as new in the early 1980s. Most of the early Series 40 aircraft have been broken up for spares, but several refurbished ex-USAF aircraft have been returned to civilian use from storage.

Country of origin:	USA
Engines:	two Garrett AirResearch TFE731-3-1D turbofans of 1676kg (3700lb) thrust each
Wingspan:	15.37m (50ft 5in)
Length:	14.30m (46ft 11in)
Height:	4.88m (16ft)
Weight loaded:	10,432kg (23,000lb)
Cruising speed:	901km/h (560mph)
Service ceiling:	13,715m (45,000ft)
Range:	5393km (3351 miles)
Passengers + crew:	10 + 2

North American Aviation Carrier Pigeon

Following the end of World War I, aviation in the United States, civil and military alike, slipped into the doldrums, mainly through lack of funding. There was little incentive to develop new types of aircraft; after 1918, the market was flooded with thousands of surplus military machines. Then, in 1925, Congress passed an Air Mail Act, which allowed private contractors to bid for the carriage of air mail. The US Post Office launched a competition in which aviation constructors were invited to submit designs for a fast mailplane. North American Aviation's response was the Carrier Pigeon, a single-engined sesquiplane equipped with a wide-track undercarriage for operations from rough and unprepared strips. Fifteen were built, 10 of them serving with National Air Transport. Much modified, the Carrier Pigeon II entered service in 1929.

Country of origin:	USA
Engine:	one 400hp Liberty 12 in-line
Wingspan:	12.78m (41ft 11in)
Length:	8.78m (28ft 9in)
Height:	3.68m (12ft 1in)
Weight loaded:	2549kg (5620lb)
Cruising speed:	177km/h (110mph)
Ceiling:	3900m (12,800ft)
Range:	845km (525 miles)
Crew:	1

Piper Cheyenne III

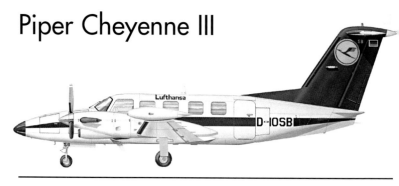

The Piper Cheyenne III and IV executive aircraft represent the ultimate in development from the original Piper PA-31 Navaho, which made its first flight on 30 September 1964, offered in two versions, and entering service in March 1967. The aircraft seen here, D-IOSB, is a Cheyenne IIIA, used by Lufthansa to train airline crews. A feature of the Cheyenne series is the wingtip tanks, which in the IIIA combine with six wing cells to provide an internal capacity of 1552 litres (410 gallons). An optional 322 litres (85 gallons) can be carried in a fuel tank in the rear of each engine nacelle. A new designation, PA-42, was introduced for the Cheyenne III, reflecting several radical changes, which included a lengthened fuselage and increased span, 720hp PT6A-41 engines and a T-tail. The later Cheyenne IV was powered by a pair of Garrett TPE331 turboprops.

Country of origin:	USA
Engines:	two 720hp Pratt & Whitney PT6A-61 turboprops
Wingspan:	14.53m (47ft 8in)
Length:	13.23m (43ft 5in)
Height:	4.50m (14ft 9in)
Weight loaded:	5119kg (11,285lb)
Cruising speed:	565km/h (350mph)
Service ceiling:	10,925m (35,840ft)
Range:	4150km (2580 miles)
Passengers + crew:	11 + 1–2

Piper J3C-65 Cub

The Piper L-21 Army co-operation aircraft was developed from the PA-18 Super Cub, and was powered by a 135hp Continental O290-D2 engine. Of very similar layout to the commercial Super Cub 135, the L-21 was supplied to various NATO armed forces under the Military Aid Program. The lower-powered L-18 was made available, with customers including Belgium, Italy and France. A mixture of L-18Cs, L-21As and L-21Bs were provided to the Dutch Army, and operated by Nos 298, 299 and 300 Squadrons. Deliveries began in February 1955, with 34 aircraft being written off in service. This machine was an L-21B with No 299 Squadron, based at Deelen. Many military Super Cubs were sold to civil users after their service lives were over. The Piper Cub and its variants, both civil and military, were developed from the L-4 Grasshopper, widely used during World War II.

Country of origin:	USA
Engine:	one 65hp Continental A-65
Wingspan:	10.74m (35ft 3in)
Length:	6.78m (22ft 3in)
Height:	2.03m (6ft 8in)
Weight loaded:	499kg (1100lb)
Cruising speed:	132km/h (82mph)
Service ceiling:	3658m (12,000ft)
Range:	402km (250 miles)
Passengers + crew:	1 + 1

Piper PA-28-236 Cherokee Dakota

In June 1972, the Piper Aircraft Corporation, builders of the classic Cherokee range of light aircraft since 1960, began design work on a new four-seat 150hp model that was eventually to introduce a significant change to the entire range. Publicly launched on 26 October 1973, the PA-28-151 Warrior, which featured an entirely new, long-span wing with a semi-tapered planform. The new wing design was introduced on the 180hp Cherokee Archer in 1976 as the Cherokee Archer II, and two years later on the 235hp Cherokee Pathfinder, which became the PA-236 Cherokee Dakota. By 1 January 1991, 742 examples of this variant had been sold. Shortly afterwards, Piper suspended production of most of its single-engined aircraft pending an upturn in the company's financial position. It recovered from its bankrupt state in 1995 when sales of the Cherokee range resumed.

Country of origin:	USA
Engine:	one 235hp Textron Lycoming 0-540-J3A5D 6-cylinder
Wingspan:	10.67m (35ft)
Length:	7.54m (24ft 9in)
Height:	2.18m (7ft 2in)
Weight loaded:	1361kg (3000lb)
Cruising speed:	260km/h (160mph) at 3050m (10,000ft)
Service ceiling:	5335m (17,500ft)
Range:	1500km (935 miles)
Passengers + crew:	1 + 3

Pitts Special

The Pitts Special, which first flew as long ago as 1947, was for many years almost the universal mount of the world's aerobatic teams. Many, such as the Toyota team, flew the versatile two-seat S-2 model as it allowed them to carry passengers on orientation and demonstration rides. The aircraft seen here, single-seater S-1S G-BOOK, was the first Pitts Special to be acquired by international display pilot, Brian Lecomber. A former member of the Rothmans team, he went solo in a Pitts S-1T in 1978, and soon modified the aircraft extensively, fitting it with a 260hp Lycoming engine and a three-bladed propeller. The basic S-1T has symmetrical wings, like the preceding S-1S, and is fitted with a 180hp engine. This was the first version to be factory-built, as the Pitts had previously been sold in kit form for home assembly by aircraft enthusiasts.

Country of origin:	USA
Engine:	one 180hp Lycoming IO-360-B4A
Wingspan:	6.09m (20ft)
Length:	5.76m (18ft 9in)
Height:	2.04m (6ft 7in)
Weight loaded:	521.6kg (1150lb)
Cruising speed:	225km/h (140mph)
Service ceiling:	6797m (22,300ft)
Range:	507km (315 miles)
Crew:	1

Rockwell Thrush Commander

Since the early 1950s, American aircraft designers have produced a bewildering array of aircraft intended for the aerial crop-spraying role. Typical of the family, this is one of the many Thrush Commanders built by the Rockwell agricultural division, virtually all of which were finished in yellow house colours, a scheme deliberately chosen for its high visibility. Key features of the aircraft were its broad wing, which allowed a good load to be lifted, while retaining a low enough wing loading to permit high manoeuvrability, an essential attribute for all crop dusters. Large flying surfaces enhanced the degree of control, ensuring that the design was more than adequate for agricultural work. Note the graduated scale on the hopper tank just forward of the cockpit. It continued in production for 10 ten years until the aircraft certificate was sold to the Ayres Corporation.

Country of origin:	USA
Engine:	one 600hp Pratt & Whitney R-1340 9-cylinder radial
Wingspan:	13.54m (44ft 5in)
Length:	8.95m (29ft 4in)
Height:	2.79m (9ft 2in)
Weight loaded:	3130kg (6900lb)
Cruising speed:	177km/h (110mph)
Service ceiling:	not applicable
Range:	676km (420 miles)
Crew:	1

Saab 340B

Before 1982, the last airliner built by Saab was the Scandia of 1946, but after nearly 40 years of successful military aircraft design, the Swedish company felt that it had a world-beating civil aircraft to offer. The result was the SF (Saab Fairchild) 340, which first flew in January 1983. Saab saw a considerable market for the 340 in the United States, where the type was aimed at the commuter airlines and feeder networks. They were rewarded with several important sales, including aircraft for the regional networks of American, Eastern, Northwest and Continental, one of whose aircraft, a 340B, is pictured here. Six leased aircraft served with Bar Harbor Airlines at various locations on the eastern seaboard, but the Saabs were returned when the airline ceased operations in January 1991. The rest of the fleet continued to operate under Continental Express ownership.

Country of origin:	Sweden
Engines:	two 1870hp General Electric CT7-9B turboprops
Wingspan:	21.45m (70ft 4in)
Length:	19.75m (64ft 8in)
Height:	6.89m (22ft 6in)
Weight loaded:	12,928kg (28,500lb)
Cruising speed:	522km/h (325mph) at 4575m (15,000ft)
Service ceiling:	9449m (31,000ft)
Range:	1810km (1125 miles)
Passengers + crew:	37 + 2

Saro SR.45 Princess

The end of the commercial flying boat era was heralded by the cancellation of the Saunders-Roe (Saro) Princess flying-boat programme. Three of these giant aircraft were built, but only one was ever flown. Saunders-Roe had received a specification from the British Overseas Airways Corporation (BOAC) for a flying boat that could accommodate 200 passengers on transcontinental flights, and in May 1946 an order was placed for three prototypes. However, the construction programme ran into difficulties and fell behind schedule, and in 1951, BOAC announced that it no longer intended to adopt a new flying boat to replace its Short C-Class boats, having opted to use only landplanes in its future fleet. All attempts to sell the Princesses to other operators failed, and the flying boats remained in a cocooned state for some years before being broken up.

Country of origin:	GB
Engines:	ten 2500hp Bristol Proteus 600 turboprops (inner pairs coupled)
Wingspan:	66.9m (219ft 6in)
Length:	45.11m (148ft)
Height:	16.99m (55ft 9in)
Weight loaded:	156,492kg (345,000lb)
Cruising speed:	576km/h (358mph)
Ceiling:	not established
Range:	9720km (6040 miles)
Passengers + crew:	220 + 6

Short S.23 C-Class flying boat

In the years between the wars, the speedy carriage of mail was the key to commercial aviation development. Imperial Airways' aspirations in this field centred on the Short C-Class flying boat, designed in 1935 to meet the demands of the Empire Air Mail Scheme. Two versions were produced, the S.30 for transatlantic operation (nine built), and the earlier S.23, which did not have the range for transatlantic flying, but which proved very successful on the England–Australia mail service. Two S.30s and two S.23s served with the RAF's No 119 Squadron during World War II. Forty-two 'Empire' boats were built in total; 'Caledonia', shown here, surveyed the first leg of the proposed transatlantic route, flying from Hythe to the Azores on 5 July 1937. She was the last to serve on the African routes, and returned to the United Kingdom in March 1947 to be broken up.

Country of origin:	GB
Engines:	four 920hp Bristol Pegasus XC radials
Wingspan:	34.75m (114ft)
Length:	26.82m (88ft)
Height:	9.7m (31ft 10in)
Weight loaded:	18,370kg (40,500lb)
Cruising speed:	274km/h (170mph) at 1676m (5500ft)
Service ceiling:	6095m (20,000ft)
Range:	1223km (760 miles)
Passengers + crew:	24 + 4

Short-Mayo Composite

The Short-Mayo Composite was a considerable success for its time, and provided one of the more remarkable chapters in commercial aviation history. The S.21 Maia first flew on 27 July 1937, followed by the S.20 Mercury on 5 September. The composite flew as a complete two-aircraft unit on 20 January 1930, and achieved the first (uneventful) separation on 6 February. On 21 July 1938, Mercury was launched over Foynes, Ireland, with a load of newspapers, newsreels and press photographs, landing at Boucherville, Montreal, 20 hours later. Other proving flights were made, including one to South Africa, and some services were flown for BOAC. The outbreak of WWII brought any further development of this promising long-range, mail and passenger concept to an end; Mercury was scrapped, and Maia destroyed by German bombs at Poole, Dorset.

Country of origin:	GB
Engines:	four 910hp Bristol Pegasus XC radials
Wingspan:	34.7m (114ft)
Length:	25.9m (84ft 11in)
Height:	9.95m (32ft 7in)
Weight loaded:	17,237kg (38,000lb)
Cruising speed:	265km/h (165mph) at 1524m (5000ft)
Service ceiling:	6100m (20,000ft)
Range:	1360km (850 miles)
Passengers + crew:	20 + 5

Short 330

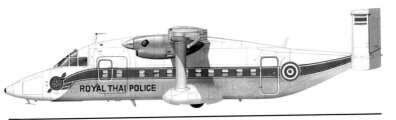

ROYAL THAI POLICE

Atypical outgrowth from the successful Skyvan utility transport, the Short 330 was in the vanguard of the turboprop feeder-liner revolution. Although it has been overtaken in recent years by more advanced designs, it is still in fairly widespread service, and has gained popularity as a light freighter in both civil and military use. The Short 330 project was first announced at the September 1974 Farnborough Air Show. The prototype, G-BSBH, had already flown on 22 August under the designation SD3-30, and eight days later won its first order from Command Airways of Poughkeepsie, New York. The 330 was primarily intended for short-range, regional and commuter air routes in the United States, but the aircraft sold well in other countries too, in both civil and military guises. The aircraft illustrated is one of four used by the Thai police and army.

Country of origin:	GB
Engines:	two 1200shp Pratt & Whitney Canada PT6A-45R turboprops
Wingspan:	22.8m (74ft 8in)
Length:	17.7m (58ft)
Height:	4.95m (16.25ft)
Weight loaded:	10,400kg (22,930lb)
Cruising speed:	350km/h (217mph) at 3050m (10,000ft)
Service ceiling:	not known
Range:	875km (545 miles)
Passengers + crew:	30 + 2

Short 330

The history of the Short organization dates from April 1901, when two brothers, Oswald and Eustace Short, first set up in business at Hove in Sussex as manufacturers of aerial balloons. In 1908, they were joined by their brother Horace, and at a new base at Shellbeach on the Isle of Sheppey near London began building, under licence, six of Orville and Wilbur Wright's biplanes. The main production facilities were moved to Belfast in Northern Ireland in the late 1930s. Production began with a contract to build 50 Bristol Bombays, followed by 150 Handley Page Herefords; then came production runs that included over 1200 Stirling bombers, and 130 Sunderland flying boats. With the factory located in Belfast, Short has been a major employer in Ulster for many years. The Short 330 has been operated by Aer Lingus Commuter, part of Eire's national airline.

Country of origin:	GB
Engines:	two 1200hp Pratt & Whitney Canada PT6A-45R turboprops
Wingspan:	22.8m (74ft 8in)
Length:	17.7m (58ft)
Height:	4.95m (16ft 3in)
Weight loaded:	10,400kg (22,930lb)
Cruising speed:	350km/h (220mph) at 3050m (10,000ft)
Service ceiling:	not known
Range:	875km (545 miles)
Passengers + crew:	30 + 2

Short 330

Although the initial order for the Short 330 came from Command Airways in California, the first aircraft to enter revenue-earning service was that delivered to the Canadian domestic operator Time Air, which is based at Lethbridge in Alberta. The first service was inaugurated on 24 August 1976. The United States proved to be the most lucrative market for Shorts, where commuter lines operated significant fleets of small aircraft between cities and outlying airfields. Mississipi Valley Airlines was a major 330 operator, although it is now defunct. So is Air Puerto Rico, which ceased operations in 1987, having flown the Short 330 on services around the island, and to the neighbouring Bahamas. Some airlines operating short-haul services have now replaced their Short 330 fleets with the Saab 340.

Country of origin:	GB
Engines:	two 1200hp Pratt & Whitney Canada PT6A-45R turboprops
Wingspan:	22.8m (74ft 8in)
Length:	17.7m (58ft)
Height:	4.95m (16ft 3in)
Weight loaded:	10,400kg (22,930lb)
Cruising speed:	350km/h (220mph) at 3050m (10,000ft)
Service ceiling:	not known
Range:	875km (545 miles)
Passengers + crew:	30 + 2

Short 330-100

The Short 330 series aircraft have become increasingly popular throughout the 1990s in both Europe and the United States. One of the main operators in Europe is Olympic Aviation, a subsidiary of Olympic Airways, which operates the 330-100 extensively from Athens to the Greek Islands scattered throughout the Aegean Sea. The operator has five aircraft and the first, SX-BGA (pictured here), was delivered on 22 May 1980. Several British operators have also adopted the type for regional transport. In the United States, carriers such as Midnite Express and Mountain Air Cargo have used them for transportation on a small package service. In Great Britain, they were used as freighters by Talair and National Airways, among others. One of the type's main attractions, apart from its load-carrying capacity, is its short take-off and landing ability.

Country of origin:	GB
Engines:	two 1200hp Pratt & Whitney Canada PT6A-45R turboprops
Wingspan:	22.8m (74ft 8in)
Length:	17.7m (58ft)
Height:	4.95m (16.25ft)
Weight loaded:	10,400kg (22,930lb)
Cruising speed:	350km/h (220mph) at 3050m (10,000ft)
Service ceiling:	not known
Range:	875km (545 miles)
Passengers + crew:	30 + 2

Short 360-100

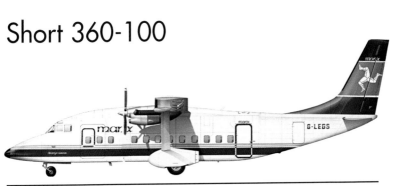

The success of the smaller Short 330, plus a rising demand from the market, encouraged Shorts to stretch and refine the design to produce the even more capable 360. Sturdy and straightforward, economic and reliable, the 360 proved to be a benchmark commuter airliner, and achieved fair sales outside its primary markets in the United Kingdom and United States. One user is Manx Airlines, part of the Airlines of Britain Group, which is involved principally in providing passenger services linking the Isle of Man to destinations in mainland Britain and Ireland. The three Short 360s are used in the 36-passenger configuration during the day, but can be quickly reconfigured for night operations, carrying freight on the mainland. This aircraft is registered G-LEGS, in honour of the Isle of Man's famous symbol, which it carries on its fin.

Country of origin:	GB
Engines:	two 1173hp Pratt & Whitney Canada PT6A-67R turboprops
Wingspan:	22.8m (74ft 9in)
Length:	21.6m (70ft 10in)
Height:	7.3m (23ft 10in)
Weight loaded:	11,793kg (26,0000lb)
Cruising speed:	393km/h (244mph)
Service ceiling:	not known
Range:	1697km (1055 miles)
Passengers + crew:	36 + 2

Short Skyvan 3

Design of the Short SC.7 Skyvan utility transport was begun as a private venture in 1959, and construction of the first prototype began in 1960. This aircraft (G-ASCN) flew for the first time on 17 January 1963, with two 390hp Continental piston engines, and completed its flight trials by mid-1963. It was re-engined with Astazou turboprops, and first flew in this new form on 2 October 1963. The Skyvan 3, which flew on 15 December 1967, became the standard version. The Skyvan's high-aspect-ratio wing was based on that of the French Hurel-Dubois designs, via research undertaken by the Miles Aircraft Company. Coupled with large and powerful flaps, it gave it exceptional STOL capability, while the large and widely spaced tail fins provided good rudder authority at low speeds. The upward-hinged, rear-loading ramp allowed it to carry bulky cargo.

Country of origin:	GB
Engines:	two 715hp Garrett AirResearch 331-201 turboprops
Wingspan:	19.79m (64ft 11in)
Length:	12.21m (40ft 1in)
Height:	4.60m (15ft 1in)
Weight loaded:	5670kg (12,500lb)
Cruising speed:	323km/h (201mph) at 3050m (10,000ft)
Service ceiling:	6858m (22,500ft)
Range:	1070km (665 miles)
Passengers + crew:	19 + 1–2

Sikorsky S-38

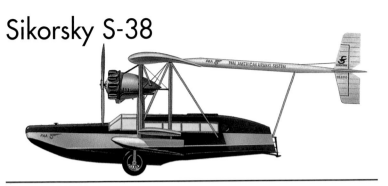

The Sikorsky S-38 was a twin-engined amphibian produced for operations in the Caribbean in 1928. It was derived from an earlier amphibian, the S-36, but was faster and had an increased range and capacity. There were two main variants, the S-36A and S-36B. Pan American received a total of 39 Sikorsky S-38s, these aircraft being used in the Caribbean and by the airline's Latin American subsidiaries. Charles Lindbergh flew the S-38 for PAA on a number of inaugural and survey flights. Pan American took delivery of the second aircraft in October 1928, and became by far the largest user. The last S-38s were not retired until 1940. The type was also used by the Curtiss Flying Service, and NYRBA (New York-Rio-Buenos Aires) Line operated one, although this was a very short-lived company, and lasted only a year before being taken over by Pan American.

Country of origin:	USA
Engines:	two 420hp Pratt & Whitney Wasp 9-cylinder radials
Wingspan:	21.84m (71ft 8in)
Length:	12.26m (40ft 3in)
Height:	4.24m (13ft 10in)
Weight loaded:	4753kg (10,440lb)
Cruising speed:	165km/h (103mph)
Service ceiling:	4900m (16,000ft)
Range:	805km (500 miles)
Passengers + crew:	10 + 2

Sikorsky S-42

On 25 January 1946, an agreement was signed between Pan American Airways and Imperial Airways, against fierce opposition from the French, Germans and Dutch, for joint operations on the transatlantic route. The American aircraft involved in this agreement was the Sikorsky S.42, 10 of which had been ordered by Pan American in 1931. The S.42 entered service from April 1943, operating first on the San Francisco–Hawaii, and later on the New York–Bermuda, Miami-South America and Manila–Hong Kong routes. However, the standard S.42's range was found to be insufficient for transatlantic flying, which in the event was undertaken by the Boeing 314 Clipper, ordered by Pan American in 1936. The S.42 was fitted with extra tanks, re-designated S.42B, and operated with success on the Pacific routes until the outbreak of the Pacific war in December 1941.

Country of origin:	USA
Engines:	four 70hp Pratt & Whitney Hornet S51DG 9-cylinder radials
Wingspan:	34.79m (114ft 2in)
Length:	21.08m (69ft 2in)
Height:	5.28m (17ft 4in)
Weight loaded:	19,051kg (42,000lb)
Cruising speed:	267km/h (166mph)
Service ceiling:	5790m (19,000ft)
Range:	1250km (775 miles)
Passengers + crew:	32 + 5

Stampe SV.4

The Belgian-designed Stampe et Vertongen SV.4 entered production during 1933 as a training and touring aircraft. Original Belgian-built Stampes had a 130hp de Havilland Gipsy Major engine, but those built under licence in France had a more powerful Renault engine. Considerable numbers of Stampes remain in use with private owners and flying clubs. It is similar in configuration to the Tiger Moth, but its handling is better in most respects. The twin ailerons on the upper and lower mainplanes are a significant improvement. The Stampe shown belonged to aerobatic pilot Brian Lecomber, and was one of the few to be fitted with a 145hp de Havilland Gipsy Major engine in place of the standard 140hp Renault powerplant. This gave more power and better inverted capability. The wings and tailplane are externally braced with aerofoil section wires.

Country of origin:	Belgium
Engine:	one 140hp Renault
Wingspan:	8.94m (29ft 4in)
Length:	7.29m (23ft 11in)
Height:	2.67m (8ft 9in)
Weight loaded:	828kg (1825lb)
Cruising speed:	161km/h (100mph)
Service ceiling:	4267m (14,000ft)
Range:	483km (300 miles)
Passengers + crew:	1 + 1

Supermarine S.5

In 1926, the British Air Ministry issued a specification calling for a floatplane powered by a Napier Lion engine, capable of a top speed of 426km/h (265mph) at 305m (1000ft), and with an alighting speed of not more than 145km/h (90mph), the intention being to enter the aircraft in the 1927 Schneider Trophy contest. Supermarine's response was the S.5, successor to the earlier S.4, which had crashed in the 1925 race. Three S.5s were built, and two travelled to Venice with a Royal Air Force team to take part in the 1927 contest. They took first and second places, and in 1931 the Schneider Trophy was won outright for Britain by a more advanced version, the Supermarine S.6B, powered by a Rolls-Royce engine. These all-metal, high-performance aircraft were the progenitors of one of the aircraft that won the Battle of Britain in 1940, the Supermarine Spitfire.

Country of origin:	GB
Engine:	one 875hp Napier Lion VIIB V-type
Wingspan:	8.15m (26ft 9in)
Length:	7.4m (24ft 3in)
Height:	3.38m (11ft 1in)
Weight loaded:	1470kg (3241lb)
Maximum speed:	514.29km/h (319mph)
Service ceiling:	not known
Range:	not known
Crew:	1

Supermarine Sea Lion III

The Supermarine Sea Lion I was a racing seaplane built to take part in the 1919 Schneider Trophy contest, and was one of four British seaplanes available at the time. Unfortunately, it struck an obstacle on take-off, holing its hull, and sank on alighting. For the 1922 contest, Supermarine produced the Sea Lion II, a high speed 'pusher' flying boat, which was originally the single-seat Sea King amphibian, and this overcame powerful Italian competition to win. Competition in the 1923 race became even fiercer when the Americans made a surprise entry of two Curtiss CR-3s. In response, Supermarine carried out an extensive rebuild of the Sea Lion II to produce the Sea Lion III, with cleaned-up floats and a 525hp Napier Lion engine. Although the aircraft was considerably faster than any previous race winner, it was completely outclassed by the US Navy's CR-3s.

Country of origin:	GB
Engine:	one 525hp Napier Lion III
Wingspan:	8.53m (28ft)
Length:	8.53m (28ft)
Height:	not known
Weight loaded:	1485kg (3275lb)
Maximum speed:	281.6km/h (175mph)
Service ceiling:	not known
Range:	not known
Crew:	1

Swearingen (Fairchild) Metro I

A product of Swearingen Aircraft of San Antonio, Texas, a company well known for its range of Merlin twin-engined executive aircraft, the Metro I prototype made its first flight on 26 August 1969, having been developed originally at the instigation of Fairchild Hiller. Operated by a crew of two, it can be readily converted into a cargo transport, carrying a 2268kg (5000lb) payload. FAA certification for the Metro was granted in June 1970. The first scheduled services using the Metro were begun in 1973 by Commuter Airlines, and by late 1980, nearly 200 had been ordered. Since 1966, the Metro has been one of the major feeder-liner types in the United States, offering superb safety in a small airliner. Pioneer Airlines, pictured here, operated the type alongside Beech 99s from its base at Denver, Colorado. Swearingen was taken over by Fairchild in 1982.

Country of origin:	USA
Engines:	two 940hp AirResearch TPE 331-3UW-303G turboprops
Wingspan:	14.10m (46ft 3in)
Length:	18.09m (59ft 4in)
Height:	5.08m (16ft 8in)
Weight loaded:	5670kg (12,500lb)
Cruising speed:	473km/h (294mph)
Service ceiling:	8380m (27,500ft)
Range:	805km (500 miles)
Passengers + crew:	20 + 2

Swearingen (Fairchild) Metro II

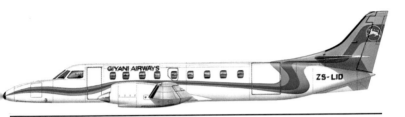

The Metro was a major effort for Swearingen, even though its workforce exceeded 900 before the end of 1968. The development and marketing of the new aircraft was a joint venture with what was then Fairchild Hiller, and the new wings and various other components were made at Fairchild's plant at Hagerstown, Maryland. To increase the potential market, Swearingen put the passenger door, with integral airstair built into the inner face, immediately aft of the flight deck, and added a wide cargo door at the rear. Sales were enhanced by the early switch of production to the Metro II, in which small portholes were replaced by upright rectangular windows. The Metro pictured here served with Giyani Airways, a small regional operator based at Tzaneen in South Africa, alongside the company's main equipment of three Cessna 404 Titans.

Country of origin:	USA
Engines:	two 940hp AirResearch TPE 331-3UW-303G turboprops
Wingspan:	14.10m (46ft 3in)
Length:	18.09m (59ft 4in)
Height:	5.08m (16ft 8in)
Weight loaded:	5670kg (12,500lb)
Cruising speed:	473km/h (294mph)
Service ceiling:	8380m (27,500ft)
Range:	805km (500 miles)
Passengers + crew:	20 + 2

Swearingen (Fairchild) Metro III

In 1981, the Metro underwent a major upgrade with the appearance of the Metro III, which featured a dramatic 3.05m (10ft) increase in wingspan, permitting an increase in useful load in accordance with FAA Special Regulations. Another important change was the use of the TPE331-11U-612G engine, rated at 1000hp or 1100hp with water/alcohol injection, and driving a four-blade McCauley propeller. The Metro III's engines are housed in more streamlined nacelles, with improved all-round-access cowlings. Tyre pressures were reduced, enabling the aircraft to make use of adequate unpaved surfaces, if necessary. The main landing doors were also redesigned. Six Metro IIIs, F-GCPG illustrated here, formed the backbone of Montpelier-based Air Littoral (previously the Compagnie Aerienne du Languedoc). Air Littoral connects towns and cities within metropolitan France.

Country of origin:	USA
Engines:	two 1000/1100hp Garrett TPE331-11U-612G turboprops
Wingspan:	17.37m (57ft)
Length:	18.09m (59ft 4in)
Height:	5.08m (16ft 8in)
Weight loaded:	6577kg (14,500lb)
Cruising speed:	515km/h (320mph) at 7620m (25,000ft)
Service ceiling:	8380m (27,500ft)
Range:	1610km (1000 miles)
Passengers + crew:	19 + 2

Tupolev Tu-104B

With the introduction of the Tu-104 on Aeroflot's Moscow–Irkutsk route on 15 September 1956, the Soviet Union became the second nation (after the United Kingdom) to provide scheduled passenger services using turbojet-powered aircraft. Advanced features of the machine included slotted trailing-edge flaps, boundary layer fences, and an anti-skid braking system on the main landing-gear units. One novel feature was a double-braking parachute pack. Successive developments over the years increased passenger capacity by more than 100 per cent, in addition to overall performance improvements, and although the airliner saw service with only two operators, its place in aviation history is assured as one of the pioneer designs. The existence of the Tu-104 became known outside the USSR when the prototype brought General Serov to London Airport on 22 March 1956.

Country of origin:	USSR
Engines:	two Mikulin AM-3M-500 turbojets of 9700kg (21,385lb) thrust each
Wingspan:	34.54m (113ft 4in)
Length:	40.05m (131ft 5in)
Height:	11.9m (39ft)
Weight loaded:	76,000kg (167,551lb)
Cruising speed:	800km/h (497mph) at 10,000m (32,800ft)
Service ceiling:	11,500m (37,730ft)
Range:	3100km (1926 miles)
Passengers + crew:	100 + 4

Tupolev Tu-114

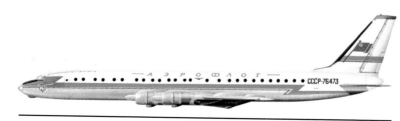

In 1957, a few days before the 40th anniversary of the Russian Revolution, the largest Soviet turboprop aircraft of the time, and the largest commercial aircraft in the world, made its first flight. It was the Tupolev Tu-114 Rossiya, Andrei Tupolev's response to a demand for an aircraft capable of spanning the globe. Based on the Tu-95 Bear Strategic bomber, using the same wing, mounted low on the fuselage so that the passenger cabin was unobstructed by the wing carry-through structure, it broke new ground in air transportation history. One of its most successful routes was the joint Aeroflot-Japan Air Lines service between Moscow and Tokyo, which was operated with mixed Russian/Japanese crews. The performance of the airliner (NATO reporting name Cleat) was not outstanding, but its load-carrying and speed made it the USSR's prestige airliner in the 1960s.

Country of origin:	USSR
Engines:	four 14,795hp Kuznetsov NK-12MV turboprops
Wingspan:	51.1m (167ft 6in)
Length:	54.1m (177ft 3in)
Height:	15.5m (50ft 11in)
Weight loaded:	171,000kg (377,000lb)
Cruising speed:	770km/h (480mph) at 9000m (29,500ft)
Service ceiling:	12,000m (39,370ft)
Range:	8950km (5560 miles)
Passengers + crew:	170 + 5

Tupolev Tu-114D

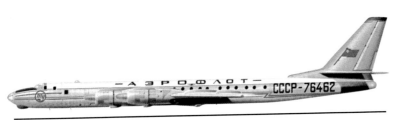

From September 1967, the Ilyushin Il-62 jet airliner began to replace the Tu-114, but the process took until 1975 to complete. One Tu-114 was converted into an airborne, early-warning and control (AWACS) aircraft, with a large, surveillance radar in a rotating dome mounted on a pylon above the rear fuselage; this became the prototype of the Tu-126 AWACS, at least 12 of which were operated by the Soviet Naval Air Arm from 1971 to 1990. Pictured here is the Tu-114D variant, three of which were built to undertake very long-range, mail and cargo flights. The first Tu-114D wore full Aeroflot colours and a civil registration, while the other two had military markings. Windows were incorporated in the rear fuselage, which was otherwise identical to that of the Tu-95 bomber (the early-model Bear) except that the rear gun turret was faired over.

Country of origin:	USSR
Engines:	four 14,795hp Kuznetsov NK-12MV turboprops
Wingspan:	51.1m (167ft 6in)
Length:	54.1m (177ft 3in)
Height:	15.5m (50ft 11in)
Weight loaded:	171,000kg (377,000lb)
Cruising speed:	770km/h (480mph) at 9000m (29,500ft)
Service ceiling:	12,000m (39,370ft)
Range:	10,500km (6520 miles)
Passengers + crew:	20 + 5

Tupolev Tu-134A

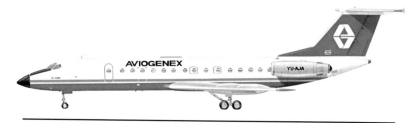

Although the Tu-134A (known to NATO as Crusty) was based on that of the earlier Tu-104 and Tu-124, and was initially designated Tu-124A, it incorporated so many changes that an entirely new bureau number was allocated. Work on the Tu-134A project began in June 1962, and the prototype flew in December 1963, being followed by five pre-production aircraft. The type entered service with Aeroflot on internal routes in 1966, and began international operations in September 1967 on the Moscow–Stockholm service. The original 64-seat Tu-134 was followed in 1968 by a stretched version, the 80-seat Tu-134A. In general terms, the Tu-134 was the Russian equivalent of the BAC OneEleven and the Douglas DC-9. Seen here is a Tu-134A of Aviogenex, the air transport division of the Yugoslavian General Export organization.

Country of origin:	USSR
Engines:	two Soloviev D-30 turbofans of 6790kg (14,990lb) thrust each
Wingspan:	29m (95ft 2in)
Length:	37.05m (121ft 6´in)
Height:	9.14m (30ft)
Weight loaded:	47,00kg (103,600lb)
Cruising speed:	885km/h (550mph)
Service ceiling:	11,900m (39,000ft)
Range:	3020km (1876 miles)
Passengers + crew:	80 + 3

Tupolev Tu-144

The Tupolev Tu-144 was the world's first supersonic transport to fly, on 31 December 1968, beating the Anglo-French Concorde SST into the air by two months. Unlike Concorde, the Tu-114 programme remained in the experimental and development stage for nearly 10 years, undergoing a major redesign in the interim, receiving a new wing, relocated engine nacelles, a new undercarriage, and retractable foreplanes to improve slow-speed handling. The second production standard Tu-144 was lost in a fatal accident at the Paris Aviation Salon on 3 June 1973, breaking up in mid-air; no report on the crash was ever published by the Soviets. The Tu-144 began operating on a twice-weekly cargo service between Moscow and Alma Ata, and began carrying passengers on that route in November 1977. The aircraft was abruptly withdrawn from service in June 1978.

Country of origin:	USSR
Engines:	four Kuznetsov NK-144 turbofans of 12,983kg (28,660lb) thrust each
Wingspan:	28.80m (94ft 6in)
Length:	65.70m (215ft 6in)
Height:	12.85m (42ft 4in)
Weight loaded:	180,000kg (396,830lb)
Cruising speed:	2500km/h (1553mph or 2.5M)
Service ceiling:	16,000–18,000m (52,500–59,000ft)
Range:	6500km (4030 miles)
Passengers + crew:	140 + 3

Tupolev Tu-154M

Still in production at Kuybyshev, although ultimately to be replaced by the new-technology Tu-204, the Tu-154 is one of the world's major airliner types. In widespread service with Aeroflot on both domestic and international services, it is also the standard airliner of nations allied to the former Soviet Union. Although not competing with western types in terms of performance and fuel efficiency, the Tu-154 exhibits typical Russian characteristics in being very strong, and able to operate from semi-prepared surfaces. A notable feature of this and many other Tupolev jets are the undercarriage nacelles projecting beyond the wing trailing edge. The sturdy main units retract backwards into the nacelles, the bogies somersaulting to lie flat within the fairings. The aircraft shown here is a Tu-154M of Balkan, the national airline of Bulgaria, which has a large fleet.

Country of origin:	Russia
Engines:	three Soloviev D-30-KU turbofans of 10,591kg (23,380lb) thrust each
Wingspan:	37.55m (123ft 2in)
Length:	47.9m (157ft 1in)
Height:	11.4m (37ft 5in)
Weight loaded:	100,000kg (220,460lb)
Cruising speed:	950km/h (590mph)
Service ceiling:	11,900m (39,000ft)
Range:	2750km (1700 miles)
Passengers + crew:	151 + 3

Vickers Vanguard

In 1951, Vickers-Armstrong began design studies of an aircraft to succeed the Viscount in airline service. The result was the Type 951 Vanguard, which first flew on 20 January 1959. In the event, only 44 Vanguards were built and these were operated by just two major airlines, BEA, which had placed an order for 20 Vanguards in July 1956, and the Canadian airline TCA. The Type 951 was followed by two more variants, Types 952 and 953, which had a reduced range but increased payload; 20 Vanguard 952s were ordered by TCA in January 1957, followed by three more at a later date. BEA, meanwhile, had revised its order to six Vanguard 951s and 14 953s; the first aircraft entered service with BEA on 17 December 1960, while TCA began Vanguard operations in February 1961. The Vanguard, however, was never a success in its passenger role.

Country of origin:	GB
Engines:	four 4985hp Rolls-Royce Tyne 506 turboprops
Wingspan:	35.96m (118ft)
Length:	37.45m (122ft 10′in)
Height:	10.64m (34ft 11in)
Weight loaded:	63,956kg (141,000lb)
Cruising speed:	684km/h (425mph) at 6100m (20,000ft)
Service ceiling:	9150m (30,000ft)
Range:	3330km (2070 miles)
Passengers + crew:	126-139 + 3

Vickers Viking

The first Vickers Viking prototype flew on 22 June 1945; after an exhaustive series of operational trials, the Ministry of Aircraft placed an order for 50 aircraft in April 1946. Nineteen Viking 1As, with fabric-covered wings, were followed by the lengthened Viking 1B, which had metal-skinned wings, and which became the standard production version. Apart from the large fleet operated by British European Airways, many Vikings were exported, total production running to 163 aircraft. The major version was the Viking 1B, 113 of which were built before production ceased at the end of 1947. The last three Vikings in service were operated by the French company Europe Aero Service; they were withdrawn in 1974. One Viking was used as a test bed for the Nene jet engine, and was the first jet-powered, British transport aircraft to fly, in April 1948.

Country of origin:	GB
Engines:	two 1690hp Bristol Hercules 634 14-cylinder radials
Wingspan:	27.20m (89ft 3in)
Length:	19.86m (65ft 2in)
Height:	5.97m (19ft 7in)
Weight loaded:	15,422kg (34,000lb)
Cruising speed:	338km/h (210mph)
Service ceiling:	7240m (23,750ft)
Range:	837km (520 miles)
Passengers + crew:	24–36 + 3

Vickers Vimy Commercial

In the years after World War I, the mainstay of the RAF's bomber squadrons was the Vickers Vimy, produced too late to take part in the hostilities. The RAF's faith in the Vimy, more than 1000 examples of which were ordered during the war, led to its post-war adaptation to the commercial role. Four Vimys were initially converted for long-range passenger and freight operations, fitted with a completely redesigned fuselage capable of accommodating up to 10 passengers. The Vimy Commercial prototype made its first flight on 13 April 1919, and the best-known example, named City of London (G-EASI, illustrated), was delivered to the steamship company Instone on 30 April 1920. It operated Instone's first London–Cologne service on 1–2 October 1922, and in 1924 was passed to Imperial Airways, in whose hands it operated between Croydon and Brussels.

Country of origin:	GB
Engines:	two 360hp Rolls-Royce Eagle VIII
Wingspan:	20.47m (67ft 2in)
Length:	13m (42ft 8in)
Height:	4.76m (15ft 7in)
Weight loaded:	5670kg (12,500lb)
Cruising speed:	135km/h (84mph)
Ceiling:	3200m (10,500ft)
Range:	720km (450 miles)
Passengers + crew:	10 + 2

Vickers Viscount

The order placed by TCA (later Air Canada) for the Viscount Series 700 in November 1952 was most significant. For the first time, a British company realized that an operator outside the UK might be able to improve the product and make it more acceptable in the world market. CF-TGK, seen here, was the third aircraft purchased by TCA. Stretching the basic AV.630 into the V.700 made the aircraft more attractive, and enhanced its load-carrying capacity. The first V.700, G-AMAV, flew in the colours of British European Airways in 1950. Although it never belonged to BEA, it was named Endeavour in 1953 as a member of the airline's 'Discovery' class. With race number 23 on its tail, it took part in the air race from London to Christchurch, New Zealand, in October 1953, averaging 467km/h (290mph) over the 18,982km (11,795 mile) course.

Country of origin:	GB
Engines:	four 1400hp Rolls-Royce Dart 506 turboprops
Wingspan:	28.56m (93ft 8in)
Length:	24.73m (81ft 2in)
Height:	8.15m (26ft 9in)
Weight loaded:	27,216kg (60,000lb)
Cruising speed:	486km/h (302mph) at 6100m (20,000ft)
Service ceiling:	7250m (23,750ft)
Range:	1980km (1230 miles)
Passengers + crew:	40–63 + 2–3

Vickers Viscount 701

For 30 years between 1935 and 1965, the American dominance of the world commercial aircraft market encountered only one formidable competitor: the Vickers Viscount. The world's first true turboprop aircraft, the Viscount emerged as a superb design, offering comfort, reliability and efficiency; it consequently sold in large numbers on both sides of the Atlantic. The Viscount 630 prototype first flew on 16 July 1948, and, on 29 July 1950, British European Airways started a month's trial service on the London–Paris and London–Edinburgh routes using this aircraft. The production 700-series Viscount went into regular service from 18 April 1953, and from then, the major European and American airlines sought early delivery of their share of the 445 Viscounts built up to the beginning of 1959. The aircraft here also served with BEA, British Eagle and Channel Airways.

Country of origin:	GB
Engines:	four 1547hp Rolls-Royce Dart 505 turboprops
Wingspan:	28.56m (93ft 8in)
Length:	24.73m (81ft 2in)
Height:	8.15m (26ft 9in)
Weight loaded:	27,216kg (60,000lb)
Cruising speed:	486km/h (302mph) at 6100m (20,000ft)
Service ceiling:	7250m (23,750ft)
Range:	1980km (1230 miles)
Passengers + crew:	40–63 + 2–3

Vickers Viscount V.748

Although there were many Viscount type numbers (they signified differences in interior layouts to suit customer requirements), there were basically only three models in the 700 series. These were the original 700, with Dart 505 or 506 engines; the 700D with Dart 510s and extra fuel tankage; and the 770D, the North American equivalent of the 700D. Some of the latter aircraft were fitted with slipper fuel tanks on the wing leading edges. In total, 287 Series 700 Viscounts were built. The aircraft shown here, VP-YNC, was a V.748 for Central African Airways (CAA), and the 100th Viscount built. Flown on 24 May 1956, it was delivered two weeks later and named Mlanje. After the breakup of the Central African Federation, it was transferred to Air Rhodesia on 1 January 1969, flying in blue camouflage after a SAM attack. Air Zimbabwe took the aircraft over in 1979.

Country of origin:	GB
Engines:	four 1400hp Rolls-Royce Dart 506 turboprops
Wingspan:	28.56m (93ft 8in)
Length:	24.73m (81ft 2in)
Height:	8.15m (26ft 9in)
Weight loaded:	27,216kg (60,000lb)
Cruising speed:	486km/h (302mph) at 6100m (20,000ft)
Service ceiling:	7250m (23,750ft)
Range:	1980km (1230 miles)
Passengers + crew:	40–63 + 2–3

Vickers Viscount V.794

The Viscount 794 seen here was almost the last short-body Viscount to be built. Number 431 off the production line at Hurn, it was delivered to the national airline of Turkey, THY, in October 1958, as TC-SES. Later, with two others, it was transferred to the THK (Turkish Air Force), the three aircraft enjoying a long career as staff transports. A 'one-off' 700 Series Viscount was the V.763, which drew the attention of Howard Hughes, the celebrated pilot, aircraft manufacturer and multi-millionaire owner of the Hughes Tool Company. The specification for the single V.763 was the longest ever drawn up, and the aircraft was subjected to minute inspections by Hughes's engineers. In the end Hughes's interest waned and the aircraft, which by now was holding up the production line, was sold to TACA of El Salvador with the registration YS-09C.

Country of origin:	GB
Engines:	four 1400hp Rolls-Royce Dart 506 turboprops
Wingspan:	28.56m (93ft 8in)
Length:	24.73m (81ft 2in)
Height:	8.15m (26ft 9in)
Weight loaded:	27,216kg (60,000lb)
Cruising speed:	486km/h (302mph) at 6100m (20,000ft)
Service ceiling:	7250m (23,750ft)
Range:	1980km (1230 miles)
Passengers + crew:	40–63 + 2–3

Vickers Viscount V.810

The 444th, and last, Viscount was first flown on 2 January 1964, 438 of these being regular aircraft sold to airline customers. Several were bought new by executive owners (the first was the Canadian Department of Transport in 1954, and by air forces, the first by the Indian Air Force in 1954. Every Viscount on the second-hand market was quickly snapped up. Viscount V.810 9G-AAU, airframe number 446, was one of the last to be built, and was delivered to Ghana Airways on 26 November 1961. Note the rectangular doors swinging back on parallel arms, which in the stretched 800-series replaced the original elliptical type to improve freight loading. This aircraft subsequently served as G-BZCR with Field, BMA, Southern International and Dan-Air. Viscount construction numbers included undelivered or unfinished aircraft, number 446 being number 431 in practice.

Country of origin:	GB
Engines:	four 1800hp Rolls-Royce Dart 525 turboprops
Wingspan:	28.56m (93ft 8in)
Length:	26.11m (85ft 8in)
Height:	8.15m (26ft 9in)
Weight loaded:	29,257kg (64,500lb)
Cruising speed:	491km/h (305mph) at 6100m (20,000ft)
Service ceiling:	8230m (27,000ft)
Range:	2075km (1290 miles)
Passengers + crew:	40–63 + 2–3

Vickers Viscount V.813

In 1954, Vickers and BEA jointly reached a decision to stretch the Viscount by moving back the rear-pressure bulkhead, creating a 2.82m (111in) internal extension while making the fuselage only 1.17m (46in) longer. This aircraft appeared as the V.802, 12 of which were ordered by BEA. In 1955, Rolls-Royce offered an increase in power with the Dart 525 engine, which was installed in the considerably revised V.810 series. The V.810 sold well, the last order being placed by CAAC of the Chinese People's Republic – the first time that country had placed an order with a Western source. Typical of the smaller companies that recognized the value offered by the Viscount was Manx Airlines, which leased an 813 series aircraft, G-AZNA (shown here) from British Midland Airways; this particular airliner had, by then, been in service for over a quarter of a century.

Country of origin:	GB
Engines:	four 1800hp Rolls-Royce Dart 525 turboprops
Wingspan:	28.56m (93ft 8in)
Length:	26.11m (85ft 8in)
Height:	8.15m (26ft 9in)
Weight loaded:	29,257kg (64,500lb)
Cruising speed:	491km/h (305mph) at 6100m (20,000ft)
Service ceiling:	8230m (27,000ft)
Range:	2075km (1290 miles)
Passengers + crew:	40–63 + 2–3

Voisin-Farman I

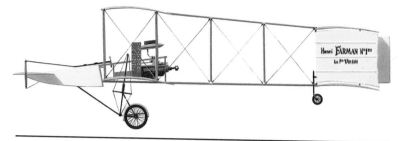

Henry Farman's early career was linked with that of two other great French aviation pioneers, Gabriel and Charles, who were the first men in Europe to build aircraft as a commercial venture. Henry Farman commissioned them to build an aeroplane on his behalf; work on it began in June 1907, and after some preliminary testing, including a few short 'hops', Farman set about making extensive modifications to the aircraft's basic configuration, particularly the structure of the wings and the elevator. The results were amazing: when the machine was flown on 26 October 1907 at Issy, it made a straight-line flight of 771m (2530ft) in 52.6 seconds, and on 5 November, it made its first turn in flight. On 13 January 1908, Farman piloted the aircraft on its first officially logged flight of more than 1km (0.62) miles, becoming the first European to achieve this.

Country of origin:	France
Engine:	one 50hp Antoinette 8-cylinder inline V
Wingspan:	10.2m (33ft 5in)
Length:	10.5m (34ft 5in)
Height:	3.35m (11ft)
Weight:	522kg (1150lb)
Speed:	55km/h (34mph)
Ceiling:	not known
Range:	27km (17 miles)
Crew:	1

Vought-Sikorsky VS-44 Excalibur

The Vought-Sikorsky VS-44 Excalibur was the last large, commercial flying boat to be built in the United States. The first VS-44A flew made its maiden flight on 18 January 1942, and was followed by two more. All three, named Excalibur, Excambia and Exeter, were operated by American Export Airlines throughout the remainder of World War II on transatlantic transport duties on behalf of the US Naval Air Transport Service. Only Excambia remained in commercial service after the war, flying until 1971, first with Avalon Air Transport, and then with Antilles Air Boats. During their wartime service, the VS-44A boats broke several speed and distance records, setting up a new transatlantic record between Europe and the United States. The withdrawal of Excambia marked the end of an era for the large flying boat, once the majestic symbol of long-range air transport.

Country of origin:	USA
Engines:	four 1200hp Pratt & Whitney R-1830-S1C3G Twin Wasp 14-cylinder radials
Wingspan:	37.79m (124ft)
Length:	24.15m (79ft 3in)
Height:	8.41m (27ft 7in)
Weight loaded:	26,082kg (57,500lb)
Cruising sped:	257km/h (160mph) at 3050m (10,000ft)
Service ceiling:	5790m (19,000ft)
Range:	5795km (3600 miles)
Passengers + crew:	16–47 + 9

Wright Flyer 3

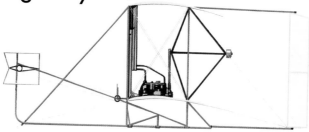

After the Wright brothers' Flyer No 1 made its first – historic – powered flight on 17 December 1903, the two pioneers built a second aircraft, Flyer No 2, which was finished in May 1904 and tested between 23 May and 9 December. The aircraft, however, was not yet totally satisfactory, and showed a tendency to stall in turns. The snags were eliminated in the Flyer No 3 of 1905, which became the first real aircraft in history. It was considerably longer than its predecessors, improving stability, and had new, more efficient propellers. Flights continued between 23 June and 16 October 1905, setting an endurance record of 38 minutes 3 seconds on 5 October. The Wrights successfully tested a derrick-and-weight-assisted take-off system, enabling the craft to become airborne irrespective of wind conditions. The Flyer 3 paved the way for the more efficient Wright Flyer.

Country of origin:	USA
Engine:	one 20hp Wright 4-cylinder water-cooled in-line
Wingspan:	12.34m (40ft 6in)
Length:	8.53m (28ft)
Height:	2.44m (8ft)
Weight loaded:	388kg (855lb)
Cruising speed:	56km/h (35mph) approx
Service ceiling:	not known
Range:	not known
Passengers + crew:	1 + 1

Index

Note: Page numbers in **bold** refer to main entries.

313

314

317

Onassis, Aristotle 21

Pacific Southwest Airlines 114
Palmer, Arnold 242
Pan American Airways 68, 69, 70, 71, 73, 80, 88, 127, 187, 216, 250, 258, 287, 288
Panair do Brasil 128
Patterson, Major Cyril 146
People Express 79
People's Republic of China see China
Percival Prentice 153
Petroleum Air Services 163
Pioneer Airlines 292
Piper
  Cheyenne III **272**
  J3C-65 Cub **273**
  PA-28-236 Cherokee Dakota **274**
Pitts Special **275**
Poland
  Antonov An-2T Antek 28
Polikarpov U-2 (Po-2) 54
Polish Air Force 37, 40
Polskie Linie Lotnicze (LOT) 34, 37, 228,
Post, Wiley 242
Pratt & Whitney 18, 19, 72, 91, 96, 121, 175, 189, 238 see also individual aircraft engine specifications
Pulitzer family 133

QANTAS 72, 111

RAF see British Air Force
Ransome Airlines 165
Reichsluftdienst (Air Service) 170
Republic Airlines 205
Riddle Airlines 45
Roberts, C.M. 155
Rockwell International 270
Rockwell Thrush Commander **276**
Roe, Alliott Verdon 58
Rolls-Royce 12, 13, 15, 57, 91, 119, 175, 188, 219, 309 see also individual aircraft specifications
Roosevelt, President F. D. 176
Royal Air Force see British Air Force
Royal Brunei Airlines 91
Royal Canadian Air Force
  see Canadian Air Force
Royal Dutch Airlines see KLM
Royal Swedish Air Force 16, 153
Russia see USSR

Saab 340 B **277**
Saab J32 Lansen 16
SABENA 80, 212, 225
SANA 175

Saro SR.45 Princess **278**
SAS (Scandinavian Airlines System) 16, 71, 261, 263
SATENA (Servicio de Aeronavegacion a Territorios Nacionales) 52
Saudi Arabian Airlines 247
Saunders-Roe 278
Scandinavian Airlines System see SAS
Scenic Airways 217
Scottish Aviation 220
Seaboard World Airlines 189
Serov, General 295
Servicio de Aeronavegacion a Territorios Nacionales (SATENA) 52
Serviciul National de Navigatie Aeriana (SNNA) 48
Severa GmbH 175
Short
  330 **281, 282, 283**
  330-100 **284**
  360-100 **285**
  S.23 C-Class flying boat **279**
  Skyvan 3 **286**
Short brothers 282
Short-Mayo Composite **280**
Sikorsky S-38 **287**
Sikorsky S-42 **288**
Silver City Airways 105
Singapore Airlines 77
Slovakian Air Force 36
Smith, Charles Kingsford 209
Smith, C. R. 177
SNNA (Serviciul National de Navigatie Aeriana) 48
Societa Aerea Mediterranea 210
Societé Tunisienne de l'Air (Tunis Air) 14
Southern Airways 257
Southern International 308
Southwest Airlines 84, 85
Soviet Air Force 37, 232, 233
Sri Lanka Air Force 35
St Petersburg and Tampa Airboat Line 7-8
Stampe SV.4 **289**
Sterling Airways 18, 20
Stout D & C Airlines 175
Sud-Aviation 13, 14, 17, 18
Sudan Airways 73
Sunflower Airlines 161
Supermarine S.5 **290**
Supermarine Sea Lion III **291**
Swearingen (Fairchild)
  Metro I **292**
  Metro II **293**
  Metro III **294**
Sweden
  Saab 340B 277